IMPERIAL JUSTICE

Imperial Justice

Africans in Empire's Court

BONNY IBHAWOH

OXFORD
UNIVERSITY PRESS

OXFORD
UNIVERSITY PRESS

Great Clarendon Street, Oxford, OX2 6DP,
United Kingdom

Oxford University Press is a department of the University of Oxford.
It furthers the University's objective of excellence in research, scholarship,
and education by publishing worldwide. Oxford is a registered trade mark of
Oxford University Press in the UK and in certain other countries

First Edition published in 2013

Impression: 1

Published in the United States of America by Oxford University Press
198 Madison Avenue, New York, NY 10016, United States of America

British Library Cataloguing in Publication Data
Data available

Library of Congress Control Number: 2013940322

ISBN 978–0–19–966484–9

Printed and bound in Great Britain by
CPI Group (UK) Ltd, Croydon, CR0 4YY

For *Ehiane*

Acknowledgements

It is difficult to describe a book in one word. But in an age of sound bites, keywords, and search terms, we are increasingly asked to describe our work in ever fewer words. The word that I find most fitting in describing this book is 'palaver'. The word 'palaver' has a uniquely African pedigree. Originally derived from the Spanish 'palabra' (talk), it became a preferred colonial colloquialism for a wide range of everyday encounters in the continent. In some contexts it signified dispute, controversy, and argument. In other contexts, it meant dialogue, discussion, and reasoning. Throughout Africa, colonial archives and oral histories tell stories of simple and complex palavers, and of communities and village elders coming together in the Palaver House or under the Palaver tree to discuss and resolve them. There were land palavers, trade palavers, clan palavers, women palavers, war palavers, and even god palavers. Some palavers were so intractable that they had to be settled overseas in the ultimate Palaver House—the Privy Council—by the 'Great white Chief' himself. Life, it seems, was a matrix of intersecting palavers that had to be resolved in an unending process of communal reasoning and dialogue.

This books concerns African palavers, the circumstances that gave rise to them and how individuals and communities sought to resolve them in the courts of Empire. Ironically, the process of researching and writing this book was itself akin to confronting an intractable intellectual palaver. Like the complicated palavers of old, it took the help of a village to unravel. Elders and youths, sages and learners, kinsmen and acquaintances offered their knowledge and counsel. In researching and writing this book, I drew often on the wisdom and generosity of many friends and colleagues within and beyond academia. I am grateful to the Social Science and Humanities Research Council of Canada which funded the research for this book. My research in five national archives was facilitated by the support and assistance of old friends and some new ones that I made along the way. I am grateful to the staff of the National Archives of Kenya, Nairobi; the South African National Archives, Pretoria; the Nigerian National Archives, Ibadan; the Public Records and Archives Administration Department of Ghana, Accra; and the National Archives of the UK in Kew. I am particularly thankful to Gabuza Langa who made my research in South Africa a delightful and rewarding experience. Gabuza, who was my student in his years of Apartheid-imposed exile in Nigeria in the early 1990s, became my patient and diligent teacher, helping me to navigate his new and exuberant South Africa. Many thanks go to the veteran archivists, Richard Ambani at the Kenyan National Archives and Abraham Elumadu at the Nigerian National Archives whose dedication and commitment to record preservation have sustained the African archives.

The voluminous and rich records of the Judicial Committee of the Privy Council (JCPC) provided an appropriate archival foundation for this study. Although its jurisdiction and influence has waned greatly from what it was at the height of the British Empire, the JCPC as at the time of writing this book is still the final court of appeal for a number of Commonwealth countries and British dependencies. Its records are considered working documents and until recently, they were stored in the JCPC library in Westminster with restricted public access. When I initiated this project, I worried that it might be difficult, if not impossible, to gain extended access to these records. This was partly because the JCPC office at No 9 Downing Street stood right opposite No 10, which is the Prime Minister's official residence. But thanks to Jackie Lindsay, then Chief Clerk of the JCPC, my research assistants and I were granted unhindered access to the uncatalogued records stored in the basement of the JCPC building. We were reminded to dress decently enough to get past Downing Street security but practically enough to work in a dusty basement. Without this access, this book would have been impossible. The later decision to transfer these records to the British National Archives will certainly improve access to these important records and engender more scholarly interest in the history of the JCPC. I thank Nandini Chatterjee and colleagues associated with the 'Judicial Committee of the Privy Council Project' at the University of Plymouth, and Jim Phillips and the Legal History Working Group at the University of Toronto. These research groups provided fitting forums to test some of the arguments presented in this book. I thank John Weaver for his insightful comments on draft chapters and Solomon Ukhuegbe for offering legal commentaries on the Privy Council jurisprudence. I am also grateful to my research assistants who worked with me on this project over the years: Sylvia Bawa, Alayna Kolodziechuk, Elliott Enns, and Zuzana Wilcox.

This project coincided with my tenure as the Director of the Centre for Peace Studies and later, as Associate Dean in the School of Graduate Studies at McMaster University. Juggling administrative duties with teaching and research travel was possible only with the support of my colleagues and staff at the University. I am particularly grateful to Wendy Benedetti, Debbie Lobban, Helena Collins, and Nancy Wells for helping to facilitate my shuttles between research commitments, teaching, and administrative responsibilities. I am also grateful to Pete and Muriel Growcott for keeping an eye on the home front during my travels.

Finally and most importantly, my thanks to Omo and our boys for tolerating my many hours of solitude in the office and for enduring my long absences from home for research. The eventual unravelling of this book *palaver* is, as always, a testament to their love and support.

Contents

List of Figures

List of Abbreviations

AIR	All India Reports
CO	Colonial Office
EACA	East Africa Court of Appeal
ECtHR	European Court of Human Rights
CCJ	Caribbean Court of Justice
CSO	Chief Secretary's Office
EALR	East African Law Reports
IR	Irish Reports
JCPC	Judicial Committee of the Privy Council
KNAN	Kenyan National Archives, Nairobi (Kenya)
LJR	Law Journal Reports
LR IA	Law Reports (Indian Appeals)
NANI	National Archives of Nigeria, Ibadan (Nigeria)
NASAP	National Archives of South Africa, Pretoria (South Africa)
NAUK	National Archives of the United Kingdom
NLR	Nigerian Law Reports
NWLR	Nigerian Weekly Law Reports
PPA	Printed Papers in Appeal
PRAADA	Public Records and Archives Administration, Accra (Ghana)
SCR	Supreme Court Reports
SR	Southern Rhodesia High Court Reports
TLR	Tanganyika Law Reports
UGCC	United Gold Coast Convention
ULR	Ugandan Law Reports
WACA	West African Court of Appeal
WNLR	Western Nigeria Law Reports

1

Africa and the Umpires of Empire

> The firmest bond, by which the cheerful submissions of a people can best be secured and their affections to Government permanently engaged, is the pure and impartial administration of justice.[1]

British imperial justice reached a milestone in 1921. In that year, the Judicial Committee of the Privy Council (JCPC), the final Court of Appeal for all legal disputes throughout the British Empire, passed judgment in a landmark case (the '*Amodu Tijani*' case) that was to reverberate across the Empire because of the precedent it set on the question of indigenous land rights. The appeal was brought before the Privy Council by an African Chief, Chief Oluwa, against the colonial government in Nigeria demanding compensation for the 'illegal' expropriation of his ancestral lands. At the heart of the matter was the Treaty of Cession signed between Britain and one of Chief Oluwa's forebears, King Docemo, in 1861. The colonial government claimed that, under the terms of that treaty, the British Crown had acquired ownership of all lands in the colony of Lagos, including lands claimed by Chief Oluwa. Indeed, the 1861 treaty states that King Docemo agreed to transfer to the Queen of Great Britain, 'her heirs and successors forever', the Island of Lagos, 'freely, fully, entirely and absolutely'.[2]

Although the wording of the Treaty unambiguously attests to the transfer of legal rights over Lagos lands from King Docemo to the British Crown, the legitimacy of the surrender was tainted from the beginning. The British officer negotiating the Treaty in 1860 faced a revolt by other Chiefs, who claimed that King Docemo did not have absolute customary or legal authority over 'all the lands in Lagos', which he had supposedly ceded to the Queen of England.[3] Even in his capacity as the paramount Chief of Lagos, they contended, Docemo had neither 'feudal authority' and 'seigniorial rights' over his Chiefs, nor absolute rights over the land held in trust by them.[4] Half

[1] Hebert Macaulay, 'Petition to the Colonial Secretary', National Archives of Nigeria (hereinafter NANI) Chief Secretary's Office (hereinafter CSO) 33115 Vol 1, Ibadan-West African Court of Appeal Judgments of 1936.

[2] Robert Sydney Smith, *The Lagos Consulate, 1851–1861* (Berkeley: University of California Press, 1979) 140.

[3] M. P. Cowen and R. W. Shenton, 'British Neo-Hegelian Idealism and Official Colonial Practice in Africa: the Oluwa Land Case of 1921' (1994) 22 *Journal of Imperial and Commonwealth History* 234.

[4] The European terms 'feudal authority' and 'seigniorial rights' were used extensively in the litigation of *Amodu Tijani*. See *Amodu Tijani v Secretary, Southern Provinces* 3 NLR 31 and *Amodu Tijani v Secretary of Southern Nigeria* [1921] 2 AC 399.

a century later, Chief Oluwa's petition to the Privy Council hinged on the position that, despite the Treaty's provisions, King Docemo really had nothing to transfer to the British.[5]

The key question was whether Chief Oluwa [Amodu Tijani] was entitled to compensation under the provisions of the Public Lands Ordinance of 1903 which permitted compulsory acquisition of land but required compensation to be paid to all persons with interest in the land. At the end of a protracted case, the Privy Council ruled that, as the trustee of the lands of his native community, Chief Oluwa was entitled to be compensated for the lands expropriated by the government. Whatever concession his forebears may have made to the British Crown was made under the assumption that the property rights of the inhabitants were to be fully respected.[6] The simple assertion of British authority did not, and could not, serve to extinguish the legal rights of the aboriginal people to their traditional territories. Although this was a long established colonial principle applied where the indigenous peoples were in occupation of the land and using it, the ruling by the highest court in the Empire was significant. With this ruling, there was no more doubt that primary ownership of Lagos lands rested not with the British Crown, but with the indigenous inhabitants of Lagos.

Beyond its legal import, the Privy Council's decision in the *Amodu Tijani* case also had great political and symbolic significance for many Africans. One local newspaper editorialized that the victory was a 'boon for all West Africans', proclaiming: 'Today, the dictum that "white men and Government make no mistake" has been exploded and proved to be erroneous and untrue'.[7] The news of the decision occasioned over two weeks of popular celebrations and festivities in the streets of Lagos. On his return journey from London, where he had gone to witness the case, Chief Oluwa received congratulatory messages from African leaders and learned elites at every port of call on the West African coast, from Freetown in Sierra Leone to Sekondi and Accra in the Gold Coast.[8] Forty thousand people turned out at a ceremony to welcome the victorious Chief Oluwa and his entourage when they arrived on the Lagos shore on the morning of 25 August 1921.[9]

Only two years earlier, the Judicial Committee of the Privy Council had delivered a starkly contrary ruling in *Re Southern Rhodesia*, another African case that has been described as the 'greatest land case in British history'.[10] In a decision that upheld the supremacy of Crown title, the JCPC ruled that the Matabele and the Mashona could not have lost land rights against the Crown or the British South

[5] Olawole Elias, *The Nigerian Legal System* (London: Routledge & Kegan Paul, 1963) 324.
[6] *Amodu Tijani v Secretary of Southern Nigeria* [1921] 2 AC 399 at 404–6.
[7] *Daily Telegraph* (1 August 1921).
[8] *Lagos Weekly Record* (10 September 1921).
[9] *Daily Telegraph* (1 August 1921).
[10] This case was championed by the Anti-Slavery and Aborigines Protection Society. See John H. Harris, *The Greatest Land Case in British History: The Struggle for Native Rights in Rhodesia before the Judicial Committee of His Majesty's Privy Council* (London: Anti-Slavery and Aborigines Protection Society, 1918).

African Company.[11] They never had any in the first place. The premise for the ruling was that 'some tribes are so low in the scale of social organization that their usages and conceptions of rights and duties are not to be reconciled with the institutions or the legal ideas of civilized society'.[12]

The ruling in *Amodu Tijani* therefore challenged what was considered the settled imperial law on aboriginal land title. It set a legal precedent that would shape colonial land policies across the British Empire, and held significant ramifications for colonial administration and imperial jurisprudence. What was true of the Lagos colony applied a fortiori to the rest of Africa and presumably throughout the Empire. The significance of the case went beyond the unlikely victory of an African Chief in a case against a colonial government in the highest court of the Empire. As colonial governments across the Empire grappled with aboriginal land claims, this case originating in the tropical Empire became an authoritative reference point for cases dealing with the effect of treaties ceding overseas territories to the British Crown, the Crown's radical title, and the nature of customary aboriginal land tenures.[13]

Written in a generic way to be equally applicable throughout the British Empire, the Privy Council's ruling in Chief Oluwa's case became a *locus classicus* on the nature of Crown ownership of colonial lands.[14] It served to bolster dramatically the legal and political merit of outstanding aboriginal land claims in Canada, Australia, New Zealand, and elsewhere in the Empire.[15] The *Mabo* judgments, which granted indigenous land rights in Australia, drew partly on the doctrine of native title as developed in *Amodu Tijani* and in a series of other decisions by the Privy Council that arose from appeals from West Africa in the first half of the twentieth century.[16] In Canada, where there had been longstanding demands for Provincial and Dominion governments to acknowledge aboriginal title, the federal government became increasingly concerned about the prospect of Indians pressing land claims before the Privy Council based on the precedent of *Amodu Tijani* and took steps to prevent this. One such step was the passage of the Indian Act by the Canadian parliament in 1927, which made it a criminal offence to solicit funds without permission, for the purposes of pursuing Indian land claims against the government.

[11] The supremacy of the Crown's radical title was upheld in *Amodu Tijani* as well, but in that case there was an ordinance entitling Chief Oluwa to compensation that did not exist in the *Southern Rhodesia* case.

[12] *Re Southern Rhodesia* [1919] AC 211 at 233.

[13] Omoniyi Adewoye, 'The Tijani Land Case 1915–1921: A Study in British Colonial Justice' (1976) 13 *Odu* 24.

[14] Omoniyi Adewoye, *The Judicial System in Southern Nigeria 1854–1954* (London: Longman, 1977).

[15] See, for example, Michael Asch, *Aboriginal and Treaty Rights in Canada: Essays on Law, Equity, and Respect for Difference* (Vancouver: University of British Columbia Press, 1997) 136, and Marcia Langton, *Honour Among Nations? Treaties and Agreements with Indigenous People* (Melbourne: Melbourne University Publishing, 2004) 18.

[16] Ben Silverstein, 'The Rule of Native Title: A View of Mabo in the British Empire' (2007) 16(1) *Griffith Law Review* 55. The differences of judicial opinion arose mainly over whether that radical title of the Crown included or excluded on-going native customary rights and that depended greatly on the facts of each case and presence or absence of relevant statutes.

The evident aim was to forestall Indian land claims before the Privy Council following the *Amodu Tijani* decision.[17]

What circumstances made it possible for an African Chief in this part of the British Empire to successfully challenge a powerful colonial government in the highest court in the Empire? How could a case dealing with a small group of natives in one of Britain's tropical outposts influence imperial jurisprudence? What do such cases tell us about imperial legal universalism and the construction of colonial difference?[18] Moreover, what were the broader implications of these judgments and of the judicial precedents they set for colonizers and the Africans who brought these appeals before imperial appellate courts? These are the central questions that this book addresses.

This book examines the imperial control of the administration of justice and, what I term the 'adjudication of colonial difference'. Focusing on the Judicial Committee of the Privy Council and the colonial regional Courts of Appeal for West Africa and East Africa, it explores the ways in which the local judicial discourses of native difference and imperial universalism influenced the practices of power in colonial settings, and shaped the evolving jurisprudence of Empire. The central argument here is that Imperial Courts of Appeal were key sites where colonial legal modernity was fashioned. This process was underscored by a tension that permeated the colonial legal system—that between upholding the basic standards of British justice and, at the same time, allowing for local customary divergence that was thought essential for achieving that justice. The 'civilizing' and modernizing mission of British justice could only truly be achieved through the recognition of local exceptionality and difference. Natives who appealed to the Courts of Empire were entitled to the same standards of justice as their 'civilized' colonists, yet the boundaries of racial, ethnic, and cultural difference somehow had to be recognized and maintained. This epitomized the central paradox of imperial liberalism noted by Martin Wiener—the endemic tension between everyday racial inequality evident throughout the Empire and the deep rooted liberal premise of British justice that extended everywhere in the Empire.[19]

Confronting and working through this paradox required adaptability and flexibility in colonial law-making, as in the administration of justice. Imperial justice was therefore simultaneously driven by the homogenizing impulses of English law and by the imperatives of maintaining colonial difference. In the paradox of integration and differentiation, imperial power and local cultures were not always in conflict, but were at times complementary and mutually reinforcing. This paradox and the opportunities it provided for various groups to advance competing interests accounts for the enduring legacies of British colonial law, more so than Empire's crushing power.

[17] Paul Tennant, *Aboriginal People and Politics* (Vancouver: University of British Columbia Press, 1990) 111–12, and Christian W. McMillen, *Making Indian Law: The Hualapai Land Case and the Birth of Ethnohistory* (New Haven: Yale University Press, 2007) 97.

[18] 'Universalism' is used here in the loose sense of the search for commonality.

[19] Martin Wiener, *An Empire on Trial: Race, Murder, and Justice under British Rule, 1870–1935* (New York: Cambridge University Press, 2009) viii.

This book offers broad interpretations of the processes of adjudicating colonial 'otherness' and the ways in which notions of African difference figured in imperial understanding and implementation of universal justice. The idea of justice was the centrepiece of British self-representation, and the administration of justice was a carefully protected imperial prerogative.[20] The Judicial Committee of the Privy Council (JCPC) was the foundation of the Empire's authoritative status in the realm of imperial justice and its administration. To a lesser extent, colonial regional appeal courts also fulfilled this task. The JCPC was unique among British imperial institutions. Since 1833, it had become the statutory supreme appellate court of the British Empire and later the Commonwealth. It received appeals from across the British Empire and from those countries where British subjects had been granted extra-territorial rights. It became the key organ for the interpretation and expansion English common law exported to a very large part of the world.[21]

In exercising its power of final judicial review in all British overseas possessions, the JCPC created a centripetal jurisprudence through standardization of legal interpretation and conformity with imperial ideals of justice. A crucial element in this process was the common law tradition of judicial precedent, the principle of *stare decisis*, which obliges judges to respect the precedents established by prior decisions and the judicial interpretations of statutes in ways that may be different from their original legislative intent. This made the decisions of the JCPC strictly binding in colonial courts across the British Empire. Local courts were bound to follow its decisions even if they were rendered on appeals from other jurisdictions.[22] Only the JCPC enjoyed this dominant status in the colonies. The case laws of domestic English Courts and the House of Lords were treated with respect but were not considered strictly binding in colonial courts.[23] Unlike the House of Lords, the JCPC was not bound by its previous decisions on similar cases based on the same consideration.[24] The JCPC therefore enjoyed an unprecedented influence in the administration of justice in the colonies. As the final Court of Appeal for legal disputes from all corners of the British colonial world, it played a pivotal role in the homogenization of local legal cultures through the application of precedents from communities and contexts across the Empire. Its role as the ultimate appellate judicial authority is an enduring legacy of British colonial rule.

Exploring the imperial role of the JCPC and of the regional appeal courts in Britain's African empire, this book also focuses on the reciprocal place of Africa in

[20] The same points have been made about imperial Venice and the Ottoman Empire. See Ergene Boğaç, *Local Court, Provincial Society and Justice in the Ottoman Empire: Legal Practice and Dispute Resolution in Çankırı and Kastomonu 1652–1744* (Leiden: Brill, 2003) 190, and Monique O'Connel, *Men of Empire: Power and Negotiation in Venice's Maritime State* (Baltimore: Johns Hopkins University Press, 2009) 75.

[21] J. N. Matson, 'The Common Law Abroad: English and Indigenous Laws in the British Commonwealth' (1993) 42(3) *The International and Comparative Law Quarterly* 754.

[22] J. W. Harris, 'The Privy Council and the Common Law' (1990) 106 *The Law Quarterly Review* 583.

[23] John A. Harrington and Ambreena Manji, 'The Emergence of African Law as an Academic Discipline in Britain' (2003) 102(406) *African Affairs* 120.

[24] Per Lord Porter, *Gideon Nkambule v The King* [1950] AC 379.

shaping British imperial legal culture through examination of African appeals to the Privy Council. The JCPC was more than simply a colonial court. It was the quintessential imperial court. With its primary mandate to uphold British standards of justice in the colonies and dominions, its jurisdiction went beyond national and regional boundaries and would ultimately cover more than a quarter of the world.[25] The JCPC was a veritable clearing house of conflicting legal codes, demands, disputes, and hence a gateway to both local processes and imperial regulation.[26] It comprised metropolitan judges who, having limited knowledge of the laws they were expected to interpret and of the customs of the litigants who came before them from the colonies, struggled to find the right balance between promoting a common British standard of justice while allowing for some degree of local autonomy and difference.

The revered Lords of the JCPC saw themselves less as part of the imperial political order and more as *umpires* of the Empire or, as one African writer put it, the 'Daniels of the British realm'[27]—impartial arbiters and exponents of the universality of British justice. One visitor to the JCPC chambers in Westminster in 1928 was in awe of these imperial judges and their work of adjudicating the Empire:

> Nobody can appreciate the power and the ramifications of the British Empire until he visits the book-lined room of the Privy Council which is something between the British Museum and a Police Court... All the queer cases that occur in strange lands beyond the seas are settled by judges in this library. All the quaint laws and customs governing old world people, from primitive tribes to ancient civilizations are settled in these quiet rooms. For everything there is a book. Ushers spend their lives climbing ladders and bringing down books for the Law Lords who are the *umpires of Empire*.[28]

The present study of the JCPC offers insights into the complex modes of engagement between the colonial subjects in the peripheries of the Empire and the metropolitan institutions. It can help us better understand how colonial and imperial courts grappled with the tension between the aspiration toward imperial legal universalism and the 'othering' of non-European subjects that was so central to maintaining the colonial order. If, as others have argued, law lay at the heart of the British imperial enterprise and the English legal system is one of the most enduring global legacies of British colonial rule,[29] the JCPC more than any other

[25] Paul Magrath, 'British Justice International Plc?' (2003) 3 *Incorporated Council for Law Reporting Newsletter* 4.

[26] Nandini Chatterjee and Charlotte Smith, 'Communities-in-Law: Self, Sociality and the Legal Process in the British Empire, 1790–1950', *Communities of Law Research Network Proposal* (Plymouth: University of Plymouth, 2011) 2.

[27] *West African Pilot* (2 July 1963) 6.

[28] R. E. Corder, 'Umpires of Empire: The Privy Council Judges at Work', *The Singapore Free Press and Mercantile Advertiser* (13 June 1928) 3. My emphasis.

[29] See Martin Chanock, 'The Law Market: The Legal Encounter in British East and Central Africa' in W. J. Mommsen and J. A. De Moor, eds, *European Expansion and Law: The Encounter of European and Indigenous Law in the 19th and 20th Century Africa and Asia* (New York: Oxford, 1992) 279; H. F. Morris, 'The Award of Blood Money in East African Manslaughter Cases' (1974) 18(1) *Journal of African Law* 25.

imperial institution shaped this legacy at the broadest levels. As a unique institution at the imperial core, charged with adjudicating appeals from colonial outposts on the dual basis of local laws and universalist imperial standards of justice, it allows us to rethink both the role of law in the imperial context and the place of subaltern agency in the making of imperial legal cultures.

Although this book focuses primarily on appellate justice and the imperial control of judicial governance in Africa through the agency of the JCPC, it is not exclusively about the JCPC. It also explores broadly, the workings of British colonial legal systems in Africa, specifically the regional Courts of Appeal for West Africa and East Africa, whence most African appeal cases came to the JCPC. One cannot fully assess the imperial role of the JCPC at the centre of the Empire without some understanding of the workings of the local and regional courts beneath it in the colonial court hierarchy. The West African Court of Appeal (WACA) and the East African Court of Appeal (EACA)[30] provide the local and regional contexts for this study.

Like the JCPC, the WACA and EACA had imperial mandates. They were supranational appellate courts whose jurisdictions transcended colonial political territorial boundaries. The West African Court of Appeal was originally set up in 1867 to hear civil and criminal appeals from the superior courts of all the British colonies in West Africa. The court was dismantled in 1874, when the administrative unification of Britain's West African colonies came to an end. It was revived in 1928 for the colonies of Nigeria, Gold Coast, Sierra Leone, and Gambia. The East African Court of Appeal had similar origins. It was established in 1902 for the British protectorates in East Africa (Kenya, Uganda, and Malawi). Over the course of the British rule in East Africa, its jurisdiction expanded to include Zanzibar, Tanganyika (Tanzania), and Somaliland. Later on, the court's jurisdiction extended beyond East Africa to include the British colonies of Aden, Seychelles and St Helena in the South Atlantic (see Figure 1.1).

This book explores the processes and outcomes of African cases before these Imperial Courts of Appeal and the ways in which they shaped colonial encounters in the continent and beyond. It is concerned with exploring the role of judicial authorities at imperial centres, in constructing colonial difference and furthering the homogenizing agendas of the Empire. This requires examining not only the cases that came before the Privy Council in London but also the related cases adjudicated in the colonies. Focusing on selected African cases heard at the Privy Council and the regional Appeal Courts in the first half of the twentieth century, this study illuminates how judicial governance at the highest level remade Africa, and how Africans—in their engagement with imperial courts—influenced colonial constructions of native difference and shaped the imperial legal culture.

[30] The name of this institution changed throughout its history. It was originally called the Eastern African Court of Appeal and later the East African Court of Appeal. By the 1950s, it became the Court of Appeal for East Africa. For consistency, 'East African Court of Appeal' is used throughout this book.

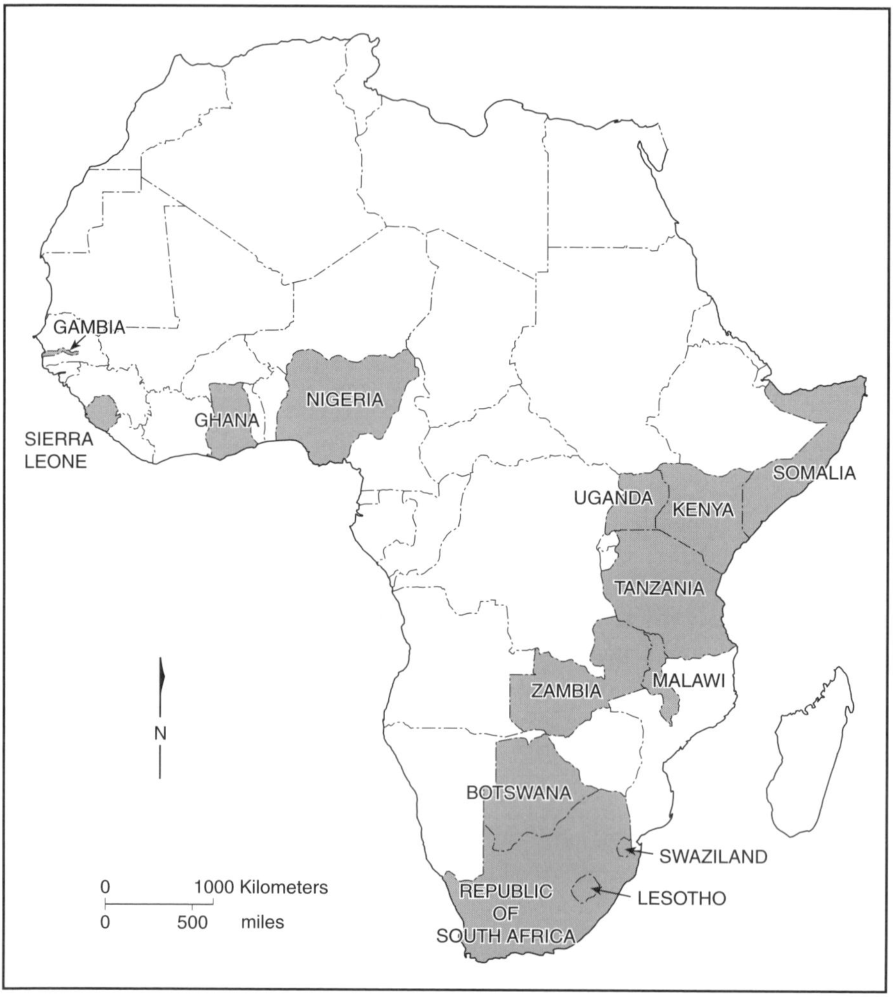

Figure 1.1: The African Jurisdiction of the JCPC, the WACA, and the EACA
Loris Gasparotto

Constructing Colonial Difference

The notion of colonial difference which, in other contexts has been described as the 'imperial politics of difference'[31] and the 'rule of colonial difference',[32] is central to this study. The ontology of colonialism has been figured as 'difference'; its production,

[31] Jane Burbank and Frederick Cooper, *Empires in World History: Power and the Politics of Difference* (Princeton: Princeton University Press, 2010) 3.

[32] Partha Chatterjee, *The Nation and its Fragments: Colonial and Postcolonial Histories* (Princeton, NJ: Princeton University Press, 1993) 10.

its management, its subversion, and its obtrusion.[33] Scholars of Empire have long recognized that the management of difference was a key device of imperial control. However, the scholarship on colonial difference has focused mainly on the political and social dynamics of colonial 'othering' and exclusion. Several studies have explored the legal and policy frameworks, within which colonial difference was constructed and maintained.[34] Few, however, extend the discussion to the construction and contestation of colonial difference within imperial judicial spaces. Maintaining colonial difference in the realm of law-making and administration of justice was essential to sustaining Empire. A uniform rule of law would have profoundly threatened the power dynamic that distinguished colonizer from the colonized, and abrogated the very foundations of the imperial project.[35]

All empires were to some degree reliant on both incorporation and differentiation.[36] The colonial states of the nineteenth and twentieth centuries self-consciously maintained the diversity and 'otherness' of the people they conquered, even as they sought to incorporate them within their homogenizing imperial orders. In British Africa, imperial politics of difference centred on claims of cultural authenticity and supremacy, but it also involved the recognition and accommodation of a multiplicity of peoples and their varied customs. This meant drawing boundaries between colonizer and colonized, civilized and uncivilized, modern and traditional, Christian and heathen. Imagery of the 'dark continent' reinforced colonial polarities and shaped modernizing agendas. The process of creating and maintaining colonial difference—particularly racial and ethnic difference—was neither settled nor conclusive however. It took work and was always an on-going process.[37] More often than not, colonial policymaking was reactive, yielding to the force of circumstances when the costs of colonial rule became too high or when colonies ran the risk of becoming 'ungovernable'.[38]

The legal spaces of the Empire were the key arenas, where the social and identity boundaries of colonial difference were fashioned and sustained. These boundaries—socially constructed and inherently unstable—were, however, continually contested and subverted. Because they operated beyond the direct purview of local colonial officialdom, Imperial Courts of Appeal were fitting sites for negotiating colonial difference. These courts were crucial not only to the constructions and contestation of colonial difference, but also to managing the tensions between native exceptionalism and imperial universalism. In the adjudication of Empire,

33 Kunal Parker, 'The Historiography of Difference' (2005) 23(3) *Law and History Review* 685.

34 Nasser Hussain, *The Jurisprudence of Emergency: Colonialism and the Rule of Law* (Ann Arbor, University of Michigan Press, 2006); Brian Owensby, *Empire of Law and Indian Justice in Colonial Mexico* (Stanford: Stanford University Press, 2008); and Lauren Benton, *Law and Colonial Cultures: Legal Regimes in World History, 1400–1900* (Cambridge: Cambridge University Press, 2002).

35 Elizabeth Kolsky, 'Codification and the Rule of Colonial Difference: Criminal Procedure in British India' (2005) 23(3) *Law and History Review* 631–84, and Chatterjee, *The Nation and its Fragments*, 9.

36 Burbank and Cooper, *Empires in World History*, 13.

37 Burbank and Cooper, *Empires in World History*, 12.

38 Jan Eckel, 'Human Rights and Decolonization: New Perspectives and Open Questions' (2010) 1(1) *Humanity* 126.

imperial courts manifested the contradictions of British law and served as venues for discourses of inclusion and exclusion—of power and restraint.

Colonialism was in a dual sense a 'regime of exception'. On one level, it was premised on the notion of basic native exceptionality. The civilizing and modernizing agenda of Empire was everywhere mediated by assumption about the essential difference of the colonized other. Colonial law, even in the aspiration towards universalist British justice, departed from the common law in its ascription of privileges, immunities, and distinctions between civilized and uncivilized.[39] On another level, it was reliant on its ability to constantly break its own rules. In the realm of law and justice, the colonial state could break its own rules on the parameters for engaging and accommodating native difference. It created legal rules such as the 'repugnancy doctrine' premised on native exceptionality to regulate the application of native African customary law in the legal system. But it could also make exceptions to these rules where local officials found it expedient to do so.

British colonialism in Africa was underscored by a proliferation of these differences and exceptionalities. The 'overriding otherness of race' was certainly evident in the judicial work of Imperial Courts of Appeal. Beyond racial otherness, imperial courts were also the sites for creating and contesting other forms of difference, particularly class, ethnic, religious, generational, and gender differences. This book explores the boundaries of difference between colonizers and colonized, but it is also concerned with judicial discourse on internal differences within colonized societies. To be sure, the need to maintain an overarching racial 'otherness' in the colonial state often meant that other forms of differences amongst Africans were hesitantly and ambiguously addressed.[40] Nonetheless, these secondary constructions of difference were manifest in African encounters with imperial courts and they shaped judicial outcomes. This book aims, therefore, at going beyond racial 'otherness' to explore other constructions of colonial difference in the administration of appellate justice.

Imperial Universalism

A related discursive framework for this study is the burgeoning scholarship on imperial universalism. Imperial judicial discourses were evidently shaped by notions of African difference. However, these notions of colonial difference were uniquely tempered by a certain universalist idealism that was perhaps less evident in other spheres of the colonial enterprise. Native 'otherness' had to be responsively accommodated within the larger homogenizing agendas of the Empire. Colonized natives, although different, somehow had to be brought within the fold of 'civilization' in fulfilment of the universally redemptive promise of Empire and to justify imperialism.

[39] Achille Mbembe, *On the Postcolony* (Berkeley: University of California Press, 2001) 29–31; Frederick Cooper, 'Provincializing France' in *Imperial Formations*, eds, Ann Laura Stoler, Carole McGranahan, and Peter C. Perdue (Santa Fe: School for Advanced Research Press, 2007) 357.

[40] Megan Vaughan, *Curing Their Ills: Colonial Power and African Illness* (Stanford: Stanford University Press, 1991) 11.

Imperial universalism may also be framed in terms of historical globalization. The premise is that European empires acted as powerful agents of globalism—in contemporary parlance 'globalization'—appropriating new lands and significant new sources of revenue, moving people, commodities, technologies, and ideas from colony to colony as well as between the imperial centre and colonial outposts. Imperial globalism was in this sense fundamental to the seismic political and cultural reorientations and transformation in cosmopolitan intellectual traditions in the twentieth century.[41] This book suggests that British imperial justice represented a globalizing agenda: it sought to square the inequities of colonial engagement with local custom while aspiring toward upholding uniform values of justice, equity, and conscience. Imperial legal universalism typified in the judicial work of the JCPC and the regional Courts of Appeal required both the accommodation and containment of African difference. The paradox of integration and differentiation in colonial constructions of globality is that imperial power and local cultures were not always in conflict, but sometimes mutually reinforcing. The JCPC forged a universalist legal culture, while at the same time helping to constitute a political and social order that divided the world by race, nationalities, cultures, and civilizations.

This study comes at a time of growing historical engagement with the concept of globalization. The initial hesitance of historians to deploy globalization as an analytical lens and interpretative framework has given way to cautious acceptance.[42] In spite of the contested meanings of the term, there is now some agreement that the concept of globalization can be a fruitful heuristic tool for historians of Empire. It engenders greater sensitivity to the structures of Empire and the ways in which the Empire acted as a globalizing force. Such an approach suggests that many parts of our globalizing moment are fundamentally entwined with imperialism, and that the momentous cultural and intellectual transformations enacted by colonialism are central to any understanding of globalization in the long run.[43] If nineteenth and twentieth-century European empires were the wheels that put our globalizing moment in motion, certain institutions served as the lynchpins that secured the wheel and kept it on its axle. This book argues that British imperial justice and the Appeal Courts within it were among such lynchpins.

Recent scholarship on colonial law indicates a growing interest in these patterns of global restructuring, with renewed awareness of the ways in which legal forms have historically migrated across the globe. For scholars who work in the intersection of law and colonial history, the focus has broadened. They seek to find new

[41] Tony Ballantyne, 'Empire, Knowledge, and Culture: From Proto-Globalization to Modern Globalization' in A. G. Hopkins, ed, *Globalization in World History* (London: W. W. Norton, 2002) 122.

[42] For example, A. G. Hopkin, ed, *Globalization in World History* (London: W. W. Norton, 2002); Jo-Anne Pemberton, *Global Metaphors: Modernity and the Quest for One World* (London: Pluto, 2001); Alex MacGillivray, *A Brief History of Globalization: The Untold Story of Our Incredible Shrinking Planet* (London: Robinson, 2006); Peter N. Stearns, *Globalization in World History* (London: Routledge, 2010); Karl Moore and David Lewis, *The Origins of Globalization* (New York: Routledge, 2009); Duncan S. A. Bell, 'History and Globalization: Reflections on Temporality' (2003) 79(4) *International Affairs* 801–14.

[43] Ballantyne, 'Empire, Knowledge, and Culture', 117.

global perspectives of understanding the large-scale transfers of legal institutions, and ways of thinking about law and justice across imperial centres and colonies. Lauren Benton states, for example, that one of the goals of her wide-ranging study, *Law and Colonial Cultures*, was to provide a historical perspective for considering some of the disruptive forces of global politics.[44] Similarly, studies of colonial law in Africa have sought to explain subaltern agency in terms of global engagement.[45] Martin Chanock has argued that the era of globalization and the transcending of the nation-state provide us an opportunity to de-emphasize state-centred histories, and to write not simply in terms of 'transplants versus independence' but with a greater awareness of the relationships between external and indigenous factors in the making of new states.[46]

Studies of globalization have nudged historians toward a search for transnational flows of ideas. Primarily, it has helped us to rehabilitate universalizing categories such as 'colonialism' and 'cosmopolitanism', which had been criticized for their tendency to ignore the difference of local cultures and the operation of power. Secondly, it implicitly raises larger historical questions. For more than a decade, historians interested in world history and globalization have attempted to periodize global integration by looking at the scope, depth, and speed of contacts and flows.[47] Colonialism is certainly a phase in global integration. If it is both a product and an agent of Eurocentric globalization, as some have argued, then a key aspect of this process was the global diffusion of legal and juridical principles regulating the relationships between states and between states and their constituents.[48]

Given that globalization, at every moment in its history, involves not only integration but also differentiation, a central question in understanding globalization as a historical process is how difference and the conceptualization of difference enter into the consciousness of globality. It is not enough to recognize that the politics or rule of difference lay at the heart of colonial enterprise; it is also imperative to appreciate that the meanings of difference were inherently unstable.[49] Ideologies of imperial inclusion and exclusion were challenged by people acting within ideological, political, and legal structures of the Empire, as well as by those who tried to defend or create a political space outside imperial structures. Equally significant is how colonial subjects and native populations who were the subjects of

[44] Benton, *Law and Colonial Cultures*, 29.

[45] Richard Roberts, *Litigants and Households: African Disputes and Colonial Courts in the French Soudan, 1895–1912* (Portsmouth: Heinemann, 2005) 14.

[46] Martin Chanock, *The Making of South African Legal Culture 1902–1936: Fear, Favour, and Prejudice* (Cambridge: Cambridge University Press, 2001) 31.

[47] C. A. Bayly, *The Birth of the Modern World, 1780–1914: Global Connections and Comparisons* (Malden, MA: Blackwell, 2004) 27–48; Hopkins, *Globalization in World History*, 45–72.

[48] Arif Dirlik, *Global Modernity: Modernity in an Age of Global Capitalism* (Boulder: Paradigm Publishers, 2007) 43.

[49] For example, Megan Vaughn has shown that even though colonial medical discourse in Africa was preoccupied with difference represented as biological 'race', more elaborate distinctions were also formulated through a process of inclusion and exclusion, and a shifting of the boundaries of difference. Anna Crozier also draws attention to the changing tone of colonial discourses on African difference. Vaughan, *Curing Their Ills*, 12, and Anna Crozier, *Practising Colonial Medicine: the Colonial Medical Service in British East Africa* (New York: I. B. Tauris, 2007).

these debates themselves dealt with shifting notions of difference. Like contemporary globalization, imperial legal universalism required both the accommodation and containment of difference.[50] At certain moments, the very idea of 'empire' accentuated the distinctiveness of the distant, colonized 'other'; at other moments, it needed to soften differentiation and enhance incorporation.[51]

The discourse on globalization presents other analytic openings. Globalization implies homogenization, but it is also a multi-centred phenomenon. It is not simply a process wherein the dominant centre acts upon lesser peripheries, but instead a process that involves the interactions of all parties.[52] Recent studies have shown how pre-twentieth century material and cultural homogenization in Africa foreshadowed contemporary globalization.[53] Generally, however, most contributors to the discourse on historical globalization have not fully appreciated how the interests of subaltern actors in the 'periphery' have affected distant societies. Even if these scholars concede that globalization is a multi-centred phenomenon, most of them have not challenged the idea of 'cores' as the determining features of global systems. Yet, it is apparent that if any part of a system has the potential to affect other parts, we should not discount the possibility that seemingly marginal actors can also significantly influence the apparently powerful ones.[54]

This study of African engagement with the Courts of the Empire offers two distinct perspectives on the discourse on historical globalization in relation to the homogenizing power of nineteenth and twentieth-century European imperialism. First, it proposes to de-emphasize the material dominance of the 'core', to explore the defining role in the globalization process of marginal actors in the periphery. Here, I am interested in what has been described as 'imperial counter-flows'—the process by which materials and ideas travelled from the imperial peripheries to the centre, and their cultural impact. Such an inquiry requires tracing the flow of knowledge within the Empire, paying close attention to the roles of indigenous learned elites in shaping and expanding the colonial knowledge base.[55] The goal is to show the broader connections in the administration of justice in Africa and to suggest how these travelled within the British Empire.

The second perspective this study offers arises from its focus on imperial justice as a unique standpoint from which we can analyse historical globalization in terms of the homogenizing impact of imperial legal culture. Although there has been an

[50] 'Universalism' is used here in the loose sense of the search for commonality.

[51] Cooper, *Colonialism in Question*, 24.

[52] A. G. Hopkins, ed, *Global History: Interactions Between the Universal and the Local* (New York: Palgrave, Macmillan, 2006) 5.

[53] Jeremy Prestholdt, *Domesticating the World: African Consumerism and the Genealogies of Globalization* (Berkeley: University of California Press, 2008); Jeremy Prestholdt, 'On the Global Repercussions of East African Consumerism' (2006) 109(3) *The American Historical Review* 755–81; and Joseph E. Inikori, 'Africa and the Globalization Process: Western Africa 1450–1850' (2007) 2 *Journal of Global History* 68–86.

[54] Prestholdt, *Domesticating the World*, 60 and 196.

[55] This approach has been adopted in several historical studies of Empire. For example, Michael Fisher, *Counterflows to Colonialism: Indian Travellers and Settlers in Britain 1600–1857* (Delhi: Permanent Black, 2006); Catherine Hall and Sonia O. Rose, eds, *At Home with the Empire: Metropolitan Culture and the Imperial World* (Cambridge: Cambridge University Press, 2006).

explosion of work on historical globalization, careful studies of the legal aspects of this transformation are few and far between.[56] Most scholars acknowledge the multi-faceted nature of globalization. Still, there remains a disproportionate concern with its material dimension in ways that exalt material culture above all other human values. In the literature on Empire, globalization has been interpreted in a narrowly material and economistic fashion, with the socio-cultural aspects of imperial globalism still largely unexplored.[57] A new focus on the universalizing impulse of imperial legal culture calls attention to the fact that globalization is not simply an economic phenomenon. It involves simultaneous processes of transformation in social, cultural, and other subjective matters. The role of the Imperial Courts of Appeal in standardizing colonial justice and maintaining uniformity in the interpretation of English common law and local statute law represents a clear example of globalization construed as a socio-cultural process.

The benefits of offering a legal perspective to understanding colonial constructions of globality are neither solely historical nor simply academic. They are also deeply relevant to contemporary legal debates about the rise of supranational adjudication by courts and other judicial institutions operating above rather than within or between states.[58] These new 'umpires' of our contemporary globalizing world order struggle with challenges that are strikingly similar to those confronted by the old 'umpires of Empire'. Like the Imperial Courts of Appeal, the jurisdiction of the new supranational judicial institutions cuts across national and cultural boundaries. Institutions such as the International Criminal Court, the International Court of Justice, and the European Court of Human Rights include judges who, like colonial judges, often have limited knowledge of the cultures and customs of litigants. As with the appellate imperial courts, they too must struggle to find the right balance between promoting contemporary universalist legal principles of human rights and transnational justice, and allowing for some degree of local autonomy and difference.

In an increasingly interdependent and globalizing world, these supranational courts play a vital role in fashioning and upholding a nascent universal legal culture founded on international human rights law both within and between states. Yet, like the Privy Council and the colonial appeal courts of old, these new institutions must grapple with the inevitable tensions between aspirations towards universal legal standards and the persistence of local difference. These processes and outcomes will engender new legal and jurisprudential universalisms as well as new and contested constructions of globality. Legal historians are in a unique position to contribute to these debates by looking back at the tensions between imperial universalism and local difference in colonial legal cultures. In doing so, they make a contribution

[56] S. E. Merry, 'From Law and Colonialism to Law and Globalization' (2003) 28 *Law & Social Inquiry* 578.

[57] Ballantyne, 'Empire, Knowledge, and Culture', 177.

[58] Alex Mills and Tim Stephens, 'Challenging the Role of Judges in Slaughter's Liberal Theory of International Law' (2005) 18 *Leiden Journal of International Law* 4.

to knowledge about the imperial past, and provide directions on how to better understand and grapple with the challenges of contemporary legal globalization.

The evidence presented in this book does not indicate that the JCPC and the regional Appeal Courts had a profoundly globalizing impact in the sense of complete jurisprudential uniformity in the interpretation of colonial law. The JCPC, the WACA, and the EACA had only limited direct impact on the daily lives of colonial subjects. Given that these courts were at the apex of a rigidly hierarchical colonial judicial system, few Africans or even colonists had opportunities to encounter them. The historical significance of these judicial institutions lies not so much in the depth of their influence but in the breadth of their influence as venues for adjudicating colonial difference across the Empire.

It is difficult to make definitive claims about the resulting balance between universalism and localism because of the changing dynamics of imperial rule—not least evident when local resistance to colonialism intensified in the twentieth century. Opposition to colonial rule, judicial opinions in London, and the regional centres of appellate justice developed over long periods of time. The relationship between English and African customary law and justice which this book captures, however, was shaped by the political changes that were occurring in Africa and in the British Empire more generally, from 1918 and gaining momentum after World War II. The vast majority of African appeals to the WACA and the JCPC came in the period between 1920 and 1950. The argument here is, therefore, not for a consciously insistent universalizing agenda on the part of imperial courts and judges, but rather for a more complex, and sometimes more fractured, universalism that was constantly tempered by overarching notions of colonial difference. In adjudicating colonial difference, Imperial Courts of Appeal constantly shifted between localism and universalist idealism. These shifts were determined as much by the judicial philosophies of imperial judges as they were by the exigencies of colonial governance.

Through judicial interpretations that continually shifted the boundaries between civil and the customary laws, imperial courts framed imperial citizenship and native difference. By doing so, they defined colonial social identities and shaped imperial encounters in varied ways. In many cases that came before the Imperial Courts of Appeal, colonial judges were called upon to interpret and rule on contested notions of colonial difference and competing assertions of imperial universalism. Taken together, the cases discussed in this book show the unstable and contested nature of colonial difference and the paradoxes of imperial legal universalism.

Imperial Justice and the Colonial Legal Order

The literature on the centrality of law and justice in European empire-building is rich and diverse, providing further discursive contexts for this study.[59] Studies in

[59] For a comprehensive review of some of the major works in this field, see Sally Engle Merry 'Law and Colonialism' (1991) 25(6) *Law and Society Review* 889–992.

law and colonialism have offered sophisticated theoretical interpretations of the nature of customary law, the dynamics of legal pluralism, and the kinds of transformations that the legal transplants of colonialism engender.[60] Many of these studies have explored the historical formation of colonial law and its fluid role in moments of transition and dispute.[61] Others have stressed the potential of the colonial legal systems to empower suppressed peoples by drawing attention to the flexible and adaptable nature of colonial law and justice.[62] Colonial law was both an instrument of domination and a site of resistance, struggles, and negotiations. Law was the primary tool for asserting imperial power abroad: the 'cutting edge of colonialism', crucial to the imperial 'civilising mission' and instrumental to justifying and legitimizing conquest and control.[63]

While coercion was often crucial for colonial conquests and expansions, law proved a more effective and enduring means of colonial administrative control.[64] European laws and legal institutions guaranteed the maintenance of social order on a scale conducive to colonial interests. In British Africa, colonial authorities sought to extend to the colonies (as far as was practicable) the same standards of law and justice as prevailed in England. The Gold Coast Supreme Court Ordinance of 1867, the first of the 'reception statutes' in British African Colonies, stipulated the enforcement of the Common Law, the Doctrines of Equity, and the Statutes of General Application that were practised in England on the date that the colony received its local legislature. Similarly, the Judicature Act, which introduced English law to East Africa in the late nineteenth century, obligated local courts to apply 'English Common Law, the doctrines of equity and the statutes of general application in force in England as at 12th August 1897' when English law officially took

[60] Merry, 'From Law and Colonialism to Law and Globalization', 69.

[61] For example, Sally Falk Moore, *Social Facts and Fabrications: 'Customary' Law on Kilimanjaro* (Cambridge: Cambridge University Press, 1986); Francis Snyder, *Capitalism and Legal Change: An African Transformation* (New York: Academic Press, 1981); and Ronen Shamir, *The Colonies of Law: Colonialism, Zionism and Law in Early Mandate Palestine* (Cambridge: Cambridge University Press, 2000).

[62] Alan Booth, 'European Courts Protect Women and Witches: Colonial Law Courts as Redistributors of Power in Swaziland 1920–1950' (1992) 18(2) *Journal of Southern African Studies* 253–75; Elizabeth Schmidt, 'Negotiated Spaces and Contested Terrain: Men, Women, and the Law in Colonial Zimbabwe, 1890–1939' (1990) 16(4) *Journal of Southern African Studies* 622–48; and Tapiwa Zimudzi, 'African Women, Violent Crime and the Criminal Law in Colonial Zimbabwe, 1900–1952' (2004) 30(3) *Journal of Southern African Studies* 499–517.

[63] See Martin Chanock, *Law, Custom, and Social Order: The Colonial Experience in Malawi and Zambia* (New York: Cambridge University Press, 1985) 4, and Merry, 'Law and Colonialism', 890.

[64] Several works have explored the use of law for colonial administrative control in Africa. See, for example, Richard Roberts and Kristin Mann, eds, *Law in Colonial Africa* (Portsmouth: Heinemann, 1991); Chanock, *Law, Custom and Social Order*; David Killingray, 'The Maintenance of Law and Order in British Colonial Africa' (1976) 85(340) *African Affairs* 411–37; Booth, 'European Courts Protect Women and Witches: Colonial Law Courts as Redistributors of Power in Swaziland 1920–1950' 253–75; Clement Ngongola, 'The State, Settlers, and Indigenes in the Evolution of Land Law and Policy in Colonial Malawi' (1990) 23(1) *The International Journal of African Historical Studies* 27–58; Inez Sutton, 'Law, Chieftaincy and Conflict in Colonial Ghana: The Ada Case' (1984) 83(330) *African Affairs* 41–62; and Benton, *Law and Colonial Cultures*.

effect in the colony.[65] However, as I point out later in this book, the vast majority of Africans came into no contact with the British courts where these rules were supposed to apply. Their matters were dealt with in native or customary tribunals.

Local customs and traditions were tolerated, however, and allowed to co-exist with the imported English legal system to the extent that they were not considered 'repugnant' to the law of England or vaguely defined principles of 'natural justice, equity and good conscience'.[66] Colonial courts were expected to enforce a curious blend of English common law principles, colonial statute law, and local African customary law within a framework of supposedly universal notions of morality and natural justice. While indigenous customary laws were tolerated, even accommodated within colonial legal systems, the ultimate goal was always to create some legal and judicial standards across the Empire that represented British ideals. The JCPC was a key agent in this task of judicial standardization by adjudicating questions of local law. It was involved more with interpreting colonial statutes and proclamations than with applying the general common law to the Empire. The diversity of legal systems in the Empire made this inevitable. For example, the local law of South Africa and Swaziland that the judges of the JCPC were called upon to interpret was not English common law but Roman-Dutch law. There was no ambition to export common law as a monolithic system. However, there was clearly an intention to uphold some common standards of judicial interpretation across the Empire founded on notions of British justice.[67]

Some of the earliest African appeals to the JCPC came from South Africa in the mid-nineteenth century, most of them commercial and land disputes involving European settlers and merchants. With the development of formal English-style legal systems in Africa in the early twentieth century, an increasing number of 'native' appeals from West Africa came before the Privy Council. Most of these appeals bordered on interpretations of local colonial statute law and on the validity of African customary laws. Many of the appeal cases suggest that, like local courts, imperial appeal courts were arenas where Africans and Europeans engaged one another; a battleground of sorts, on which they contested access to resources and labour, relationships of power and authority, and interpretations of morality and culture.[68] One of the aims of this book is to explore the role of the Privy Council not simply as a symbol of the hegemonic power of Empire but also as a contested

[65] 'Report of Legislative Council Debates', Colony and Protectorate of Kenya, LXXXVI, 1960, 384. Also see Momanyi Bwonwonga, *Procedures in Criminal Law in Kenya* (Nairobi: East African Publishers, 1994) 24.

[66] For a detailed discussion of the repugnancy doctrine in colonial law in Africa, see Bonny Ibhawoh, 'Stronger than the Maxim Gun: Law, Human Rights and British Colonial Hegemony in Nigeria' (2002) 72(1) *Africa: Journal of the International African Institute* 55–83.

[67] Roman-Dutch law as practised in South Africa was substantially influenced by English law after the British occupation of the Cape in 1806. In the South African case of *Estate Welsford v Estate Wright,* the presiding judge stated that he was constrained by the principle of precedence to follow an earlier judgment of the JCPC in a Roman-Dutch question of law that he thought was decidedly more in accordance with English Common Law than Roman-Dutch law, which the JCPC should have applied. *Estate Welsford v Estate Wright* [1930] Orange Free State Provincial Division 162 at 166, Appeals to the Privy Council, Internal Memorandum, Office of the Governor General, NASAP, GG 1845 53/592.

[68] Roberts, *Law in Colonial Africa,* 3.

terrain beyond the direct influence of colonial officialdom, where various groups of Africans, Europeans, and other settlers confronted each other in ways that shaped judicial governance in both colony and metropole. The symbolic role of the JCPC as both an advisory body to the Crown and the highest court in the Empire rendered it a privileged space, where powerful discourses of resistance could be expressed.

Nineteenth-century appeals from Africa adjudicated by the JCPC came predominantly from the Vice-Admiralty Courts of Sierra Leone that were charged with the suppression of the West African slave trade. Many of these cases, some dating back to the early nineteenth century, were petitions against the judgments issued of the Admiralty Courts brought by European merchants whose vessels had been seized under Britain's 1807 Act abolishing the Slave Trade. The work of the British Vice-Admiralty Courts foreshadowed the work of the JCPC in Africa. British Vice-Admiralty Courts mediated between international law and wartime diplomacy dealing with politically sensitive legal questions that stemmed from disputes over the international rights of maritime transport and trade. As with the JCPC, the judges of the court had to be politically astute, legally versatile, and eclectic in their judicial methods. They had to be proficient in English Common Law, Civil Law, and the Law of Nations, all the while bearing in mind the impact of their decisions on international military and diplomatic affairs.[69]

From the 1890s on, indigenous Africans began to take appeals to the JCPC. A large number of appeals came from West Africa in the 1920s and 1930s, as members of an emergent African intelligentsia began to play active roles as lawyers, clerks, interpreters, and assessors in colonial legal systems. Commercial activities in the new coastal cities of Freetown, Accra, and Lagos provided fertile ground for civil and criminal suits, some of which were appealed to the JCPC. In the white settler colonies of Eastern and Southern Africa, however, where the most extreme and explicit racial barriers to entry into the legal profession were erected, only very few indigenous lawyers practiced during this period.[70] This scarcity of local legal professionals had a direct impact on the number of indigenous appeals brought to the JCPC from these parts of the continent in the early twentieth century. At least 70 per cent of all appeals to the JCPC brought by Africans came from West Africa.[71] Nevertheless, the cases discussed in this book offer a geographically balanced view of African appeals to the JCPC.

The choice of legal cases discussed in this book is informed partly by the need to examine, for comparative purposes, African appeals from both settler and non-settler colonies where perceptions about the Privy Council were quite different. In West Africa, traditional and Western-educated indigenous elites saw the JCPC as

[69] Tara Helfman, 'The Court of Vice Admiralty at Sierra Leone and the Abolition of the West African Slave Trade' (2006) 115 *Yale Law Journal* 1126.

[70] Martin Chanock's work on the Cape Colony (now South Africa) documents the Transvaal Law Society's successful moves to keep non-white lawyers out of the profession in the first two decades of the twentieth century. Chanock, *The Making of South African Legal Culture* (Cambridge: Cambridge University Press, 2001).

[71] This is based on data from the records of the JCPC and Privy Council law reports.

the Empire's ultimate court, where they could stake competing legal claims and challenge local colonial authorities. In the settler colonies of East Africa, most Africans saw the JCPC as a 'white man's court' where the African could rarely afford to get justice. In Kenya, for example, Africans were concerned that the jurisprudence of the Privy Council reinforced legislation of segregation, and that the JCPC catered primarily to the immigrant communities who regarded English law as their law.[72] This perception was also largely true of Southern Africa, though interestingly less so in the High Commission Territories of Bechuanaland, Basutoland, and Swaziland, which produced disproportionally large numbers of 'native' appeals to the Privy Council. Generally, however, among traditional and *nouveau* elite Africans, the JCPC was viewed as an important institution of legal recourse beyond the direct influence of colonial officialdom, where imperial justice could be sought and received.

Scope and Method

Colonial legal re-ordering was fundamentally concerned with transforming the colonized society to conform to that of the colonizer. This process typically involved the large-scale transfer of laws and legal institutions from one society to another, each of which had its own distinct socio-cultural organization and legal culture. In Africa, the result of this process was a dual legal system: one for the colonized and another for the colonizers. The formal transplant of legal jurisdiction from metropolitan centres to the colonies created clear political and cultural power-infused dualities between the colonizer and the colonized, by casting only one as the possessor and interpreter of law and civility.[73] The colonizing authorities well understood that the structures of legal authorities and the creation of cultural hierarchies were inextricably interlinked. The essential inequalities of power in the colonial order should not be discounted or minimized in the quest to unravel the tentativeness of colonial law and justice. The arguments offered in this book regarding contestation and negotiation in the adjudication of colonial difference do not ignore or deny the real structural inequities of imperial power and the subordinated dualities they produced within the colonial state.

This book moves beyond what has been described as the 'sterile' and 'tendentious' debate between 'celebratory and accusatory histories of the Empire'.[74] It explores the history of African engagement with the colonial Courts of Appeal both in the context of hegemonic imperial power and in terms of the position of these

[72] Y. P. Ghai and J. P. MacAuslan, *Public Law and Political Change in Kenya* (Nairobi: Oxford University Press, 1970) 172.

[73] Benton, *Law and Colonial Cultures*, 12.

[74] Martin Wiener, *An Empire on Trial: Race, Murder, and Justice under British Rule, 1870–1935* (New York: Cambridge University Press, 2009) viii.

courts as spaces for contestations beyond the direct purview of the colonial state.[75] Additionally, it draws attention not only to the role of these judicial institutions in Africa, but also to the reciprocal place of the colonized peoples who played a formative role in shaping the development of these institutions and, ultimately, the imperial legal culture. The larger argument here is that colonialism was as much involved in the making of the metropole and the identities and ideologies of the colonizers, as it was in re-making its peripheries and colonial subjects.[76]

The circulation of persons and knowledge within the Empire not only transformed the colony and post-colony, but also altered the metropole. Legal knowledge was not exclusively transferred in linear patterns to and from the centres and peripheries, but rather took more unpredictable routes travelling throughout the Empire. The JCPC was pivotal in this process. Although it was a court of colonial appeal, it was also a valid (albeit non-binding) source of precedents for British domestic courts, serving to channel imperial legal experiences into the shaping of law and legal practice in Britain itself.[77] The story of how African encounters with colonial institutions resonated in the metropole and elsewhere in the Empire is an important one that this book tells. Relating this story is made all the more necessary by the fact that available studies of the JCPC have focused almost exclusively on the 'old Empire'—the Dominions of Canada, Australia, New Zealand, and the Irish Free States.[78] By contrast, the histories of the JCPC in India and Africa have received significantly less attention, despite recognition by legal scholars that judicial precedents set by the Privy Council cases from the 'tropical colonies' influenced imperial jurisprudence on such issues as colonial treaty rights, aboriginal land title, and validity of customary laws.[79] Part of the goal here, therefore, is to tilt the balance in the scholarship of the JCPC toward the non-Western World.

My methodology focuses on selected landmark cases rather than a multiplicity of cases. The cases discussed in this book are by no means representative of the vast variety of civil and criminal appeals from African jurisdictions heard by the JCPC and by the regional appeal courts in over half a century. Given the book's focus on universalism and localism, emphasis has been placed on cases that epitomize the

[75] This approach to the study of colonial law in Africa is evident in Elizabeth Schmidt, 'Negotiated Spaces and Contested Terrain: Men, Women, and the Law in Colonial Zimbabwe, 1890–1939' (1990) 16(4) *Journal of Southern African Studies* 622–48.

[76] For example, Shula Marks has argued that daily life in Britain—from diet to industrial discipline, from sexual mores to notions of governance—was permeated by experiences of 'empire'. Ana Davin has also shown how the imperial project created fears of race degeneration in Britain, leading to eugenic policies and changing attitudes towards the role of women in British public life. Shula Marks, 'History, the Nation and Empire: Sniping from the Periphery' (1990) 29 *History Workshop Journal* 115; Ana Davin, 'Imperialism and Womanhood', *Tensions of Empire: Colonial Cultures in a Bourgeois World*, eds Frederick Cooper and Ann Stoler (Berkeley: University of California Press, 1997) 131–5.

[77] Nandini Chatterjee et al, 'Judging Empire: The Global Reach of the Judicial Committee of the Privy Council', online: <http://www.plymouth.ac.uk/pages/view.asp?page=32920>.

[78] The JCPC's role in the development of the case law of Canada, Australia, and New Zealand has received much scholarly attention. David Swinfen, *Imperial Appeal: The Debate on the Appeal to the Privy Council, 1833–1986* (Manchester: Manchester University Press, 1987) and Richard Risk, *The Privy Council and its Scholars* (Manitoba: Canadian Legal History Project, University of Manitoba, 1992).

[79] Swinfen, *Imperial Appeal*, 36.

tensions between imported English law and indigenous customary laws. Such cases show how customary laws were invoked by litigants and interpreted by appellate judges. They also demonstrate the process of judicial incorporation and restriction of indigenous customary practices. They involve legal debates over the validity and repugnancy of African customary laws, disputes over land title and customary tenure systems, and the interpretation of statute laws and criminal procedures relating to the natives. Beyond their legal significance, these cases also had important socio-economic and political ramifications, which are most evident in high-profile cases that generated wide public interest and discussions. The need to capture these broader ramifications, rather than the quest for the dramatic or sensational, informed the selection of cases discussed in this book.

Accounts of cases heard by the JCPC, the WACA, and the EACA are available in a number of overlapping Law Reports which provide a valuable starting point for this study. Their limitations for historical research are obvious. They are selected to elucidate legal technicalities and precedential significance. The main consideration in determining which cases are reported and how they are reported is the precedential value of each case and the relevance of the judgment to lawyers and judges in future cases. These factors are less relevant to the historian, however, who must read these reports with an eye for language and context as well as patterns of change and continuity. In this study, Law Reports provided the foundation for archival research. They offered insights into legal debates and afforded a means of measuring—through citation analysis—the precedential value of appeal court decisions in African cases. For a more detailed and nuanced record of JCPC cases, however, I turned to the archives.

Colonial archives offered more information on legal cases. The African archives, where most of the research was undertaken, offered detailed administrative and legal records of Privy Council appeals.[80] The existence of these detailed records in itself indicates the significance of the JCPC in colonial legal history. For local colonial authorities, the spectre of natives taking legal appeals to the Privy Council in London was a very serious matter. Successful appeals leading to the reversal of local executive and judicial decisions were considered damaging to the prestige and authority of the government. For this reason, officials paid great attention to Privy Council cases, particularly those involving the government. Extant archival records include detailed court records, case files kept by legal officers (typically the Office of the Attorney General), and administrative files containing official circulars, memorandums, and newspaper clippings relating to Privy Council appeals.

The underexplored but rich records of the JCPC itself provided an appropriate archival base for this study. Privy Council procedures required that complete sets of printed records be produced for every case. These records designated 'Printed Papers in Appeal' included valuable details: cases for the appellant and respondent (as framed by their solicitors) and the record of proceedings from the first court of hearing upwards, including depositions, affidavits, and all submitted exhibits.

[80] The archives referred to here are the national archives of the UK, South Africa, Kenya, Tanzania, Nigeria, and Ghana.

The documents, which ran anywhere from 150 to 800 printed pages, were bound into several volumes.[81] These wide-ranging documents offered multiple and sometimes conflicting perspectives. With verbatim transcripts of JCPC proceedings, it was sometimes possible to map 'case genealogies' by following court accounts as cases progressed from local courts, through the regional appeal courts to the Privy Council. These records, which at the time of researching this book were stored in the dusty basement of the JCPC office in Downing Street, proved to be an invaluable source of information on appellate judicial processes and discourses on 'native appeals'.[82]

Despite their merit in the amount of detail they offer, court records also do not tell the whole story. They are often 'cold' documents that do not convey the atmosphere in the courtroom or the demeanour of litigants and witnesses—factors that invariably influence the outcome of cases. As one historian explains, 'We cannot hear the hesitation or inflection, or see the down cast eyes, nor do we receive any real sense of the ambience of the court room'.[83] Court records also do not reveal much about the context of the case. Why were certain cases appealed all the way to the Privy Council, while similar cases were not? What local conditions in the colonies influenced decisions to launch appeals? How did litigants and the public react to court decisions? How did these decisions affect colonial policies on the ground? Answering these questions requires going beyond the archives to excavate accounts of cases in the public domain through local newspapers, personal memoirs, and oral histories. Legal contests are in many ways social and political theatre. Privy Council appeals in particular were often complicated, long-drawn, high-stakes disputes that drew public interest and media coverage. In this book, I attempt to place the legal appeals in the social and political contexts from which they emerged. Where possible, I have drawn on popular public accounts to complement court and archival records.

I recognize the limitations of attempting to reconstruct processes of social control and interaction through a narrow and limited arena of public life, even one as crucial as appeal courts. African litigants who came before colonial courts had a collective history before their appearance in court and these relationships often persisted long after court judgments. Such social encounters that stretch beyond formal legal arenas are essential to our understanding of the engagement between the colonized peoples with the imperial law and justice. I provide social and political context for the cases discussed, but I have not primarily focused on encounters beyond the courtroom.

The story of the Imperial Appeal Courts in Africa is invariably also the story of the judges who staffed these courts, the litigants who brought appeals to the courts, and the lawyers who represented them. Indeed, it is impossible to fully understand

[81] Nandini Chatterjee et al, 'Judging Empire'.

[82] For most of its history, the records of the JCPC were considered working documents and stored at the JCPC office. Some of these records were transferred to the National Archives in 2010.

[83] Richard Rathbone, 'A Murder in the Colonial Gold Coast: Law and Politics in the 1940s' (1989) 30(3) *The Journal of African History* 450.

the cases adjudicated in the imperial Courts and the judicial and public debates they engendered without also examining the lives and personalities behind these cases. The life histories of pioneering indigenous West African lawyers who travelled from the colonies to represent clients at the JCPC in London, for example, provide fascinating insight into personal encounters with imperial justice. A close scrutiny of the network of British barristers and solicitors, who took up criminal appeals *in forma pauperis* on behalf of indigent African litigants, is similarly revealing. While these life stories offer interesting lines of inquiry, they are beyond the scope of this book. Even so, these important personal perspectives are not completely ignored here, since many of the cases discussed are framed around key historical personalities. One such personality is Richard Burdon Haldane (Lord Haldane), the British lawyer, judge, and Liberal politician who, in his long career as a JCPC judge, adjudicated many African appeals. Another historical personality that anchors the narrative in this book is Eshugbayi Eleko, the African Chief who brought successive appeals before the JCPC in the 1930s to challenge his deposition and deportation by the colonial authorities in Nigeria.[84]

Finally, a note on terminology. For the purposes of narrative coherence, I refer to the JCPC and the regional appeal courts—the WACA and the EACA—collectively as the Imperial Appeal Courts. I also make a distinction between the 'imperial judges' who staffed the appellate courts and 'colonial judges' of the lower courts in the colonies. Historically, these categories were not mutually exclusive, as colonial judges were often promoted or seconded to the JCPC. The distinction here is largely for the purposes of clarity.

Although often referred to as the highest Court of Appeal in the British Empire, the JCPC was technically not a court. It served more or less as an advisory board (one of many), which constituted the Privy Council as a body of advisors to the British Sovereign. Unlike regular courts, the JCPC did not pass a judgment or a verdict after hearing an appeal, but sent a report to the Sovereign, recommending that the appeal be allowed or denied. Most members of the JCPC were Law Lords occupying high judicial office in the United Kingdom, hence the reference in this book to the 'Lords' and 'Judges' of the Privy Council. This also explains the occasional reference to the JCPC as a 'Board' or 'Committee'. I use the terms 'Privy Council' and 'Judicial Committee of the Privy Council' (JCPC) interchangeably. 'Privy Council' is used broadly in reference to Crown advisory duties, while 'JCPC' in specific reference to the adjudicatory work of the Judicial Committee.

I use the term 'indigenous people' and 'natives' interchangeably in this book. I use the term 'native', keenly aware of the ethnocentric connotations that it implied in colonial contexts. In colonial discourse, the term as applied to indigenous people often assumed a disparaging and paternalistic sense. Sometimes, I have used the term precisely for that reason—to capture the pejorative and patronizing

[84] *Eshugbayi Eleko v Officer Administering the Government of Nigeria* [1931] AC 652; Judicial Committee of the Privy Council, *Printed Papers in Appeal* (hereinafter JCPC PPA), Vol 24 (1928) and Vol 26 (1931).

undertones of colonial legal and judicial discourse. At other times, I have used the term as a neutral descriptive expression.

The organization of this book is both thematic and chronological. Cases are discussed in order of relevance to the thematic focus of each chapter rather than strictly chronologically. Within each chapter, thematic, geographical, and chronological considerations guide the discussion. Chapter 2 traces the historical development of the JCPC, the WACA, and the EACA. Given the JCPC's dual role as Crown Advisory Board and Imperial Court, its structure and appeal procedures differed in many ways from the practices and procedures of regular courts. Understanding the broader political and juridical framework within which the JCPC operated is essential to our understanding of its imperial role. The chapter also explores the nature and scope of African appeals that came before these courts.

Chapter 3 examines the ambivalent place of African customary law in the colonial legal system, the tensions arising from conflicting systems of laws, and the role of the Imperial Appeal Courts in interpreting and applying customary law. It also explores the contested judicial discourse over the doctrine of repugnancy and the role of 'native assessors' in the colonial legal system. It focuses on the tensions arising from the fluid interpretations of the judicial role of African judicial assessors (preferred by local colonial administrators) and the more rigid definitions embraced by the metropolitan judges.

Chapter 4 studies the adjudication of criminal appeals at the Privy Council and its implications for our understanding of the homogenizing and universalizing character of colonial legal culture. 'Medicine murder' cases and debates over African 'blood money' customs provide contexts for exploring the paradox of imperial universalism and local exceptionalism in the administration of criminal justice. They show that even in the improbable realm of criminal justice, Britain's African colonies were laboratories for legal experimentation, the assertion of imperial universalism, and the production of difference.

Chapter 5 examines the place of Imperial Appeal Courts in the political and economic struggles of the late colonial period. Focusing on legal disputes over land title, native customary rights, and chieftainship authority, it considers how the appellate judicial process both enhanced and circumscribed political power in the colonial state. Finally, Chapter 6 examines the legal and political circumstances leading to the end of Privy Council appeals in Africa and the demise of the regional Appeal Courts. It also explores the relevance of the JCPC and its jurisprudence to our understanding of the emerging trends in transnational justice and supranational adjudication.

2

The Great Chief Overseas

In the first half of the twentieth century, a debate raged within British colonial officialdom over the need for a court of appeal for the entire British Empire. This topic dominated discussions at the Imperial Conferences of 1911 and 1927, and it shaped the events leading up to the 1931 Statute of Westminster. At a time when dominion governments were keen to remove the remaining vestiges of colonial status, the relevance of the JCPC became a disputed issue. Opinions were sharply divided. To many commentators in London and the colonies, the JCPC was indispensable because it provided the 'link of Empire'; the central connector between the distant constituents of the British Empire. It was a symbol of enlightened association based on Common Law, without which the Empire would be less effective. To others, however, the JCPC was seen as a symbol of outdated imperialism.[1] From Canada to Australia, from Ceylon to South Africa, administrators, judges, the press, and ordinary citizens weighed in on the subject of the relevance and legitimacy of imperial appeal courts.

In South Africa, the debate took a particularly partisan, even acrimonious turn. Members of the Afrikaner-dominated National Party, harbouring deep suspicion of British institutions, moved a motion in the House of Assembly in 1937 to abolish South Africans' right to appeal to the Privy Council in London. They argued that the South African Supreme Court was the most suitable and competent court to give final judgment in cases relating to the South African law. They also thought that the right to appeal to the Privy Council conflicted with the sovereign and independent status of the South African Union and, as one parliamentarian put it, was 'an undeserved slur on South African Judges'.[2] Pointing to Ireland, which had abolished appeals to the Privy Council, critics claimed that it was anomalous for a sovereign independent state to subject its own tribunals to the over-ruling jurisdiction of another state's court with no control over the constitution it was adjudicating. The fact that such 'judicial subjugation' was voluntary and could be terminated at any time did not, in their view, remove the anomaly.[3]

The pro-British Dominion Party countered this argument. Its leader and a staunch anglophile, Col. C. F. Stallard, deplored the bill as an attempt to sever

[1] David Swinfen, *Imperial Appeal: The Debate on the Appeal to the Privy Council, 1833–1986* (Manchester: Manchester University Press, 1987) 17.

[2] Parliamentary comments by C. R. Swart, *Daily Telegraph* (16 January 1937) 4.

[3] 'Privy Council Acts: Imperial Judicial Committee', National Archives of South Africa, Pretoria (hereinafter NASAP) GG 1845 53/592.

one of the last remaining links with Britain and break the unity in the administration of justice in the Empire.[4] The Privy Council, he argued, was ideal for South Africa, since there was no tribunal in the world capable of giving better judgment than the Judicial Committee. An appeal to the Privy Council, Stallard reminded his parliamentary colleagues, was more than simply a legal petition. It was an appeal to the King in Council, and it was a serious thing to deprive citizens of the Commonwealth, anywhere in the Empire, of the ultimate right of appeal to the Sovereign. He invoked Canada and Australia, which at the time had chosen to maintain the right of appeal to the Privy Council, as examples.[5]

It took the intervention of General Smuts, then Deputy Prime Minister, to calm the growing tension. Smuts admitted that the Privy Council sitting in London was not the ideal body to hear South African appeals, due to its distance, cost of appealing, and the lack of experience of its members in Roman-Dutch law. As long as the Nationalists and Dominionites exploited the issue for political purposes, however, his government would maintain the status quo.[6] An astute politician, Smuts was keenly aware that, in reality, the frenzied arguments over the right of appeal to the Privy Council reflected imperial and local politics, rather than a concern for law and justice. Actual legal appeals to the Privy Council from South Africa had been rare. Between 1920 and 1933 only ten Privy Council appeals from South Africa appeared, none of them particularly significant.[7]

For the Nationalists, the debate over abolishing the right of appeal to the Privy Council was a proxy cause for their longstanding opposition to British influence in South Africa. For the Dominionites, the right of appeal to the Privy Council was a crucial symbol of British imperial power and authority they sought to maintain in the Union. For the fragile 'grand coalition' government of Prime Minister Hertzog caught in the middle, the main concern was that the abolition of appeals to the Privy Council would hamper the possible incorporation into the Union of South Africa of Basutoland, Bechuanaland, and Swaziland that was being negotiated at the time with Britain.[8] In South Africa, as in many other parts of the Empire, the JCPC was more than an imperial court of appeal; it was also a lightning rod for local political battles over the scope of British imperial authority.

While politicians and administrators were divided over the utility of an imperial court of appeal, most judicial officers and legal practitioners in South Africa were convinced of its value. Writing in 1901, the Chief Judge of the Cape Colony Lord de Villiers argued passionately for the retention of an imperial court of appeal that would be a 'firm link in the chain which binds the colonies to the mother country'.[9] His colleague, Judge Innes, made an even stronger case when he stated:

[4] 'Privy Council Acts', NASAP, GG 1845 53/592.

[5] Canada abolished criminal appeals to the Privy Council in 1933 and civil appeals in 1949.

[6] *Daily Telegraph* (16 January 1937) 4.

[7] Memorandum from T. E. Water, South Africa's High Commissioner in London, to Prime Minister Hertzog, 1933, NASAP, BLO 88 PS 3/3, 1933–1937.

[8] 'Privy Council Acts', NASAP, GG 1845 53/592.

[9] Martin Chanock, *The Making of South African Legal Culture 1902–1936: Fear, Favour and Prejudice* (Cambridge: Cambridge University Press, 2001) 38.

> We want a direct appeal to the Crown's person because we think that the prerogative of the Crown, the influence of the Crown, the prestige of the Crown, is a very important factor in binding the Empire together.... I think it is valuable that the appeal should be to the Sovereign. There are many important questions involving land, areas of land, native reserves, the right of those which come before the Supreme Court. We think it very important that we should sometimes be able to tell a native Chief, that in addition to his appealing to three impartial Judges in Cape Town, he can go to *the Great Chief over the sea* and be protected.[10]

Justice Innes' views are significant because they exemplify a recurring theme in colonial political rhetoric, namely the manipulation of the aura of authority of the monarchy in securing native acceptance of colonial power.[11] The imagery of Africans bringing disputes before local Chiefs in the native tribunals, petitioning colonial officials and ultimately appealing to the 'Great Chief' overseas was a powerful one which, as the subsequent chapters of this book show, came to define the place of the Privy Council and the regional Courts of Appeal in Africa.

Impassioned debates about the relevance and legitimacy of the JCPC were not limited to South Africa or the old dominions. In the tropical colonies of Africa, where the demand for judicial autonomy was less prominent in the early twentieth century, there were similar disagreements over the imperial role of the Privy Council. Many considered the JCPC more than just another colonial institution; it represented the very essence of the Empire. To the natives who could afford to take their appeals there, the JCPC and the regional Courts of Appeal symbolized the pinnacle of British justice. Because of their place at the top of the colonial judicial hierarchy and the precedential value of their judgments, these courts were important sites where Africans encountered British justice. The physical location of the JCPC at the seat of imperial power—beyond the direct purview and influence of local colonial authorities—also made it a powerful symbol of the detached impartiality of British justice. Even though few African litigants ever had the resources or opportunity to appeal to the Great Chief overseas, knowing that this was theoretically possible provided reassurance in the colonial legal system.

This chapter examines the origins and historical evolution of the Imperial Appeal Courts: the JCPC, the WACA, and the EACA. It analyses their organizational structures and judicial procedures. The goal here is not to provide detailed accounts of the histories of these courts, but rather to offer an analysis of the imperial imperatives that drove their formation, and the conditions in the colonies that shaped their evolution. The chapter also broadly explores the ways in which African litigants engaged with these courts and, in the case of the JCPC, how official discourse regarding these imperial courts formed an integral part of the wider debate on imperial judicial governance. Understanding how and why the JCPC became so central to the administration of justice in the colonies and to the debates over identity politics requires an excursion into its origins in the early nineteenth century.

[10] Colonial Office, Confidential Prints Miscellaneous, 138: 9–10. Quoted in Chanock, *The Making of South African Legal Culture*, 39. My emphasis.

[11] Chanock, *The Making of South African Legal Culture*, 38.

An Appeal Court for the Empire

The origins of the modern JCPC date to 1833, when the British parliament passed the Judicial Committee Act as part of a broader reform of the Privy Council. The Act directed the hearing of Crown appeals to the newly formed Judicial Committee; this had been the responsibility of the Privy Council's Appeals Committee since the seventeenth century. The new JCPC's original jurisdiction derived from a customary practice of the Norman monarchs (medieval *Curia Regis*), according to which the English Crown was advised by a royal court consisting of magnates, ecclesiastics, and high officials. Subjects bearing grievances against the administration of justice by baronial and other subordinate judicial authorities were permitted to petition the Crown in Council.[12] This practice was founded on the premise that the King was the fountain of all justice throughout his dominions, and exercised judicial powers through the Privy Council acting as an advisory body of the Crown.[13] By the nineteenth century, the Privy Council came to represent British constitutional monarchism and became a symbol of the power and influence of British aristocratic principles and traditions.[14]

Although the Privy Council historically concerned itself with advising the Crown on domestic legislation and the administration of justice, growing ties between Britain and the settlements in the New World saw an expansion of this role, as an increasing number of appeals to the Crown came from the plantations and colonies. Some scholars have suggested that without the uniformity of colonial law forged by the Privy Council's judicial review in the period prior to the eighteenth century, the thirteen American colonies might never have felt a collective will to fight their revolution and remain united.[15]

By the mid-nineteenth century, it became necessary to reform and standardize the system of appeals to the Crown through the Council. The Judicial Committee Act of 1833, which formally established the JCPC, was the outcome of a protracted reform process aimed at making the old Appeals Committee of the Privy Council more efficient and relevant to the administration of appellate justice as the British Empire expanded eastwards. By the terms of the Act, the JCPC became the final court of appeal for non-domestic jurisdictions and other judicial matters not handled by existing domestic courts. Until the enactment of the Statute of Westminster in 1931, which enabled colonial dominions to assert more autonomy and discontinue appeals, the JCPC was the final court of appeal for more than a quarter

[12] P. A. Howell, *The Judicial Committee of the Privy Council 1833–1876: Its Origins, Structure, and Development* (Cambridge: Cambridge University Press, 1986) 3.

[13] Norman De Mattos Bentwich, *The Practice of the Privy Council in Judicial Matters: In Appeals from Courts of Civil, Criminal, and Admiralty Jurisdiction and in Appeals from Ecclesiastical and Prize Courts, with the Statutes, Rules and Forms of Procedure* (London: Sweet & Maxwell, 1926) 1.

[14] Almeric William Fitz Roy, *The History of the Privy Council* (London: John Murray, 1928) 285.

[15] Loren P. Beth, 'The Judicial Committee of the Privy Council and the Development of Judicial Review' (1976) 24(1) *The American Journal of Comparative Law* 42.

of the world.[16] It made final rulings and interpretations on a vast variety of laws across the Empire-Commonwealth, including Roman-Dutch law from South Africa, British Guyana, and Salome; Spanish law from Trinidad; pre-revolutionary French law from Quebec; the Napoleonic Code from Mauritius; Sardinian law from Malta; Venetian law from the Ionian islands; medieval Norman law from the Channel Islands; Muslim, Buddhist, and Hindu law from India; Ottoman law from Turkey, Cyprus, and Egypt; Chinese law from British courts in Shanghai; and diverse indigenous customary laws from across Africa.

The responsibility of the JCPC in interpreting and ruling on a wide variety of laws from across the Empire was one that its judges took seriously. Lord Watson, a long-serving judge of the JCPC, was extolled for his acumen in interpreting laws according to the spirit of the jurisprudence from which an appeal came. 'If it was a Cape appeal from South Africa, he was a Roman-Dutch lawyer; if it was an Indian case of adoption, he entered into the religious reasons for the rule to be applied; if it was a Quebec case of substitution under the old French code, or a Jersey appeal about the customs of Normandy, it was just the same.'[17] This eclectic approach to judicial governance was considered crucial to the work of this 'court of last resort' in the British Empire. The judges who served on the JCPC had to be 'jacks of all trades' and masters of all, adept at adjudicating wide-ranging legal disputes from across an Empire that was rapidly expanding and encompassed peoples with unfamiliar legal cultures. These judges circled the world on promotion within one legal service; their precedents were imperial. Unfamiliarity with local ruling culture was deemed to be a strength and a shield of impartial judgment that relied not on someone who knew the people and their ways but on objective evidence proven in court.[18]

A central figure in the creation of the JCPC was the liberal statesman and Lord Chancellor of Britain, Henry Brougham, who became famous for his unrelenting fight against the slave trade, among his other achievements. As Lord Chancellor from 1830 to 1834, Brougham initiated several domestic and colonial legal reforms aimed at speeding up judicial governance and ensuring more uniform standards in the administration of justice in the British Empire. The highlights of Brougham's tenure as Lord Chancellor included the passing of the 1832 Reform Act, which introduced wide-ranging changes to the British electoral system, and the Slavery Abolition Act of 1833 that he staunchly supported as well.

It is no coincidence that the Judicial Committee Act of 1833 establishing the JCPC was passed in the same year as the Slavery Abolition Act, which provided for the emancipation of slaves in England and its colonies. Both landmark legislations were the defining outcomes of Brougham's reformist agenda. An eloquent and passionate abolitionist, Brougham described the slave trade as 'a trade of iniquity

[16] Paul Magrath, 'British Justice International Plc?' (2003) 3 *Incorporated Council for Law Reporting Newsletter* 4.

[17] R. B. Haldane, 'Lord Watson' (1899) 9 *Juridical Review* 279.

[18] John Lonsdale, 'Kenyatta's Trials: Breaking and Making an African Nationalist', in Peter Coss, ed, *The Moral World of the Law* (London: Oxford, 2000) 200.

and shame', and charged his fellow Britons with being the 'ringleaders in the crime'.[19] After it was revealed in 1838 that the emancipation of slaves was being obstructed in the British colonies, Brougham famously stated in the House of Lords: 'The slave . . . is as fit for his freedom as any English peasant or any Lord whom I now address. I demand his rights; I demand his liberty without stint . . . I demand that your brother be no longer trampled upon as your slave.'[20]

Besides his anti-slavery advocacy, Brougham's campaigns for humanitarian causes included legal reforms relating to the freedom of speech and of the press; universal public education; women's rights; rights for Catholics, Jews, and the Irish; law and court reform; and the outlawing of corporal punishment. The vehemence of his advocacy won him admiration in the Whig party but made him the scourge of the Tories.[21] One contemporary described Brougham as the 'greatest law reformer of his time',[22] while another claims that he 'accomplished nothing as a statesman'.[23]

It is Brougham's passionate advocacy for legal reforms that concerns this book. In 1828, he introduced a comprehensive scheme of law reform in the House of Commons, exposing defects in the administration of justice in Britain and in the colonies. In a characteristically lengthy speech before the House of Commons, he argued that English law had become 'the patrimony of the rich . . . the two-edged sword of craft and oppression', where it ought to be 'the inheritance of the poor and the shield of innocence'.[24] Part of Brougham's remarks focused on the old Privy Council's Appeals Committee. Having acquired regular practice before the Committee in his early career as a barrister, he was well placed to speak about the Committee's limitations and potentials in a way that commanded the attention of his peers.

Brougham believed that the Privy Council's Appeal Committee, as then constituted, did not adequately meet the judicial governance needs of an expanding British Empire. Delays in the dispensation of justice and the long back-log of cases before the Committee were his principal concerns. Because of the distance of most colonies, the great variety of their legal systems, and the unfamiliarity of English judges with these systems, Brougham thought that any judicial tribunal in England was an extremely inadequate court of review. Distance, Brougham argued, was an unavoidable reality of the Empire, but more could be done to mitigate the adverse effects on the Privy Council's judicial work.[25] He urged the parliament to remove

[19] Chester William New, *The Life of Henry Brougham to 1830, Vol 1* (London: Clarendon Press, 1961) 24.

[20] Baron Henry Brougham and Vaux, *Lord Brougham's Speeches in 1837 & 1838* (London: Ridgway, 1837) 49.

[21] Howell, *The Judicial Committee of the Privy Council*, 14.

[22] John McGilchrist, *The Life and Career of Henry, Lord Brougham* (London: Cassell, Petter & Galpin, 1868) 138.

[23] John Campbell, *Lives of Lord Lyndhurst and Lord Brougham: Lord Chancellors and Keepers of the Great Seal of England* (London: John Murray, 1869) 214.

[24] 'Speech of Henry Brougham in the House of Commons on February 7, 1828' (1928) 2 *The Jurists: Quarterly Journal of Jurisprudence and Legislation* 6.

[25] Henry Brougham, *Speeches of Henry Lord Brougham upon Questions relating to Public Rights, Duties, and Interests* (Edinburgh: A & C Black, 1838) 537.

every unnecessary obstacle to the 'right judgment', and to provide a system that better guaranteed the British subjects' access to justice in the Empire's court of last resort.

Typical of his unconventional position on many of the issues of his day, Brougham was particularly critical of the composition of the Privy Council's Appeals Committee: it comprised councillors without legal training who had won their rank through diplomatic or parliamentary careers. Brougham considered the idea of political careerists serving as judges to be uncharacteristic of the British legal tradition. English judges handling colonial appeals, he argued, should be the most learned and experienced judges available; they should be men of the 'largest legal and general information, accustomed to study other systems of law beside those of England and associated with lawyers who have practised and presided in the colonial courts'.[26] In order to redress the difficulties of delay and cost that had characterized the old Privy Council's Appeals Committee (sitting for only nine days annually), Brougham proposed a reconstituted 'Court of Review' that would sit frequently to adjudicate colonial appeals expeditiously.[27] Membership of the new tribunal would be determined not by status or privilege but by legal training and judicial experience. Brougham argued that such a system would engender confidence in the Privy Council, enforce uniform standards of justice, and subsequently strengthen the bonds between Britain and her Empire as among the Empire's colonies.[28]

These proposals took effect in 1833, when Brougham as Lord Chancellor introduced the precursor to the Judicial Committee Act, entitled 'A Bill for the Better Administration of Justice in His Majesty's Privy Council'. Under the statute, the new tribunal consisted of all Privy Councillors who held certain senior judicial positions, including the Lord Chancellor, Chief Justice of the Court of King's Bench, Master of the Rolls, and the Chief Judges of other superior courts in Britain. The Crown could appoint two additional Councillors with legal training to the Committee, also retaining the prerogative to appoint anyone to the Privy Council and, subsequently, to the Judicial Committee.[29]

The Judicial Committee Act of 1833 significantly extended the jurisdiction and imperial influence of the Privy Council. Apart from transferring the entire appellate jurisdiction of the King in Council to the Judicial Committee, it provided that all appeals relating to law, statute, or custom brought before the King in Council regarding any sentence, rule, or court order must be referred to the Committee. The reconstituted Judicial Committee acquired jurisdiction in appeals from the forty-four colonies and plantations under the British rule or control at the time. The Committee also acquired jurisdiction over English maritime cases, making it the final appellate tribunal in cases determined by the colonial and other overseas

[26] Swinfen, *Imperial Appeal*, 6.

[27] For example, of the 517 appeals lodged before the Committee between 1815 and 1826, only 129 had been adjudicated by 1828.

[28] Howell, *The Judicial Committee of the Privy Council*, 28.

[29] Howell, *The Judicial Committee of the Privy Council*, 29.

Vice-Admiralty Courts. Many of these Vice-Admiralty Courts handled cases involving the seizures and confiscation of slave-trading ships on the West coast of Africa by ships of the British Navy in the post-abolition period.

These arrangements for imperial judicial governance were not unique to the British Empire. In the mid-nineteenth century, the German Supreme Imperial Court in Leipzig was charged with deciding constitutional matters and adjudicating matters involving German imperial subjects. The sixteenth-century Ottoman Empire also created a system of appellate courts in Egypt and elsewhere in the North African frontiers, headed by Turkish-speaking chief judges appointed by administrators in Istanbul. Assistant judges who adjudicated in these courts were locals, as were the notaries and other court employees. Like the JCPC and the other British colonial appellate courts, the Ottoman courts were sites where imperial goals, articulated both in Istanbul and by its local representatives, were implemented. They were judicial arenas where imperial mandates were forced to take account of the needs and preferences of local patrons and employees.[30] In the sixteenth century, Spain too established similar imperial administrative and judicial institutions to deal with the affairs of its rapidly expanding New World holdings. The *Consejo de Indias* (Council of the Indies) was the most important administrative organ of the Spanish Empire and, like other councils of state, it exercised a variety of administrative, fiscal, and judicial functions until the early eighteenth century.[31] Like the JCPC, the *Consejo de Indias* was considered the defender of the public good and the custodian of royal prerogative. It was the highest court of appeal for civil litigation emanating from colonial *audiencias* (appeal courts).[32]

A key feature of the JCPC that made it different from the Ottoman and Spanish imperial appeal courts was its location in the imperial metropole instead of in the colonies. Unlike the Ottoman and Spanish Courts, which operated in the imperial outposts, the JCPC dispensed justice from the imperial centre in London. Another distinguishing feature of the JCPC was the scope of its jurisdiction and its dual mandate as both a court of final appeal and Crown advisory board.

Law Court and Advisory Board

Some provisions of the Judicial Committee Act, which extended the jurisdiction of the JCPC, proved controversial from the beginning. While it was clear that the old Appeal Committee was an advisory board to the Crown similar to other Privy Council Committees, there was some ambiguity about the status of the new

[30] Najwa Al-Qattan, 'Litigants and Neighbors: The Communal Topography of Ottoman Damascus' (2002) 44(3) *Comparative Studies in Society and History* 511–33; Ergene Boğaç, *Local Court, Provincial Society and Justice in the Ottoman Empire: Legal Practice and Dispute Resolution in Çankırı and Kastomonu 1652–1744* (Leiden: Brill, 2003) 190.

[31] William Walton, *Present State of the Spanish Colonies Including a Particular Report of Hispañola, or the Spanish Part of Santo Domingo, Vol 2* (London: Longman, 1810) 115.

[32] Charles R. Cutter, *The Legal Culture of Northern New Spain, 1700–1810* (Albuquerque: UNM Press, 2001) 49.

JCPC. The confusion was whether the reconstituted Judicial Committee remained a Crown advisory board or whether, given its composition and expanded authority, it was a full-fledged court of law. In a parliamentary session on this subject in 1872, Lord Cairns, a former Lord Chancellor who did not share Brougham's ambitious vision, claimed that the JCPC had no real judicial authority and was merely a consultative body. Other contemporaries disagreed, insisting that the JCPC was a court insofar as the Crown in Council had no constitutional power to interfere with its 'judgments'.[33]

As was customary with matters referred by the Crown to the Privy Council, the 1833 Judicial Committee Act provided for the JCPC to make its recommendation to the King in Council for a final decision, after hearing and considering any matter referred to it. The premise was that the Sovereign was the judge, and the Councillors his advisers. Every aspect of the Judicial Committee's work, as indeed those of the larger Privy Council, therefore derived its authority and efficacy solely from the direct official action of the Sovereign.

Notwithstanding this customary constitutional position, certain provisions of the Judicial Committee Act suggested that it possessed the full adjudicatory powers of a regular court of law. For example, unlike the old Appeals Committee, the reconstituted Judicial Committee comprised experienced senior judges empowered to summon and subpoena witnesses to testify under oath before the Board. Like regular appeal courts, the JCPC could also refer cases back to lower courts for retrial. Most significant from a legal standpoint was the provision in the Act that the Committee shall 'have and enjoy in all respects the same power of punishing contempt and compelling appearances... as are exercised by the High Court of Chancery or the Court of King's Bench'.[34] This clause implied that the JCPC was more than an advisory committee of the King's Privy Council, as was customary. In practice, the JCPC served as an imperial appeal court, exercising independent judicial function more as an appellate tribunal than as an advisory board to the Crown. As one legal scholar put it, 'in form it merely advises His Majesty, but in reality its hearings constitute judicial proceedings and its "advice" binding decisions of His Majesty's Appeal Court of the British Empire'.[35] Still, the uncertainty about the constitutional status of the JCPC would continue to define the debates over its judicial and imperial role in Africa as elsewhere in the Empire.

The practice and procedures of appeals to the JCPC as they evolved in the late nineteenth century underscore its dual role as both the Crown advisory board and the Empire's Court of Appeal. At the conclusion of each appeal case, the Board produced two documents: the formal report to the Privy Council and an opinion, or 'Judgement', embodying the reasons for that report; the latter was read in the JCPC chambers in the presence of the parties or their lawyers. Concise and generic, the reports to the Crown were couched in terms of humble advice. They simply

[33] Swinfen, *Imperial Appeal*, 18.

[34] 'Section 28, Judicial Committee Act 1833', *The Statute of Great Britain and Ireland*, Vol XVI, Part 1 (London: Her Majesty's Printers, 1843) 702.

[35] 'Privy Council Acts', NASAP, GG 1845 53/592.

stated that the Board had taken the appellant's petition into consideration and, having heard counsel, reports that the judgment of the lower court from which the case was appealed ought to be affirmed or reversed.[36] The report contained no reasons for the Board's decisions, the details of the case, or the legal arguments presented before it. On the basis of this report the King issued an 'Order in Council', which put the Board's decision into effect. The published opinions or judgments of the JCPC, on the other hand, were detailed legal documents that analysed the legal arguments presented before the Board and the reasons for its decision.

Another distinguishing feature of the JCPC was that, unlike traditional British appellate courts, it did not acknowledge or publish dissenting judicial opinion.[37] Its decisions were presented as the unanimous views of all its members. The historical rationale for this practice was that the Sovereign should not be troubled with conflicting advice.[38] Another reason was to maintain the prestige of the JCPC among colonial subjects. When proposals were put forward in 1901 to publish the dissenting opinions of JCPC judges, Lord Chancellor Selborne worried that dissent might create discontent in the colonies and negatively affect the prestige of the JCPC in the eyes of the local British subjects. He was particularly concerned about the difficulty of satisfying public opinion in India, where the opinion of dissenting judges might become the subject of 'great and critical discussion'. While criticism of the JCPC might be permissible in England, he argued, it was ill-advised among 'half-educated Hindoo lawyers'.[39] It was crucial to maintain finality of litigation and this was better secured without the uncertainty and ambiguities imposed by the publication of dissenting judicial opinion. Imperial justice was anchored in perceptions of infallibility as much as it was by the rule of law.

For reasons of cost and distance, few colonial subjects ever directly encountered the JCPC. This lack of direct engagement does not necessarily indicate the JCPC's limited influence in the colonies. The imperial role of the JCPC is best measured in the breadth rather than the depth of its reach, in the high precedential value of its judgments, and in the ways they shaped colonial law and the administration of justice in the British Empire. The JCPC adjudicated a wide range of legal disputes from diverse jurisdictions affecting everyday life in the colonies. These colonial appeals involved questions of nationality rights, treaty rights and obligations, the validity of customary law and colonial statute law, the scope and limits of executive power, the power of the Crown to annex territories, as well as a variety of commercial and private legal matters.

Colonial appeals constituted the largest category of cases that came before the JCPC between 1833 and 1966. Before 1860, most of these appeals came from

[36] Howell, *The Judicial Committee of the Privy Council*, 38.

[37] The JCPC did eventually introduce the practice of publishing dissenting opinions of its members in 1966.

[38] George Rankin, 'The Judicial Committee of the Privy Council' (1930) 7(2) *Cambridge Law Journal* 8.

[39] Quoted in Robert Bocking Stevens, *The Independence of the Judiciary: The View from the Lord Chancellor's Office* (London: Clarendon Press, 1993) 19.

British colonies and plantations in the Americas, Australia, New Zealand, the Irish Free State, and India. However, with the strengthening of British colonial presence in Africa and the spread of English law in the late nineteenth century, an increasing number of 'native appeals' from Africa and the Indian subcontinent came before the JCPC. To put it in a position to adjudicate appeals from different legal systems within the Empire, reforms were introduced in 1913 and 1928 that allowed for colonial judges who were members of the Privy Council to sit on the JCPC.[40] Further reforms allowed for the appointment of Judicial Assessors, who were sometimes drawn from the ranks of retired colonial judges and provided advice on local conditions and local law. In spite of this theoretical composition of the JCPC, the three or five judges who sat to hear any one appeal were often United Kingdom judges.[41] This was usually the case also with the WACA and the EACA whose benches were dominated by senior British colonial judges drawn from the courts' jurisdiction.

The Regional Courts of Appeal

Beneath the JCPC in the colonial court hierarchy was a complex system of English Courts charged with enforcing English law, and native tribunals implementing customary law. Appeals could be brought to the JCPC only after litigants had exhausted all local legal remedies. This often meant that cases would have been previously adjudicated at other levels of the judicial hierarchy below the JCPC—native courts, provincial and district courts, High Courts, Supreme Courts, and in some cases the regional Courts of Appeal. The regional Appeal Courts—the WACA and the EACA—were the penultimate courts of review in British Africa. Many of the cases adjudicated by the JCPC came on appeal from these regional Appeal Courts.[42]

Established as 'His Britannic Majesty's Court of Appeal for Eastern Africa' in 1902, the EACA administered appellate justice in British East Africa throughout the colonial period. The court's mandate, as per the Order-in-Council that had established it, was to 'exercise appellate jurisdiction and powers over the High Courts and other courts in the Protectorates'.[43] The Protectorates in question included The East Africa Protectorate (Kenya), Uganda, and the British Central African Protectorate (Malawi). The court emerged from a broader process of inter-territorial political cooperation, and was a part of the British attempt to amalgamate its three East African territories into a single administrative unit. At its inception,

[40] 'Imperial Conference 1930: Judicial Committee: Privy Council Proposed', NASAP, BLO 88 PS12/2/24.

[41] 'Appointment of Colonial Judges', National Archives of the United Kingdom (hereinafter NAUK) CO/1026/114.

[42] West African Court of Appeal Judgments, 1938 Session, National Archives of Nigeria Ibadan (hereinafter NANI) CSO 33115, vol 3.

[43] 1902 Order in Council. Cited in J. W. Katende and George W. Kanyeihamba, 'Legalism and Politics in East Africa: The Dilemma of the Court of Appeal for East Africa' (1973) 43 *Transition* 44.

the court was staffed by three British colonial judges appointed by the Governor of Kenya. In 1910, the court was reconstituted and renamed 'The Court of Appeal for Eastern Africa', and included the chief judges of the constituent colonies.[44] By 1921, the jurisdiction of the court had extended to the island of Zanzibar on the East African coast and to the former German Colony of Tanganyika, which was mandated to Britain after World War I. The court's jurisdiction over Nyasaland (Malawi) was terminated in 1947, but by then it had extended to Aden, St Helena, the Islands of Seychelles, and the Somaliland Protectorate.[45] The court's East African jurisdiction in Tanganyika, Uganda, and Kenya was concretized in 1947, with the establishment of the British East African Commission. The Commission provided the political framework for the court's operation until its demise in the 1960s, when the constituent countries gained independence.

The West African Court of Appeal (WACA) had a similar history. Originally established in 1867 for all the West African colonies, the WACA was a product of British attempts to unify its West African possessions for administrative and economic reasons. The court was originally located in Freetown, Sierra Leone, and was mandated to hear civil and criminal appeals from the superior courts of all British colonies in West Africa. The original Court was short-lived, however. The administrative unification of the West African colonies came to an end in 1874, when Lagos and the Gold Coast were amalgamated into a single British colony. The WACA was thereafter revived in 1928 for the autonomous British dependencies in West Africa. Its jurisdiction included the Gold Coast, Nigeria, Sierra Leone, and Gambia.

The territories covered by the WACA did not form a contiguous geographical unit, but were dispersed along the West African Coast. This had obvious implications for logistical arrangements and other practical matters.[46] Unlike the EACA, which operated within the framework of a regional colonial administrative authority, the WACA was not a component part of the region's administrative structure.[47] It was the quintessential supranational appeal court in that its jurisdiction covered administratively autonomous colonial territories.

Although they were charged with adjudicating civil and criminal appeals, the regional Appeal Courts typically heard more criminal appeals than civil appeals. For example, out of the sixty-one appeals heard by the EACA in 1936, fifty-four were criminal appeals. Many of these were high-stakes appeals against convictions for capital offences. Civil appeals mostly involved land and commercial disputes.[48] One observer of the EACA's circuit in 1937 described the appeals that came before the court as a reflection of the intrigues and complexities of social life in the colonies.

44 The Eastern Africa Protectorates (Court of Appeal) Order in Council 1901.

45 *The East African Standard* (18 February 1937) 4.

46 Frans Viljoen, 'The Realisation of Human Rights in Africa through Sub-Regional Institutions' in Abdulqawi A. Yusuf, ed, *African Yearbook of International Law Vol 7* (The Hague: Kluwer Law International, 1999) 195.

47 West African Court of Appeal Judgments, 1936 Session, NANI, CSO 33115, vol 2.

48 *The Tanganyika Standard* (19 November 1936).

Life has been at stake for many people. Domestic tragedies have been retold, stripped of the appeal of sentiments, reduced to the examination of facts. The Chief Justices have dealt with murder, with grievous assault, with a rare case of cannibalism, with intricate maritime law on the African lakes, with the position of some of the older generations of African on the golf course playground of the white man, with the status of those who produce and act in stage dramas for the entertainment of the public, and with many other sections of the drama of human life as it is lived in this continent in the twentieth century.[49]

Like the JCPC, the regional Appeal Courts were key arenas of high-stakes legal battles over authority and power, economic resources, and interpretations of morality and culture. The fact that these Courts were more accessible to ordinary Africans than the JCPC made them even more crucial sites of judicial governance and the administration of imperial appellate justice.

'The Daniels of the British Realm'

Between 1890 and the early 1960s, about three hundred and fifty African appeals were adjudicated by the JCPC. Most of these were 'native' appeals, about two-thirds of which came from West Africa.[50] Given that the JCPC met infrequently and heard only an average of seventy-six cases from across the Empire in any calendar year, this number is significant.[51] The litigant in a colony who sought to appeal to the JCPC could proceed in one of two ways. The first was by requesting 'Leave of Appeal' from the Supreme Court or Appeal Court in the colony to take his case to the JCPC. This legal right of appeal was derived from the ancient privilege of the British subjects to seek redress of grievance at the foot of the throne. This right existed only where it had been specifically created by a statute, however, and was subject to local colonial legislation. This was the case in all the British colonies in Africa.

When a litigant failed to obtain 'leave as of right' from the local court of appeal, he could still apply for a 'Special Leave of Appeal' directly from the JCPC. The JCPC's prerogative to grant special leave of appeal derived from the inherent prerogative of the Sovereign to hear appeals from all his subjects. In such cases, it was up to the JCPC—acting on behalf of the Crown—to decide whether or not to

[49] *The East African Standard* (18 February 1937).

[50] The term 'Native African appeals', as used here, refers to appeals initiated by Africans, which were distinct from appeals by Europeans, other non-Africans, or corporate entities. Included in this figure are appeals that were fully adjudicated and also the applications for a 'Leave of Appeal' that were rejected by the JCPC. This figure is inexact because of the inherent difficulty of definitively identifying which appellants were Africans and which were not, since some Africans bore English names. This figure comes from analysis of Law Reports and the *Printed Papers in Appeal* at the JCPC. Most West African appeals to the JCPC are reported in Olisa Chukura, ed, *Privy Council Judgments: Opinions of the Judicial Committee of the Privy Council in Appeals from West Africa, 1841 to 1973* (London: Gilford, 1981) and Harry Robert Frederick Butterfield, *Index Digest of the Reported Cases Determined by the Court of Appeal for Eastern Africa and on Appeal Therefrom by the Judicial Committee of the Privy Council, 1900–1952* (Nairobi: Government Printer, 1954).

[51] Howell, *The Judicial Committee of the Privy Council*, 63–4.

accept the appeal. The Committee then made a decision by asking whether the case involved 'some great principle' or 'some very wide public interest'.[52] Special intervention was not granted indiscriminately or freely. The threshold was set very high. As Lord Watsons indicated in one JCPC judgment, 'Her Majesty will not review or interfere with the cause of proceedings, unless it is shown that, by a disregard of the forms of legal process, or by some violations of the principles of natural justice, or otherwise, *substantial and grave injustice* has been done'.[53] Lord Dunedin made the same point when he stated that in order to warrant the JCPC's intervention in a case: 'There must be something so irregular, or so outrageous, as to shake the very basis of justice'.[54]

Who were these imperial judges of the JCPC—the 'Daniels of the British realm' as one African newspaper described them—who sat in judgement over colonial subjects?[55] One of them was Lord Richard Haldane. A liberal imperialist and Labour politician who served as the British Secretary of State for War and as Lord Chancellor in the 1920s, Haldane was the archetypal imperial judge. By his own admission, he 'lived' most of his life at the JCPC, first as a lawyer and later as a judge for three decades. He presided over some of the most significant dominion and colonial appeals brought to the JCPC between 1910 and 1930. On Canadian constitutional appeals alone, he sat on thirty-two cases and gave judgment in nineteen of them.[56] A firm believer in imperial partnership, Haldane held the view that the JCPC should be the only institution in the Empire to exercise complete control and centralized power. He also believed that this authority should expand to include permanent representation from the colonies. His close association with representatives of colonial governments through his early years of legal practice convinced him that the two chief factors for keeping the empire together were the Crown and the Law.[57] The JCPC, he argued, was a 'real and most important portion of the silken bonds which with so little friction holds our great Empire together'.[58] It was an institution for the Empire and not just for Britain. As he put it: 'It is no more an English body than it is an Indian body, or a Canadian body, or a South African body, or . . . an Irish Free State body.'[59] These notions of imperial unity and collective ownership of the Empire's institutions were central to Haldane's judicial philosophy and were evident in many of these judgments at the JCPC.

[52] Rankin, 'The Judicial Committee of the Privy Council', 16.

[53] *Re Dillet* [1887] 12 AC 459 at 467. My emphasis.

[54] *Mohinder Singh v The King-Emperor* [1932] AIR 103. Cited in Hedley H. Marshall, *Natural Justice* (London: Sweet & Maxwell, 1959) 94.

[55] Editorial, *West African Pilot* (2 July 1963) 6. This phrase undoubtedly alludes to the biblical character Daniel, who was attributed with having fine powers of judgement. Daniel 5:14 (KJV).

[56] Jean Graham Hall and Douglas F. Martin, *Haldane: Statesman, Lawyer, Philosopher* (London: Barry Rose Law Publishers, 1996) 176.

[57] Hall and Martin, *Haldane: Statesman, Lawyer, Philosopher*, 43.

[58] R. B. Haldane, 'The Work for the Empire of the Judicial Committee of the Privy Council' (1922) 1(2) *Cambridge Law Journal* 143.

[59] Lord Haldane, *Alexander E. Hull & Co. v M'Kenna* [1926] IR 402.

Another JCPC judge presiding over several African appeals later on was Lord James Atkin. A liberal lawyer of Welsh origin, Lord Atkin has been described as 'one of the greatest of all English common law lawyers'.[60] He became a High Court judge in 1913, and was appointed Lord Justice of Appeal and JCPC judge in 1919. He soon gained a reputation for his liberal interpretation of the law and for his unique approach to interpreting dominion constitutional appeals.[61] Lord Atkin's judgment in the famous case of *Donoghue v Stevenson* became the foundation of the modern law of negligence in the common law world. He was also reputed for his strict position on protecting civil liberties and limiting executive power. His dissenting judgment in the case of *Liversidge v Anderson* asserted the courts' right to question the wide discretionary powers of British security services to detain aliens during wartime.[62] Lord Atkin delivered the judgment in the Privy Council appeal of the African Chief Eshugbayi Eleko against his deposition and deportation by the British colonial authorities in Nigeria. In that case, he famously stated:

> In accordance with British jurisprudence, no member of the executive can interfere with the liberty or property of a British subject except on condition that he can support the legality of his actions before a court of justice. And it is the tradition of British justice that judges should not shrink form deciding such issue in the face of the executive.[63]

The judgment became the *locus classicus* on successive *habeas corpus* applications in common law jurisdictions.

The judicial and extrajudicial work of Lord Haldane, Lord Atkin, and other prominent judges who presided over colonial appeals illustrate the judicial thought of JCPC judges more generally. However I recognize that the views of these judges, however dominant, cannot fully represent the varied judicial philosophies of the judges who sat on the JCPC. It is difficult to imagine that there were not disagreements among these judges especially on questions of indigenous customary law in adjudicating colonial appeals. The difficulty with identifying the divergences in the judicial philosophies of JCPC judges arises from the fact that dissenting opinions were not countenanced on the Committee. This tended to shroud differences among the judges that there might have been.

Just as crucial to the administration of imperial justice at the JCPC were the lawyers who appeared before the Committee. Barristers appearing before the JCPC were not required to be members of the English bar; they needed only to be qualified to practise before the originating court. Even so, most of the lawyers or 'Privy Council Agents' who litigated colonial appeals at the JCPC were British lawyers with established practice in the United Kingdom. Similarly, the lawyers who litigated appeals at the regional Appeal Courts in Africa were mostly expatriate

[60] Geoffrey Lewis, *Lord Atkin* (London: Hart, 1999) 4.

[61] Frederick Morton, *Law, Politics and the Judicial Process in Canada* (Calgary: University of Calgary Press, 1984) 427.

[62] *Liversidge v Anderson* [1942] AC 206.

[63] *Eshugbayi Eleko v Officer Administering the Government of Nigeria* [1931] AC 652; Judicial Committee of the Privy Council, *Printed Papers in Appeal* (hereinafter JCPC PPA), Vol 24 (1928) and Vol 26 (1931).

British lawyers who dominated the legal profession in these colonies. In addition, a small but active group of indigenous African lawyers played important roles in theses judicial processes and in the colonial legal system generally. This was particularly true of the West African colonies of Nigeria, the Gold Coast, Sierra Leone, and Gambia. By the late 1920s, there were as many as sixty African lawyers in the Gold Coast and about as many in Nigeria.[64] Among these pioneering African lawyers were the Gold Coast lawyers, John Mensah Sarbah and Joseph Casely-Hayford, who were called to the English bar in 1887 and in 1896 respectively. Both lawyers pioneered legal studies in African customary law.

In Nigeria, the community of indigenous lawyers included Sapara Williams, the first fully qualified African legal practitioner in Nigeria who was called to the English bar in 1879. By the 1930s, the ranks of indigenous lawyers in West Africa swelled with the likes of Nash Williams, Joseph Egerton Shyngle, Eric Moore, G. H. Savage, Henry Carr, and Kitoyi Ajasa, all of whom were also actively involved in nationalist politics.[65] These indigenous lawyers struggled to establish their reputation in a professional landscape initially dominated by British lawyers and judicial officers.

Some of these indigenous lawyers, for example R. A. Doherty, Adetokunbo Ademola, Olumuyiwa Jibowu, and Steven Bankole Rhodes, occupied important positions as magistrates and judges in the colonial judiciary.[66] Other lawyers litigated appeals at the regional Appeal Courts and at the JCPC. The Gold Coast lawyer Awoonor-Renner and the Nigerian lawyer Joseph Egerton-Shyngle litigated the famous *Amodu Tijani* land appeal in 1921.[67] Adeyemo Alakija litigated a similar land appeal against the government in 1950.[68] Egerton Shyngle and Eric Moore represented the African Chief, Eshugbayi Eleko, in his appeal against his deposition and deportation by the British authorities in Nigeria.[69] Another lawyer, Adetokunbo Ademola, would later be appointed a judge of the JCPC in 1963.

In some cases, African lawyers partnered with British barristers and 'Privy Council Agents' to litigate appeals at the JCPC. A network of British lawyers specialized in litigating colonial appeals at the JCPC developed in London. In the 1930s and 1940s, British lawyers such as Lionel Edwards, Bruce Campbell, Henry Salt, the law firms of A. W. Burchell and A. L. Bryden, and the London-based Canadian lawyer Frank Gahan, gained a reputation among colonial officials and

[64] Andrew Roberts, 'African Cross Currents' in Andrew Roberts, ed, *The Colonial Moment in Africa: Essays on the Movement of Minds and Materials, 1900–1940* (Cambridge: Cambridge University Press, 1990) 229.

[65] Anthony Olden, 'Alan Burns, the Lagos Library, and the Commencement of Carnegie Support for Library Development in British West Africa' (1987) 22(4) *The Journal of Library History* 402.

[66] Omoniyi Adewoye, *The Judicial System in Southern Nigeria, 1854–1954: Law and Justice in a Dependency* (Atlantic Highlands, NJ: Humanities Press, 1977) 247.

[67] Patrick Cole, *Modern and Traditional Elites in the Politics of Lagos* (New York: Cambridge University Press, 1973) 126.

[68] Adeyemo Alakija, Notice of Petition to the Privy Council (*Akinola Maja v The Chief Secretary to the Government*) 6 January 1950, NANI CSO 26/2/19439.

[69] *Daily Telegraph* (1 August 1921); Adewoye, *The Judicial System in Southern Nigeria*, 291.

African elites for their expertise in litigating colonial appeals at the JCPC.[70] In East Africa, the Nairobi-based Indian solicitor M. H. Malik litigated several criminal appeals *pro bono* for African clients on behalf of humanitarian organizations such as the London-based Howard League for Penal Reform.[71]

Unlike the JCPC bench, which comprised jurists who held high judicial office in Britain and the Dominions, the WACA and EACA were staffed by career colonial judicial officers. The WACA bench comprised the Chief Justices and Puisne Judges of all the territories under the court's jurisdiction. In 1948, the court was reconstituted with the appointment of a permanent president. Some of the court's more prominent judges included Sir James Henley Coussey, who was appointed in 1949 to draw up a Constitution for the Gold Coast, and Sir Hector Hearne who previously served as Chief Judge of Kenya and Jamaica.[72] In the 1930s and 40s, a number of Africans were appointed to the WACA bench as part of a broader policy to open up the colonial judiciary to indigenous legal practitioners. Among these were the Sierra Leonean judge Sir Ernest Beoku-Betts who was appointed to the WACA bench in 1947.[73] Although staffed by judges from the constituent colonial territories, the WACA, like the EACA, operated beyond the direct purview of territorial colonial authorities. Local administrators worried about the 'frequently unsatisfactory' judgments delivered by the WACA in cases involving the government.[74]

Africans were significantly less involved in the colonial legal systems in East Africa and Southern Africa, where greater racial barriers prevented the entry of Africans into the legal profession.[75] The legal profession in East Africa was almost entirely non-African until the 1960s.[76] As late as 1962, there were only thirteen African attorneys in practice in the whole of South Africa, and no advocates. Even then, a number of these lawyers involved in politics, most prominently Oliver Tambo and Nelson Mandela, were either imprisoned, placed under banning orders, or were forced into exile.[77]

Assessing the role of these indigenous lawyers and judges in the colonial legal systems can be difficult. Rather than reading them as villainous collaborators or as heroes exercising agency, the trend in recent scholarship has been to see them as 'intellectual middlemen' and law interpreters moulding colonial forms of

70 *The Times* (13 October 1954) 9; *Rex v Kwame Bempah*, 29 June 1937, PRAADA CSO 15/3/42.

71 Appeals by Natives Convicted of Criminal Charge, KNAN, AP/1/619.

72 West African Court of Appeal Judgments, 1938 Session, NANI, CSO 33115, vol 3.

73 C. Magbaily Fyle, *Historical Dictionary of Sierra Leone* (Oxford: Rowman and Littlefield, 2006) 20.

74 Lionel Brett, Confidential Internal Memorandum, Office of the Solicitor General, NANI CS0 26/2/19439/S.15.

75 Martin Chanock's work on the Cape Colony documents the Transvaal Law Society's successful moves to keep non-white lawyers out of the profession in the first two decades of the twentieth century. See Chanock, *The Making of South African Legal Culture*.

76 Henry Morris and James Read, *Indirect Rule and the Search for Justice: Essays in East African Legal History* (London: Clarendon Press, 1972) 181.

77 Albie Sachs, *Justice in South Africa* (Berkeley: University of California Press, 1973) 211.

ethnographic knowledge and collective self-image.[78] The relevant point for our purpose is that the lawyers who litigated colonial appeals and also the men who sat in judgment over Africans in colonial courts were not always Europeans or non-Africans. In the mid and late colonial period, some of these lawyers and judges were Africans.[79]

Judicial Uniformity and Colonial Difference

Imperial appeal courts had the implicit mandate of maintaining consistency and uniformity in the exercise of their powers of judicial review. The JCPC's role in maintaining jurisprudential homogeneity is demonstrated most clearly in its exercise of the power of judicial review. The basis of that power lay in the principle that all colonial legislatures were subordinate to the Crown and that colonial law and justice must conform to British standards.[80] In the Atlantic Empires of the sixteenth and seventeenth centuries, it was taken for granted that European settlers took English law with them, and a unitary system of English common law was assumed to extend wholesale to the colonies. This changed significantly with the expansion of Europe's empires into the tropical regions. Where new lands were already populated by indigenous peoples, judicial governance had to reconcile the competing claims of old and new law. The main difference between the early Atlantic colonies and the later tropical colonies in Asia and Africa was that, in the former, the legal system remained essentially European and unified, while in the latter the law had to grapple with the problem of organized indigenous communities, each with its own body of laws.[81]

But even in the tropical Empire, colonial English-style courts were expected to serve no lesser function than the courts in England. Their purpose was to deal with disputes in terms of clear-cut rights and duties, established by objective investigation of only those events deemed relevant to each case. Strict rules of evidence limited the content of testimony that the courts could hear. Cases were treated as involving a 'right' and a 'wrong' with judges making final decisions, sometimes after consultation with local experts and 'native assessors'. These principles were key elements of the British colonial legal system, and extended to Africa in the late nineteenth and early twentieth century.

The JCPC forged imperial unity through universalist interpretations of divergent colonial statute laws and indigenous customary laws. Jurisprudential standardization was guided by the need to maintain law and order in the colonies in a way that

78 Mitra Sharafi, 'Review: A New History of Colonial Lawyering: Likhovski and Legal Identities in the British Empire' (2007) 32(4) *Law & Social Inquiry* 1084.

79 Although no Africans were appointed to the JCPC until the 1960s, African judges sat on territorial Supreme Courts and the regional Appeal Courts from the 1930s.

80 Alpheus Todd, *Parliamentary Government in the British Colonies* (Boston: Little, Brown, 1880) 14.

81 J. N. Matson, 'The Common Law Abroad: English and Indigenous Laws in the British Commonwealth' (1993) 42(3) *The International and Comparative Law Quarterly* 753.

allowed for the Empire's overarching administrative and economic interests to be met.[82] In 1879, the JCPC stated in a landmark judgment: 'It is of the utmost importance that in all parts of the Empire where English law prevails, the interpretation of that law by the courts should be as nearly as possible the same.'[83] Writing in 1922, Lord Haldane stressed the JCPC's quest for judicial uniformity even in cases involving non-English law:

> We sit there to administer Buddhist law, or Hindu Law, or Mohammedan Law, one after the other. We administer Roman-Dutch law from South Africa or from Ceylon, or French law from Quebec, or the common law of England for Ontario . . . [We] try to look for the *common principle* underlying systems of jurisprudence of differing kinds. [We] know that the form often veils over a very similar substance. We are constantly finding that, where great broad principles of justice are concerned, you find—veiled, but still there and only distinguished by technicalities—the same substance as belongs to other systems.[84]

Another long-serving judge of the JCPC, Lord Atkin, described the JCPC as 'the only agency for securing any measure of uniformity in legal development over the whole of this vast Empire'.[85] The JCPC's quest for uniformity and standardization in the adjudication of colonial appeal reflects the Empire's universalist impulse in judicial governance.

There were, however, limits to the JCPC's ability to pursue legal uniformity due to the regular need for the Board to apply non-English law. As Lord Haldane put it, the jurisdiction of the JCPC was a 'very delicate one'.[86] The Crown could not always be safely advised to interfere with matters involving the constitutions or systems of governments of the Empire's colonies and dominions. The object of the JCPC adjudication, Haldane stated, was to 'make the part of the Empire from which the appeal comes have the sense of seeing that there has been a mistake, if one has been made'.[87] The process of appeals adjudication had to reflect the law and the spirit of the country from which the appeal was brought, as well as adhere to the laws and traditions of that country. In other words, even in its quest for judicial uniformity and standardization, the exigencies of imperial governance made it necessary for the JCPC judges to recognize and accommodate divergence and difference.

Faced with the tenuousness of the imported English law and the resilience of traditional customary laws, colonial administrative and judicial officers sought to accommodate both systems of law. It was necessary to temper the initial insistence on imperial unity of the English law with the development of a plural system of laws and with the mixture of common law and indigenous customary law. While the former was more universal in nature, the latter varied considerably.[88] In many parts of British Africa, indigenous customary laws were allowed to exist alongside English

[82] Swinfen, *Imperial Appeal*, 14. [83] *Trimble v Hill* [1879] 5 AC 342 at 345.
[84] Haldane, 'The Work for the Empire', 154. My emphasis.
[85] Lewis, *Lord Atkin*, 94.
[86] Haldane, 'The Work for the Empire', 143.
[87] Haldane, 'The Work for the Empire', 143.
[88] Matson, 'The Common Law Abroad', 753.

law, provided they met certain conditions. Native customary laws, however, were recognized only in subordination to colonial law, and were denied such recognition where they conflicted with local statute law or with the presumed universalist standards of British justice.[89]

The JCPC and the regional Appeal Courts played a decisive role in delineating the threshold for accommodating indigenous customary laws within the colonial legal system. These Imperial Appeal Courts were frequently called upon to interpret colonial laws and make decisions on disputes arising from the conflicts between English law and African customary laws. In adjudicating these cases, imperial courts addressed the central tension in colonial judicial governance in Africa—that between upholding uniform standards of colonial justice based on Common Law traditions and simultaneously allowing for some degree of local customary divergence. This balance was thought to be essential for achieving justice. Imperial judges also recognized that to achieve justice in the colonies, some flexibility was required in interpreting colonial statute law and indigenous customary laws.

A cursory analysis of the *West African Court of Appeal Reports* indicates that the court was preoccupied with disputes arising from conflict of laws and from the interpretation of divergent customary laws. A considerable number of reported disputes required the court to determine whether English or Customary Law should be applied. Even more problematic were cases that involved internal conflict of customary laws, where litigants invoked contradictory customary laws in disputes over land, personal law matters, or commercial transactions. In the Gold Coast case of *Ghamson v Wobill*, for example, the WACA was faced with the problem of choosing between several systems of customary law applicable to an intestate succession dispute between litigants who invoked conflicting customary succession laws.[90] In adjudicating such cases, colonial appellate judges sometimes had to resort to rules of Private International Law, as they applied in England, to indicate the appropriate law to apply.[91] The judicial processes by which appellate judges sought to address these conflicts in specific cases are examined in the subsequent chapters of this book.

Seeking Imperial Justice

The JCPC was decidedly non-interventionist. Presiding over an Indian appeal in 1941, Viscount Simon enunciated a cardinal principle that guided the JCPC's adjudication of colonial appeals. He stated that the JCPC would only interfere where there has been an infringement of the 'essential principles of justice'.[92] Another rule of practice was that the JCPC would not disturb concurrent findings

[89] Peter Fitzpatrick, 'Terminal Legality: Imperialism and the (De)composition of Law' in Diane Kirkby and Catharine Coleborne, eds, *Law, History, Colonialism: The Reach of Empire* (Manchester: Manchester University Press, 2001) 21.

[90] *Ghamson and ors v Wobill* [1947] 12 WACA 181.

[91] 'West African Court of Appeal' (1957) 1(1) *Journal of African Law* 51.

[92] *Muhammad Nawaz v The King-Emperor* [1941] LR 68 IA 126.

of fact, arrived at by the courts overseas. This was not an inflexible rule, but strong reasons were required to induce the Board to go outside the limits imposed by this rule.[93]

The JCPC was not a 'theatre of legal performance' in the same way that regular colonial courts were. It did not often provide opportunities for a dramatic use of the 'dock-as-platform' by the otherwise silenced colonial subjects, to call attention to their cause or make impassioned calls to public action.[94] When adjudicating cases, the JCPC did not re-try the case. Instead, it decided cases by applying purely legal principles to the facts already ascertained during previous trials—a practice similar to most appeal courts. It relied mainly on the record of the case prepared by the court appealed from, and on the argument of the lawyers representing the parties in the case. It also typically did not hear oral testimonies, and there was no requirement for the litigants themselves to be physically present at the JCPC chambers for the hearings. Some litigants travelled from the colonies to London, however, to witness the hearing of their cases. Speaking before a group of law students in 1922, Lord Haldane described the scene at the JCPC Chambers. On a typical day, he stated, a visitor could experience the rich diversity of the British Empire, encountering 'white men, some of whom look as if they had come from the far West, and may be of American appearance; yellow men, some of whom come from Hong Kong; Burmese, who come from Burma; Hindus and Mohammedans from India; Dutch from South Africa or a mixed race from Ceylon'.[95] One visitor to the JCPC wrote: 'Natives from four continents come to the back rooms of Downing Street with their domestic troubles to receive justice dispensed by all the majesty of the British Empire.'[96] One of such natives was the Yoruba Chief Oluwa who in 1921 travelled with an entourage from Nigeria to the JCPC in London, to witness his land appeal against the colonial government. The trip turned out to be a carefully planned publicity exercise. While in London, Chief Oluwa attended Court hearings in his chiefly regalia, with an assistant carrying in front of him a silver-mounted Staff of Office presented to the *Oba* (King) of Lagos by Queen Victoria in 1852. The pictures of the African Chief and his retinue in Western and 'exotic native attires' at the JCPC Chambers soon appeared in British and West African newspapers, drawing public attention to the case[97] (see Figure 2.1).

Colonial subjects who travelled to London to witness appeals at the JCPC may not have been very impressed with what they saw. Even at the height of its influence in the 1930s, the JCPC office on Downing Street hardly conveyed the stately grandeur that litigants would have expected of the highest court in the British

93 Rankin, 'The Judicial Committee of the Privy Council', 18.

94 John L. Comaroff, 'Colonialism, Culture, and the Law: A Foreword' (2001) 26(2) *Law & Social Inquiry* 307.

95 Haldane, 'The Work for the Empire', 144.

96 R. E. Corder, 'Umpires of Empire: The Privy Council Judges at Work', *The Singapore Free Press and Mercantile Advertiser* (13 June 1928) 3.

97 Herbert Macaulay to Lord Passfield, 13 January 1930, NANI CSO 33115. These photographs are reproduced in *West Africa*, 31 July 1920 and Tekena N. Tamuno, *Herbert Macaulay: Nigerian Patriot* (London: Heinemann, 1975) 25.

Figure 2.1: Chief Oluwa and his entourage at the JCPC, 1921
West Africa, July, 1931

Empire. Lord Haldane described a 'very dirty' door and a 'dilapidated staircase' leading to the modest oak-panelled boardroom of the JCPC.[98] Although legal practitioners appearing before it were required to wear the wig and gown, its judges wore no robes or wigs. They sat in what one writer described as 'formal sober lounge suits' and looked more like a board of directors of some old-fashioned English company than the judges of the ultimate court of the British Empire.[99]

Although a trip to London was not required to bring an appeal to the JCPC, prosecuting an appeal in the highest court of the Empire was still a very expensive and laborious undertaking. After exhausting all legal appeal remedies in the colony, an appellant typically had to retain a solicitor in the colony and a barrister or 'Privy Council Agent' in London, in order to prosecute an appeal at the JCPC. Apart from lawyers' fees, litigants also had to bear incidental costs that might be incurred in the course of what was often a slow and lengthy appeal process. A frequent complaint against the JCPC was that appeals involved inordinate expense and delay, making it a 'rich man's court' that the poorer litigant could not afford. Even Privy Councillors expressed concern about the administrative expense of appeals, which included the cost of producing copies of the court's proceedings in the concerned colonies. These transcripts could run to several thousand folios and cost as much as a thousand pounds.[100]

[98] Haldane, 'The Work for the Empire', 155.
[99] Magrath, 'British Justice International Plc?' 4.
[100] Swinfen, *Imperial Appeal*, 10.

Although it was theoretically possible for indigent colonial subjects to bring appeals before the JCPC *in forma pauperis* at no cost, few African litigants were able to do so.[101] A petitioner seeking to bring an appeal before the JCPC *in forma pauperis* had to present an affidavit stating that, apart from his wearing apparel, he was not worth more than £5 (later increased to £25). Even so, the status of appealing *in forma pauperis* relieved the poor litigant only of the fees due to the Privy Council office and from the liability of paying costs if he lost the case.[102] The poor litigant still had to bear the incidental costs of retaining lawyers to litigate the appeal *pro bono*. The cases of Africans appealing to the JCPC *in forma pauperis* were therefore few and far between.

Apart from criticism that the Privy Council appeals system was costly, favoured rich litigants, and involved considerable delays, there were also concerns about the quality of justice it dispensed. Questions were frequently raised within the African intelligentsia about the competence of the JCPC to adjudicate appeals from African colonies, given the judges' limited knowledge of local laws and customs. Writing in 1906, the Gold Coast lawyer, John Mensah Sarbah, wondered if it was possible for the Crown legal and judicial officers in England to make satisfactory decisions about Africans whose habits and lifestyles they knew little about.[103]

Indeed, a key criticism of the JCPC in the colonies was that it could not match the local practitioners' knowledge of local law and conditions, because it was composed almost entirely of English judges.[104] Many in both Whitehall and in the colonies questioned whether a tribunal so physically and culturally remote from Africa could effectively administer justice that would be as acceptable to the Africans as the justice traditionally dispensed by local officials in daily contact with them. In South Africa, officials complained about the hardship litigants faced as a result of the JCPC judges' unfamiliarity with Roman-Dutch Law used in the country.[105] These concerns were partly responsible for the eventual decline of the JCPC's influence in the mid-twentieth century.

Merchants and Native Agitators

The Africans who brought appeals before the Imperial Courts of Appeal in the twentieth century followed a long tradition of resolving disputes in colonial courts. Some early British officials accused the Africans of being lawless and over-litigious.[106] The British merchant Brodie Cruickshank, who served for many

[101] G. L. Hove to Chief Secretary to the Government (Nigeria), 28 May 1947, NANI CSO 26/2/9814.

[102] 'Judicial Committee Rules of the Privy Council 1925', KNAN, AP/1/1430; *Rex v Kwaku Mensah*, 10–15 May 1943, PRAADA, Accra, CSO 15/3/213.

[103] John Mensah Sabah, *Fante National Constitution* (London: Cass, 1968) ix.

[104] Swinfen, *Imperial Appeal*, 11.

[105] 'Privy Council Acts: Imperial Judicial Committee', NASAP, GG 1845 53/592.

[106] Claude George, *The Rise of British West Africa* (London: Frank Cass, 1904) 173; also see Brodie Cruickshank, *Eighteen Years on the Gold Coast of Africa, Vol 1* (London: Hurst and Blackett, 1853) 276; Sachs, *Justice in South Africa*, 111.

years as a magistrate in the Gold Coast, asserted that colonial courts fostered the litigious disposition of the natives.[107] Commenting on the proliferation of court cases in the Gold Coast in the 1930s, Governor Sir Hugh Clifford attributed it to the 'naturally litigious character of the [Gold Coast] people'.[108] Others explained the presumed African proclivity for litigation in terms of primordial cultural traits. 'Law', wrote one official, held a fascination for the West African, particularly among natives of the 'warrior tribes'. Modern conditions had forced them to beat their swords into ploughshares, but the fighting instinct was still strong in them, and the best way they could give it expression was to enter the legal arena with an opponent.[109] African litigiousness was explained in terms of the tribal and the primitive, the same attributes that were considered antithetical to enlightened Euro-modernity.

Most Africans encountered colonial justice in local native tribunals applying customary law. Appellate justice at the JCPC and at the regional Courts of Appeal was often the preserve of the elite. In the mid-nineteenth century, many of the early appeals from Africa to the JCPC were petitions by European merchants against sentences of the British Admiralty Courts in Sierra Leone—courts charged with the suppression of the slave trade. Others were commercial disputes brought to the Privy Council from South Africa; these mostly involved Afrikaners, Europeans, and Indian merchants. Of the thirty-nine African appeals heard by the JCPC between 1861 and 1890, thirty-five were from South Africa. By the 1900s, Africans were also bringing appeals before the JCPC.[110] Who were these nineteenth-century Africans seeking imperial justice at the JCPC? Two West African cases offer some insight.

In 1890, Shitta, a Yoruba 'native merchant, financier and money lender' in the colony of Lagos, was a respondent in a JCPC appeal over a dispute with a European merchant to whom he had loaned £6,000. The case involved technical legal questions relating to the English law of contract—specifically whether the appellant had the authority to borrow money on behalf of his employers, according to the terms and rates agreed upon. At the end of a lengthy case, the appeal was dismissed with an order for the appellant to pay Shitta the cost of the appeal. Part of the issue that arose in the course of the trial was whether the native merchant, Shitta, understood the terms of the contract he had purportedly entered into with the European merchant. In his judgment, the presiding judge of the JCPC, Lord Herschell, noted that Shitta did not appear to have 'thoroughly understood the English language, or to have been able to read it'.[111]

Another early case in 1896 involved an African lawyer, Peter Awoonor-Renner, who appealed to the JCPC against a judgment of the Supreme Court of the Gold

[107] Brodie Cruickshank, *Eighteen Years on the Gold Coast of Africa, Vol 1* (London: Hurst and Blackett, 1853) 276.

[108] Roger Gocking, 'A Chieftaincy Dispute and Ritual Murder in Elmina, Ghana, 1945–6' (2000) 41(2) *The Journal of African History* 218.

[109] *The Gold Coast Observer* (20 August 1943).

[110] The figures are from the record of cases compiled by the staff of the JCPC Office shared with the author in the course of research at the JCPC.

[111] *Montaignac v Shitta* [1890] 15 AC 357.

Coast Colony, which had barred him from legal practice in the colony on account of fraud and professional misconduct. After a lengthy trial, the JCPC held that no case of fraud or professional misconduct had been established against him, and ruled that he should be permitted to practise law in the Colony.[112]

The cases of Shitta and Renner exemplify the early African appeal cases at the JCPC. The litigants also typify the type of Africans involved in these appeals. Shitta, the native merchant, was a man of means who—though illiterate and unfamiliar with the complexities of English legal system—could use his influence and resources to seek justice in the highest court of Empire. Awoonor-Renner typifies another category of African litigants. Born in the late nineteenth century to a Sierra Leonean father and a mother of Dutch ancestry, he was educated in England and Germany. He was called to the bar at Lincoln's Inn in 1883, and practised law in the Gold Coast until the 1930s.[113] Awoonor-Renner belonged to a small but active group of Western educated African lawyers who could challenge European and colonial authorities in the arena that they had mastered—that of colonial law. By appealing to the Imperial Courts, they could call to question the legal powers of the state and the state's use of those powers. They could use the legal arena—particularly those beyond the direct influence of the local officials—to successfully challenge and defy local colonial power. Colonial authorities in Africa charged with British 'pacification' agendas in the early twentieth century saw this group of Western-educated Africans as a nuisance. These were the 'trousered negros of the coast', and 'professional agitators' keen on inciting excitable native populations to resist and defy order and Crown authority in the colonies.[114]

The attitudes of colonial officials towards indigenous lawyers masked a well-founded concern about maintaining colonial authority. As British authority became entrenched and confidence in traditional authority weakened, Africans looked to these lawyers as a counterpoise of sorts to the alien administration. Lawyers could enjoy popular support and a high media profile, filling the vacuum left when the legitimacy of traditional authorities was questioned.[115] This fear of expatriate and indigenous lawyers was manifested in the sustained antagonism toward the legal profession and the restrictions on their professional activities.

In 1925, a group of senior administrative officers in Kenya wrote to the Governor to complain about the increasing activities of lawyers in native cases. They stated that they considered this a 'matter of grave danger to the administration of justice'. According to the officers, the employment of lawyers in native cases caused too much stress to be laid on technicalities and procedures with resulting delays and lessened the chance of justice being done. Moreover, the

112 *Judgments of the Judicial Committee of the Privy Council on Appeal from the Gold Coast Colony 1874–1928* (Accra: Government Printing Office, 1929) 8.

113 For a discussion of the life and times of Peter Awoonor Renner, see Christopher Fyfe, *A History of Sierra Leone 1400–1787* (Cambridge: Cambridge University Press, 1962).

114 Ade Adefuye, Babatunde Agiri, and Akinjide Osuntokun, *History of the Peoples of Lagos State* (Lagos: Lantern Books, 1987) 267.

115 Chidi Oguamanam and Wesley W. Pue, 'Lawyers' Professionalism, Colonialism, State Formation' (2007) 13(6) *Social Identities* 777.

involvement of lawyers weighted the scales of justice heavily against natives who could not afford legal assistance. 'A district officer,' they noted 'does his best to absolutely impartially to get to the truth of any case while a lawyer endeavors to confuse the issue and get a verdict for his own client irrespective of the real rights of the case.'[116] As one District Commissioner stated, 'I do not want *my* natives to waste their money on lawyer's fees. It is enough that their cases are subject to revision by the District Commissioner and the Senior Commissioner.'[117]

Neither the wealth and influence of Shitta, nor the education and sophistication of Awoonor-Renner wholly explain why some African disputes were appealed all the way to the JCPC, while others were not. Some JCPC appeals were brought by litigants of modest means, influence, and education. Given the cost and procedural complexities involved, only high-stakes disputes of utmost importance went as far as the JCPC. If a case was considered important enough, people of modest means pooled their resources to bring appeals before the JCPC. Typical of such high-stakes cases were communal land disputes, disputes over chieftaincy succession, and cases involving capital convictions.

One such case was *Kwaku Mensah v King,* which appeared before the Privy Council in 1941.[118] The appeal was against a conviction of murder—a charge imposed on the appellant by a court in the Gold Coast. The murder occurred in the course of a dispute between two villages. The appellant had led the fight on behalf of his community, and claimed that he shot and killed the deceased in the course of defending his community from theft. The appeal against the murder conviction was funded largely though contributions from the appellant's community which saw the litigation as a communal cause. Several appeals to the JCPC and the EACA from the British Somaliland Protectorate arising from tribal disputes and vendettas were prosecuted through clan contributions.[119]

Okusanya v Akanwo was a costly and protracted land appeal at the JCPC funded largely through communal contributions and levies that had been put in place by the elders and Chiefs of disputing Ake and Ijesha communities in Western Nigeria.[120] The successive appeals by Chief Oluwa in the 1920s over land expropriated by the colonial government in Nigeria were also funded entirely through contributions and subscriptions by his subjects and supporters. Similarly, the appeal by the Yoruba Chief Eshugbayi Eleko against his deposition and deportation by colonial authorities was prosecuted with funds contributed by his supporters within the class of traditional and Western-educated African elites in colonial Lagos. Some contributors sold their properties and mortgaged their houses for

[116] 'Employment of Lawyers by Natives', Internal Memorandum, 16 December 1925, KNAN, AP/1/1445.

[117] J. Combes, Internal Memorandum, 16 December 1925, KNAN, AP/1/1445.

[118] *Kwaku Mensah v The King* [1946] 83 AC 91–2.

[119] For example, *Mohamed Sugal Esa Mamasan Rer Alalah v The King* [1946] AC 57; *Adan Haji Jama v The King* [1948] AC 225; JCPC *Printed Papers in Appeal* 1948 Vol 15.

[120] *Okusanya v Akanwo* [1941] 6 WACA 1; *West African Pilot* (6 September 1941).

loans to fund Eleko's case in both the local courts and at the Privy Council.[121] Eleko also received contributions from religious groups, trade associations, and market women who saw his deposition and deportation by the government as an affront on traditional political authority.[122] Communal litigation of Privy Council appeals created unease among colonial officials in West Africa and elsewhere in the Empire. In Nigeria, officials attempted to enact measures preventing litigants from raising funds from the public for the purposes of JCPC appeals against the government.[123] Similar concerns led the authorities in Canada to introduce legislation in 1927, effectively making it illegal for aboriginal communities to raise money in the community to pursue land claims against the government.[124]

The JCPC was a powerful symbol of British imperial authority, even if the JCPC judges themselves saw their role as that of impartial adjudicators of the Empire, charged with upholding the unity and integrity of British justice. For African litigants, the JCPC offered a unique platform to challenge colonial power and local judicial authority. More than just an imperial court, it was an elevated legal arena beyond the direct influence of colonial officialdom. At the JCPC and the regional Courts of Appeal, traditional and Westernised African elites could assert their rights, contest access to resources, negotiate relationships of power and authority, and influence interpretations of custom and culture. As the next chapter shows, African engagement with the JCPC—particularly regarding the conflict of laws and the interpretation of customary law—generated crucial jurisprudential debates and shaped the processes and outcomes of imperial justice.

[121] J. E. Flood at the Colonial Office, 27 May 1930, NAUK, CO 538/173; 'Eshugbayi Eleko: Costs in Privy Council Appeals', NANI CSO 26/2; Cole, *Modern and Traditional Elites*, 137.

[122] Richard Sklar, *Nigerian Political Parties: Power in an Emergent African Nation* (Princeton: Princeton University Press, 1963) 47.

[123] J. E. Flood, Eleko Appeal to the Privy Council: Minute by Assistant Secretary at the Colonial Office, 17 June 1929, NAUK, CO 583/166/2.

[124] Christian W. McMillen, *Making Indian Law: The Hualapai Land Case and the Birth of Ethnohistory* (New Haven: Yale University Press, 2007) 97.

3

Repugnant Customs and Alien Courts

Adjudicating African appeals posed a unique challenge to the JCPC. The sheer diversity and complexity of African customary laws that their Lordships were called upon to interpret was compounded by their unfamiliarity with these customs. Lord Haldane observed in 1928 that as 'native territories' within the Empire became organized under local colonial governments, their laws assumed more complex and crystallized forms. Custom was becoming law with the aid of Crown Ordinances, and the JCPC was venturing into uncharted territory when interpreting these laws. Haldane was particularly concerned about West African customary law. Some of the legal questions arising from West Africa, he noted, were of 'exceptional difficulty' because of the novelty of the customs embodied in the native laws which he considered highly divergent from English common law traditions.[1] To Haldane and his colleagues on the JCPC bench, the challenge posed by African customary law was an existential one, requiring an adaptive JCPC and a flexible imperial legal system. Just as native customs were evolving into English-style laws, Haldane argued, so too must the JCPC evolve and reposition itself to adjudicate appeals arising from diverse and unfamiliar African customary laws.

Haldane's observations were affirmed in *Effuah Amissah v Effuah Krabah* where the JCPC acknowledged the difficulty of adjudicating West African Appeals involving customary law and solicited the assistance of local courts. Delivering judgment in this case, Lord Maugham stated that it would be 'very convenient if the Courts in West Africa, in suitable cases, would rule as to the native customs of which they think it proper to take judicial notice specifying, of course, the tribes (or districts) concerned and taking steps to see that these rulings are reported in a readily accessible form'.[2] This call for guidance from local courts became necessary because in the first half of the twentieth century, some of the most contentious African appeals before the JCPC concerned interpretations of customary law and the quality of justice dispensed on such matters.

This chapter examines the ambivalent place of African customary law in the colonial legal system, the tensions arising from conflicting systems of laws, and the role of the JCPC and the regional Courts of Appeal in interpreting and applying

[1] R. B. Haldane, 'Judicial Committee of the Privy Council', ed, R. B. Haldane, *Selected Addresses and Essays* (Freeport, NY: Books for Libraries Press, 1970 [1928]) 224.

[2] *Effuah Amissah v Effuah Krabah* [1936] reported in *Privy Council Judgments: Opinions of the Judicial Committee of the Privy Council in Appeals from West Africa, 1841 to 1973,* Olisa Chukura, ed, (London: Gilford, 1981) 280.

African customary laws. Focusing on debates over 'native assessors' in the colonial courts and the 'doctrine of repugnancy', it explores how the tension between imperial universalism and local exceptionalism played out in contested judicial discourse over the role of customary law in imperial justice. It investigates how imperial appeal courts, in dealing with questions of African customary law sought to uphold two frequently conflicting agendas: maintaining fundamental principles of British justice thought to be crucial to legitimizing the Empire, while simultaneously accommodating African customary law considered indispensable to achieving imperial justice.

The role of imperial appeal courts in judicial discourses about African customary law is best understood when examined within the broader framework of British colonial legal system in Africa. In administering its African colonies, British authorities generally sought to extend, as far as practicable, the same principles of law and justice as prevailed in England. In the colonies, however, it was not intended that the received English law should necessarily be applied in its English purity. Rather, English law was to be applied only so far as the local circumstances of each territory permitted, and subject to modifications as circumstances rendered necessary.

Court Ordinances, which introduced English law to many parts of British Africa in the late nineteenth century, stipulated that the Common Law, the Doctrines of Equity, and the Statutes of General Application would be enforced under the jurisdiction of these Courts as they were in England on the date of each colony's obtaining its local legislature.[3] Although the primary law administered in most British colonial courts was English law, local African customary laws were often allowed to exist alongside the imported English legal system. The assumption was that wholesale imposition of English statutes or the Common Law would be destructive to native societies and would be met with local opposition. As the Under Secretary of State for Colonies put it in 1926, 'nothing can be more undermining of native traditions, society, and organisation more than the substitution of European for native legal forms'.[4]

Customary Law and Native Courts

The tensions between imperial universalism and colonial difference were most evident in differential colonial policies in urban, cosmopolitan civic spaces and rural, traditional customary spaces. Under the British system of indirect rule, colonial policies tended to be culturally assimilationist in the civic sphere, with English culture considered the hallmark of civilization and modernity. In the civic spheres of the Empire, Europeans and Western-educated African elites could avail

[3] William Brandford Griffith, *Ordinances of the Settlements on the Gold Coast and of the Gold Coast Colony* (London: Waterlow, 1887) 47.

[4] W. G. A. Ormsby-Gore, 'Report by the Hon. W. G. A. Ormsby-Gore on his visit to West Africa' (1927) 69 *The Geographical Journal* 509.

themselves of the benefits of codified English law. They could seek justice in urban British courts presided over by mostly British or expatriate judges and magistrates.

In contrast, colonial policy in the customary sphere was firmly grounded in the principle of difference. The Native Administrative Authorities and the native tribunals, where the majority of Africans encountered colonial justice, produced and reified racial and ethnic differences. These native tribunals, headed by traditional Chiefs or elders appointed by British administrators, had jurisdiction only over Africans and in some cases only over particular 'tribes'. Their jurisdiction was also restricted mostly to civil cases, as spelt out in the Kenyan Native Tribunal Ordinance of 1930, which empowered the Governor to establish native tribunals with jurisdiction limited to civil matters and certain categories of criminal matters relating to natives and consenting Arabs.[5] Professional lawyers who practised in the British courts were barred from appearing before native tribunals. The rationale was that the technicalities of professional legal advocacy would undermine the simple customary justice administered in these tribunals.[6]

Conceptualizing 'customary law', which native tribunals were expected to apply, was problematic from the beginning. The term 'African Customary Law' implied a distinction between indigenous African law and colonial statute law. The JCPC's decision in *Eshuabavi Eleko v Government of Nigeria*[7] outlined what was generally considered to be the main characteristics of the 'native law and custom', namely: acceptance of the customary norm by the community, its adaptability, flexibility, uncertainty and divergence, and its multiplicity and unwritten nature. Flexibility and adaptability made customary laws useful instruments for preserving administrative control and strengthening recognized African authorities under the indirect rule system.[8] In colonial courts, however, the imprecision and uncertainty of customary law also complicated adjudicatory processes.

Evidently, most Africans encountered colonial justice in the native tribunals charged with enforcing indigenous law or 'customary law', rather than in British courts applying English law.[9] These native tribunals adjudicated primarily civil cases, applying customary law to matters of personal law, such as marriage, divorce, guardianship, and succession. They dealt mostly with disputes arising out of the ownership and possession of land, customary marriage, fetishism, witchcraft, and debt cases. These were issues that the British courts could not adjudicate or would have adjudicated with an English Common Law bias, making them unattractive

[5] 'Kenyan Native Tribunal Ordinance of 1930', *Gazette of the Colony and Protectorate of Kenya*, Nairobi, Section 4 (20 June 1930).

[6] For example, the Ashanti Administration Ordinance of 1902 provided that 'in no cause or matter, criminal or civil, shall the employment of a barrister or solicitor be allowed'. *Ordinances of the Gold Coast, Ashanti, Northern Territories, and Togoland under British Mandate* (Accra: Government Printer, 1936) 118.

[7] *Eshugbayi Eleko v Officer Administering the Government of Nigeria* [1931] AC 662.

[8] H. F. Morris and James S. Read, *Indirect Rule and the Search for Justice: Essays in East African Legal History* (Oxford: Clarendon Press, 1972) 168.

[9] Judicial Department Annual Reports (1932), KNAN, AP/1/1681; (1933) AP/1/1681; (1934) AP/1/1717.

venues for such litigation.[10] However, were possible from native tribunals through a hierarchy of British colonial courts. In the Gold Coast, for example, appeals were allowed from the native tribunals to the District Commissioner's Court, from where further appeals could be made to the Provincial Commissioner's Court, the Divisional Courts, the High Court, the WACA, and ultimately all the way to the JCPC in England. This meant that the native tribunal system and the English Court system were interlinked and the seemingly rigid boundary between customary and common law was far less so in practice than it was in theory.[11]

In both the native tribunal and British courts, native customary laws were admissible in judicial proceedings only if they met certain conditions. First, they could only be applied in cases where the cause of a legal suit was 'known to customary law'.[12] It was held, for example, that 'modern' transactions such as mortgage agreements or even the charging of interest on a loan were transactions unknown to native law.[13] This law was intended to prevent the application of existing customary rules by adaptation to transactions that are essentially different because of their novelty in Africa.[14]

Another condition for the judicial application of customary law was that such laws must not be 'repugnant to natural justice, equity and good conscience'.[15] African customary rules were recognized only in subordination to colonial law, and were denied such recognition where they were considered repugnant or contrary to the 'general principles of humanity'.[16] Crown Ordinances throughout British Africa included this proviso, which became known as the 'doctrine of repugnancy' and, in judicial application, the 'repugnancy test'.

The Doctrine of Repugnancy

The imperial role of colonial courts was demonstrated most clearly in the exercise of the power of judicial review. The basis of that power historically lay in the principle that all colonial legislatures were subordinate to the imperial parliament and that colonial legislation must conform to English standards and not be *repugnant* to the laws of England.[17] In Britain's African Empire, this repugnancy principle took on new meaning. A classic example of the repugnancy clause is the colonial law that

[10] Roger Gocking, 'British Justice and the Native Tribunals of the Southern Gold Coast Colony' (1993) 34(1) *The Journal of African History* 97.

[11] Gocking, 'British Justice and the Native Tribunals of the Southern Gold Coast Colony', 95.

[12] High Court Laws of Nigeria, Section 34 (1955).

[13] Martin Chanock, *The Making of South African Legal Culture 1902–1936: Fear, Favour and Prejudice* (Cambridge: Cambridge University Press, 2001) 318.

[14] *Salau v Aderibigbe* [1963] WNLR 80 at 87. In this case, the question before the court was whether a lease-purchase agreement for a truck was governed by customary law or whether it constituted a transaction 'unknown to customary law' because of the novelty of the transaction.

[15] See, for example, the Gold Coast Supreme Court Ordinance No 4 (1876).

[16] Peter Fitzpatrick, 'Terminal Legality: Imperialism and the (De)composition of Law' in Diane Kirkby and Catharine Coleborne, eds, *Law, History, Colonialism: The Reach of Empire* (Manchester: Manchester University Press, 2001) 21.

[17] Alpheus Todd, *Parliamentary Government in the British Colonies* (Boston: Little, Brown, 1880) 14.

introduced English law to Nigeria in the late nineteenth century. Parts of the law stated:

> The High Courts shall observe and enforce the observance of every native law and custom which is applicable and *not repugnant to natural justice, equity and good conscience*, nor incompatible either directly or by implication with any law for the time being in force, and nothing in this Act shall deprive any person of the benefit of any such native law and custom.[18]

The Gold Coast Supreme Court Ordinance of 1876 included similar repugnancy provisions, as did the Orders in Council establishing the East African High Courts.[19] The latter stipulated that in all cases to which natives were parties, the court was to be guided by native law, so far as such laws were not 'repugnant to natural justice and morality'.[20] The Concession Treaty of 1887, by which the British East African Association obtained territorial concession from the Sultan of Zanzibar, contained similar repugnancy provisions.[21]

The phrase associated with the repugnancy doctrine—'justice, equity, and good conscience'—is not a term of art in the Common Law. Terms like these were put into statutes and ordinances as tests allowing colonial officials to strike down local laws and practices they considered 'uncivilized' and wished to weed out.[22] This process of legal inclusion and exclusion was not unique to British Africa. The notion of 'equity' has historically been used as a set of rules applicable where the Common Law is silent or where the formal law recognizes some rights but does not provide adequate relief. The principle was concerned with facilitating a higher form of justice, allowing judges to modify formal legal positions where the existing law does not take sufficient account of specific facts and circumstances.[23]

In colonial contexts, applying the principles of the repugnancy doctrine allowed judges to decide cases virtually as they saw fit, and became grounds for colonial courts to apply English law rather than local law. 'Natural justice and Equity' as residual sources of law in relation to repugnancy clauses were defining features of the colonial legal system in Britain's Atlantic Empire. Pre-constitutional American law and legal culture developed within the framework of an evolving, unwritten transatlantic constitution underscored by the doctrine of repugnancy. The central tenet of this constitution was that colonial laws and customs could diverge for local

[18] Supreme Court Ordinance, Section 19 (1876); Section 27(1), High Court of Lagos, Cap. 80. Cited in Lakshman Marasinghe, 'Third World Jurisprudence for the Twenty First Century' in *Legal Visions of the 21st Century: Essays in Honour of Judge Christopher Weeramantry*, eds, C. G. Weeramantry, Antony Anghie, and Garry Sturgess (The Hague: Martinus Nijhoff Publishers, 1998) 52.

[19] Fitzpatrick, 'Terminal Legality', 21.

[20] H. F. Morris, *Some Perspectives of East African Legal History Vol 3* (Uppsala: Scandinavian Institute of African Studies, 1970) 12.

[21] R. W. Hamilton, *The Origin and Growth of British Jurisdiction and of the Judicial System of the East African Protectorate* (Nairobi: Government Printer, 1918) 16.

[22] Morris and Read, *Indirect Rule*, 171.

[23] Werner F. Menski, 'Justice, Equity and Good Conscience', *The Oxford International Encyclopedia of Legal History, Vol 3*, ed, Stanley N. Katz (New York: Oxford University Press, 2009) 445.

circumstances but could not be repugnant to the laws of England.[24] In Australia, the doctrine of repugnancy provided the legal basis on which Australian laws considered inconsistent with the enactments of the British imperial parliament were rendered invalid.[25]

The doctrine of repugnancy became a primary means of accommodating and regulating customary law in India, where British authorities first faced the problems of large non-European communities with their own systems of laws. In colonial Anglo-Indian law, the basic rule was that a court must decide a case according to 'justice, equity, and good conscience' in the absence of a rule from statute, written sources of personal law, custom, or case law. The Bengali regulations of 1781, for example, required Provincial Court judges to act according to justice, equity, and good conscience. This expression encapsulated generally accepted notions of justice defined to coincide with English law.[26] The principle became a residual source of law for all cases and contexts in which either the Hindu or the Muslim personal law was silent or could not be applied.

In British Africa, the centrality of customary law to colonial legal systems gave renewed relevance to the repugnancy doctrine. Nowhere else within the Empire did indigenous law play a more pivotal role in the imperial legal system than it did in Africa.[27] Recognizing and accommodating African customary law within the colonial legal system was one thing, but enforcing it was quite another. At a practical level, the unfamiliarity of most colonial judges and administrators with African customs was complicated by the multiplicity of African ethnic, linguistic, and cultural groups brought together under colonial legal and administrative systems. At a 1932 conference of East African Governors, senior colonial administrators acknowledged that the customs of the various tribes of East Africa were 'imperfectly known' and that enforcing these customs was a particularly difficult undertaking.[28] Determining which customs were repugnant to natural justice and equity, or what constituted the 'general principles of humanity' was one of such difficulties. In theory, 'natural justice' was equated with English justice. In practice, it underscored the attempt to universalize the principles of English justice.[29]

[24] Mary Sarah Bilder, *The Transatlantic Constitution: Colonial Legal Culture and the Empire* (Cambridge, MA: Harvard University Press, 2004) 3.

[25] Gerard Carney, *The Constitutional Systems of the Australian States and Territories* (Cambridge: Cambridge University Press, 2006) 136.

[26] J. D. M. Derrett, 'Justice, Equity and Good Conscience' in Lauren Benton, ed, *Law and Colonial Cultures: Legal Regimes in World History 1400–1900* (Cambridge: Cambridge University Press, 2002) 139.

[27] Unlike the cases in West and East Africa, where by express statute customary law was *prima facie* applicable to Africans, Britain's approach to conflicting systems of law in China was more guarded. For example, while the practice of polygamy was generally recognized under African customary law, colonial judges in the Settlements and Hong Kong were reluctant to accord such recognition to the Chinese practice of *tsip* or 'secondary wife'. J. N. Matson, 'The Common Law Abroad: English and Indigenous Laws in the British Commonwealth' (1993) 42(3) *The International and Comparative Law Quarterly* 765.

[28] Proceedings of the conference of East African Governors, Nairobi, 1932, Kenyan National Archives, Nairobi (hereinafter KNAN) AP/1/1659.

[29] David Swinfen, *Imperial Control of Colonial Legislation, 1813–1865: A Study of British Policy Towards Colonial Legislative Powers* (Oxford: Clarendon Press, 1970) 44.

The nonspecific meanings of terms such as 'natural justice' and 'good conscience' allowed for highly subjective interpretations. Colonial judges bred in the English tradition invariably interpreted these terms in ways that reflected their social and legal backgrounds. Administrators and judicial officials at every level of the colonial legal system struggled with the scope and meaning of the repugnancy doctrine but applied it nonetheless. Chief Justice Edwin Speed of Nigeria noted in 1908 that although it would not be difficult to hold that many of the 'ancient customs of the barbaric times' are repugnant under the repugnancy provisions, it was difficult to offer a strict and accurate definition of the terms.[30]

Of all the restrictions on the application of customary laws during the colonial period, the test of repugnancy 'to justice or morality' was potentially the most sweeping. Customary laws could hardly be repugnant to the traditional sense of justice or morality of the community that still accepted them. It was therefore clear that the justice or morality of the colonial power was to provide the standard to be applied.[31] Sir Kenneth Roberts-Wray, who served as a legal adviser at the Colonial Office in the 1940s and 50s, explained how colonial officials interpreted the repugnancy doctrine.

> It is claimed that in an African society due regard should be had to their own conception of what is right and proper. But there is an obvious caveat. Where the Courts are not to give effect to a rule of customary law if it is repugnant to good conscience, they cannot necessarily accept as a persuasive argument that the conscience of the community concerned sees nothing wrong with the rule.[32]

In Roberts-Wray's view (as of his many contemporaries within the colonial legal and judicial establishment), the test of repugnancy could not be the conscience of the native community practising a custom. Repugnancy had to be measured against 'higher' and more universal standards of British justice. The repugnancy doctrine was applied unevenly. It has been suggested that although the vagueness of the repugnancy provisions complicated its applications in Southern Africa, colonial courts exercised 'remarkable restraint' in invoking it. In 1922, a Southern Rhodesian court held that the repugnancy proviso applied only 'to such customs as inherently impress us with some abhorrence or are obviously immoral in their incidence'.[33] As a result of this view, customary law was only declared repugnant in relatively few cases. These were mainly cases concerned with matters of personal liberty, 'sexual immorality', and succession by 'illegitimate children'.[34] In contrast to Southern and Eastern Africa, the repugnancy clause was invoked quite extensively in the District, Provincial, and Supreme Courts of West Africa.[35]

[30] *Lewis v Bankole* [1908] 1 NLR 82, per E. Speed at 84–5.

[31] Morris and Read, *Indirect Rule*, 171.

[32] Kenneth Roberts-Wray, *Commonwealth and Colonial Law* (New York: F.A. Praeger, 1966) 578.

[33] *Chiduku v Chidano* [1922] SR 55 at 58, cited in T. W. Bennett, *Customary Law in South Africa* (Lansdowne: Juta, 2004) 68.

[34] T. W. Bennett, *Customary Law in South Africa*, 68.

[35] Omoniyi Adewoye, *The Judicial System in Southern Nigeria 1854–1954: Law and Justice in a Dependency* (Atlantic Highlands, NJ: Humanities Press, 1977) 267.

It was sometimes difficult to decide what ought to be the true morality in a particular colony's conditions. A constant judicial dilemma was how to strike a balance between what was reasonably tolerable and what was considered essentially below the minimum standard of civilized values in the contemporary world. The judgments of the JCPC and the regional Courts of Appeal contain relatively few cases in which judges found it necessary to outlaw African custom on grounds of English morality. These cases were however of high precedential value. The repugnancy doctrine was invoked more often by administrative officers in the course of reviewing the decisions of native tribunals.[36] In British Courts, the repugnancy doctrine was often invoked when modifying the procedure in the native courts to conform to English notions of due process and fair trial procedure.

Invariably, in the course of judicial review, some African customary rules failed the repugnancy test and colonial officials decided such cases on the basis of presumed universalist standards of natural justice, equity, and conscience. Some guidance as to what constituted repugnant African customs was provided in an official memorandum on native courts in Tanganyika. The murder of twins and trials by ordeal were customs that 'a civilized Government has no option but to prohibit, and enforce their prohibition with penal sanctions'.[37] The repugnancy provision was applied not only to a particular rule of customary law, but to the operation of such a rule in the circumstances of a particular case. In 1938, a Tanganyika High Court followed this course in the case of *Gwao bin Kilimo*, where a man had been held responsible under native law and custom for a judgment penalty against his son. The presiding judge held that the alleged native law had not been adequately proven, but continued:

> I have no doubt whatever that the only standard of justice and morality which a British Court in Africa can apply is its own British standard. Otherwise we should find ourselves in certain circumstances having to condone such things, for example the institution of slavery...It is certainly contrary to the principles of British justice that the sins of the sons should be visited on the fathers, when the sons are themselves fully responsible persons in law.[38]

Contemporary scholars were divided in their appraisal of the doctrine of repugnancy. While some interpreted it as a means of subordinating indigenous law to English law, others saw it as a transformative legal doctrine. The subjugation theorists asserted the inherent subjectivity in determining what is 'repugnant to natural justice, equity and good conscience' by officials who were unfamiliar with local customs in diverse multi-ethnic settings with varying perceptions of justice and morality.[39] Other scholars argued that the repugnancy doctrine was an effective

[36] Morris and Read, *Indirect Rule*, 177.

[37] 'Native Courts', *Tanganyika Territory Native Administration Memoranda, No 2* (Government Printer, Dar es Salaam, 1930) para 24.

[38] 1 TLR 403 at 405.

[39] A. P. Anyebe, *Customary Law: The War Without Arms* (Enugu: New Dimension, 1995) 7; Adetoun Ilumoka, 'Legal Imperialism and Chauvinism: Lessons from Africa' (2005) 48(1) *Publications of the Swiss Institute of Comparative Law* 11.

means of reforming some of the more obnoxious and barbarous customary rules.[40] The consensus, however, was that the doctrine fostered judicial discretion and differential application of African customary law in the adjudicatory processes.

In colonial courts, the repugnancy doctrine became an important part of the discussions about human rights within the colonial legal system. It became a useful principle with which the colonial authorities, through the courts, abrogated customs relating to slavery, human sacrifice, trials by ordeal, and forced marriages. It provided the colonial authorities with one of the most effective legal instruments for social re-engineering of African societies. This provided a foundation for later discourse on universal human rights in the period of decolonization.[41] Until the formal introduction of constitutional rights and other specific human rights laws in the post-World War II period, the doctrine of repugnancy provided a legal framework for protecting individual and collective rights.

The bulk of the work of interpreting and applying African customary law in the colonies was done in native tribunals. British courts in the colonies and the Imperial Appeal Courts, however, were crucial arenas where the broad frameworks for ascertaining the validity or repugnancy of customary law were framed and contested. In interpreting repugnancy provisions in colonial statutes, the line between valid and unacceptable African customary rules was often ill-defined and uncertain. Decisions of the Imperial Appeal Courts provided guidance to colonial judges and administrators who grappled with the difficulties of ascertaining and validating African customary laws in local courts. Unlike local courts, which tended to draw narrowly on English law in interpreting 'justice, equity and good conscience', the JCPC took recourse to many different legal systems in its interpretation.[42] In some cases, its pronouncements on the repugnancy doctrine tended to reinforce colonial difference. At other moments, the repugnancy doctrine was invoked to uphold universal ideals of justice and equity, thereby softening colonial difference.

The selective and ambivalent application of the repugnancy doctrine is evident in several landmark judgments of the JCPC. The facts of each of these cases are different, and the judicial interpretation of the repugnancy clause was certainly shaped by the peculiar circumstances of each case. Still, it is possible to identify certain trends and patterns in appellate judicial discourse on the repugnancy doctrine.

In *Eshugbayi Eleko v Officer Administering the Government of Nigeria*, which case came before the JCPC in 1931, one of the questions that arose concerned the circumstances under which a court may enforce a custom necessitating the killing of a deposed Chief or its milder alternative requiring banishment. The colonial administration in Nigeria had sought to invoke this custom to justify its decision to banish an intransigent Chief.[43] In a judgment delivered by Lord Atkin, the JCPC

[40] T. O. Elias, 'The Judicial Development of Customary Law in Nigeria', eds, T. O. Elias et al (Enugu: Government Printer, 1975) 16; A. G. Karibi-Whyte, *The Relevance of the Judiciary in the Polity: A Historical Perspective* (Lagos: Nigerian Institute of Advanced Legal Studies, 1987) 34–40.

[41] Bonny Ibhawoh, *Imperialism and Human Rights: Colonial Discourses of Rights and Liberties in African History* (Albany: State University of New York Press, 2007).

[42] Menski, 'Justice, Equity and Good Conscience', 446.

[43] Appeal to Privy Council by Eshugbayi Eleko, 1931, CO 583/177/9.

ruled that the court could not itself transform a barbarous custom into a milder one. 'If a custom stood in its barbarous character,' Lord Atkin ruled, 'it must be rejected as repugnant to natural justice, equity and good conscience.'[44]

Their Lordships acknowledged the possibility that 'barbarous' ancient African customs may become milder under the influences of 'civilization', without losing their essential character as custom. In such cases, they held, it was then essential for the party invoking custom to show that, in their milder form, such practices were still recognized in the native community as customs. As Lord Atkin stated, 'it is the assent of the native community that gives a custom its validity and therefore, barbarous or mild, it must be shown to be recognised by the native community whose conduct it is supposed to regulate'.[45] Juridical foundation for the enforcement of customary laws lay in the support they enjoyed from the people.[46] Colonial officers, the JCPC argued, could not presume what constituted native customary law. It had to be proven that particular customary practices met the two criteria for judicially ascertaining customary law: the assent of local communities and the force of law for the natives. This required making the distinction between customs that had the force of law and those that, though having moral or religious sanction, did not have legal force within native communities.[47]

Following the precedent in *Eshugbayi Eleko*, the Gambian Supreme Court held in the later case of *Koykoy Jatta v Menna Camara* that, under Gambian statutes, it was repugnant to natural justice, equity, and good conscience to import the custom of female circumcision into a tribe that did not practise it, even though this was the custom of the place where the act of circumcision occurred.[48] In a Gold Coast appeal involving a dispute over the succession to a chieftainship 'stool' (throne), the WACA held that a customary rule requiring the consent of the decision-making councillors of the stool, before an aggrieved Chief could take action in the courts, made the councillors judges in their own cause. This was held to be 'contrary to public policy and repugnant to natural justice' under the Gold Coast Courts Ordinance.[49]

Another case that illustrates judicial discourse on the repugnancy doctrine in the Imperial Appeal Courts is *Yisa Dawodu v Sowebatu Danmole*.[50] This case arose from a family dispute over the division of the estate of the patriarch of one prominent family in Lagos, Suberu Dawodu, who died intestate in 1940. First heard at the High Court in Western Nigeria, the case was subsequently appealed to the Supreme Court of Nigeria and ultimately to the JCPC in 1960. One of the questions before the courts was determining the validity of African customary law in dividing the estate of the deceased among his nine children from four wives. Evidence was tendered at trial that, under Yoruba customary law that applied to the

[44] *Eshugbayi Eleko v The Officer administrating the Government of Nigeria* [1931] AC 662.
[45] *Eshugbayi Eleko v The Officer administrating the Government of Nigeria*, 8.
[46] Morris and Read, *Indirect Rule*, 168.
[47] Appeal to Privy Council by Eshugbayi Eleko, 1931, CO 583/177/9.
[48] 'Koykoy Jatta v. Menna Camara' (1964) 8(1) *Journal of African Law* 35.
[49] 'Quansah v. Yankum' [1957] 1(2) *Journal of African Law* 128.
[50] *Yisa Dawodu and Others v Suwebatu Danmole and Others* [1962] UKPC 20.

litigants, the division of estates among the children of the deceased could be done in either of two ways. The first custom was division *per stirpe* among the deceased individual's four wives. Under this customary rule, known as *Idi Igi*, each wife would respectively receive one-fourth of the estate, irrespective of how many children she had with the deceased. Under this rule, an only child from a wife got the same share as many children from another wife, the children subsequently not receiving equal shares of their father's estate. In contrast, under the second customary rule, known as *Ori Ojori,* the estate would be divided equally among the children of each wife.

In this case, division into fourths favoured the plaintiffs, while division into ninths favoured the defendants. When the family opted for the custom of division *per stirpe* among the wives of the deceased, the defendants instituted a lawsuit challenging the decision. At the High Court, the presiding Judge Jibowu, an African, referred to the Supreme Court Ordinance, which made native law and custom applicable in such circumstances only if such native law and custom was not 'repugnant to natural justice, equity and good conscience'. He decided that the repugnancy clause was applicable in this circumstance, and that the Yoruba native law of *Idi Igi* (division by stirpes) was inequitable and did not pass the repugnancy test. The judge accordingly made an order for division of the estate into nine parts to be shared equally among the children.

The case was subsequently appealed to the Supreme Court, which held that the custom of *Idi Igi* was *not* contrary to natural justice, equity, or good conscience, and reversed the earlier judgment of the High Court. The court made a counter order for the division of the contested estate into fourth parts shared among the wives, rather than nine parts shared equally among the children. This led to a further appeal to the JCPC, which upheld the position that the customary rule of division of estates by stirpes among the wives was not contrary to natural justice, equity or good conscience. In a judgment delivered by Lord Evershed, the JCPC held that the native family law of *Idi Igi* (division among wives rather than individual children) was a valid part of the Yoruba native law and custom on succession, even though it might not be considered so in other communities. Lord Evershed stated: 'The principles of natural justice, equity and good conscience applicable in a country where polygamy is generally accepted should not in a matter of this kind be readily equated with those applicable to a community governed by the rule of monogamy.'[51]

The judicial discourse on the repugnancy doctrine in both the *Eleko* and *Dawodu* cases, if not the judgments, suggests a tendency toward accommodating and reinforcing African difference. As Lord Evershed made clear, the principles of equity and good conscience could not be applied with universal normative objectivity. In African societies, where polygamy was generally accepted, notions of repugnancy had to be construed differently than they would be in societies where monogamy prevailed. Such clarity on social differentiation and exceptionalism in

[51] *Yisa Dawodu v Suwebatu Danmole*, 20.

interpreting repugnancy clauses was not always evident in JCPC decisions. In some other cases, the judicial discourse on the repugnancy clause was less assertive of native difference.

In *Idewu Inasa v Chief Sakariyawo Oshodi*, the JCPC gave judicial sanction to a customary rule that permitted a Chief to evict an offending family member and his relatives who had supported him in a dispute against the Chief.[52] It rejected the claim that the customary rule in question was repugnant to natural justice, equity, and good conscience. This case concerned a dispute over the ownership of a family house in Western Nigeria, from which the appellants had been forcibly evicted. The appellants challenged their eviction on the grounds that they possessed a customary right to live in the house. They invoked native custom to the effect that, where a Chief had evicted a family member for misconduct, he was entitled to also evict all the relatives supporting the offending family member. This custom, counsel argued on their behalf, amounted to collective punishment, which made it repugnant to natural justice, equity, and good conscience, and therefore unenforceable under the prevailing statute law. Both the local High Court and Supreme Court disagreed with this claim, however, and found that the custom in question was not repugnant to natural justice, equity, and good conscience.

The case was subsequently appealed to the JCPC, which upheld the decision of the courts in the colony and recommended that the appeal be dismissed. In dismissing the appeal, Lord Blanesburgh restated the JCPC's longstanding principle of deferring to local courts on matters relating to the interpretation and enforcement of native law and customs. He stressed that the Lords of the JCPC were not in a position to uphold any native custom in the matter beyond what had already been decided by the local courts. These courts were deemed more suitable to determine the validity or repugnancy of local customs, as they were in closer proximity to the litigants.[53] This decision marked a departure from the *Dawodu* case, where the JCPC intervened to affirm native difference by drawing a distinction between the definitions of 'repugnancy' in polygamous Africa and in monogamous societies. In *Idewu Inasa*, the Lords of the JCPC were content to defer to the local colonial courts.

The endurance of the repugnancy doctrine beyond colonial rule is a testament to the lasting influence of British colonial legal systems. Although most African countries repealed repugnancy provisions when they attained independence, the principle continued to be invoked in African Courts. As late as 1997, the repugnancy doctrine was applied in the Nigerian case of *Mojekwu v Mojekwu*, where the courts rejected as 'repugnant to natural justice equity and good conscience' a local custom that disentitled a daughter from inheriting the property of the father where no son survived him.[54]

52 *Idewu Inasa and others v Chief Sakariyawo Oshodi* [1934] AC 99; Taslim Olawale Elias, *Nigerian Land Law and Custom* (London: Routledge & Kegan Paul, 1962) 132.

53 *Idewu Inasa and others v Chief Sakariyawo Oshodi* [1934] AC 99.

54 *Mojekwu v Mojekwu* [1997] 7 NWLR (Pt 512) 283.

These cases convey the uncertainty in the jurisprudence on the repugnancy doctrine. The imprecise meaning of terms such as 'natural justice, equity, and good conscience' in colonial statute law invariably gave colonial and metropolitan judges much flexibility in constructing African difference. For African litigants it offered a framework for negotiating the boundaries of colonial difference to serve their interests in the courts. The repugnancy clause could be invoked and interpreted in ways that reinforced African difference at certain moments; in other cases it was construed in ways that softened difference. Such flexibility and adaptability was also evident in the jurisprudence and judicial discourse on proving and ascertaining African customary law in the courts.

Ascertaining Customary Law

A key challenge for British authorities in administering imperial justice was ascertaining what customary rules and practices should be applied in the courts. In discriminating between customs that had the force of law and those that did not, colonial authorities transferred the power of judicial interpretation from the local communities to the colonial courts and administrative institutions. Colonial judicial authorities gave themselves leeway to select in which situations to recognize and use customary law rules to introduce new relations of power and production.

Cases involving customary law rarely reached the British courts originally. Rather, they were done by way of appeal, since Africans were normally required to commence proceedings in the lowest courts, which were the native tribunals. This meant that before they reached British courts, disputes between Africans would already have been adjudicated by a court that treated customary law as a matter of law, rather than a matter of fact or evidence. In the British courts, however, it was required that customary law had to be pleaded as a fact.[55]

Addressing this question in *Angu v Atta*, a prominent case appealed to the British courts from the Gold Coast in 1916, the JCPC laid down the rule for ascertaining customary law. The Board held that if a particular customary law had been proven frequently before a court and by witnesses or assessors sufficiently acquainted with the native custom that it became 'notorious', the court was obliged to take 'judicial notice' of that custom.[56] The opinions on particular customs frequently presented before a court thus effectively became understood as customary law and required no further proof. Of course, such customs still had to pass the 'repugnancy test' and meet the requirements of British 'justice, equity, and good conscience'. Moreover, the JCPC's ruling raised concerns within colonial officialdom about the misrepresentation of customary law by African assessors due to ignorance, bias,

[55] Bas de Gaay Fortman and Paschal Mihyo, 'A False Start: Law and Development in the Context of a Colonial Legacy', *International Institute of Social Studies Working Paper, Vol 112* (Erasmus University, 1991) 11.

[56] 'Angu v. Atta', *Gold Coast Privy Council Judgments 1874–1928* (Accra: Government Printers, 1929) 43.

or corruption. There were concerns about a tendency on the part of some native assessors to idealize customary law, and to present 'what it ought to be instead of what it really is'.[57] Since native assessors were used mainly in criminal trials, officials feared the spectre of grave and widespread miscarriages of justice that could arise if idealized or distorted customs were given permanent judicial recognition, such that they could no longer be challenged in the courts.[58]

The doctrine of judicial notice, as expounded in *Angu v Atta*, served progressively to incorporate the rules of customary law in the fabric of colonial law. This doctrine did not completely resolve the question of ascertaining the validity of African customary laws, however. In the Gold Coast case, *Ababio II v Nsemfoo*, heard in 1947, the WACA was called upon to determine whether the JCPC rule in *Angu v Atta* applied only to the process of ascertaining customary law in British courts, or whether it also applied to native tribunals that operated essentially on the basis of native customary law.[59] The WACA held that the rule in *Angu v Attah* did not apply to native tribunals. The need to ascertain or prove which customary law was applicable in any given case could only be relevant in a British court. There was no ground for extending the rule to native tribunals, whose members are already well versed in their own native customary law. The WACA also held that while litigants in native 'courts' or tribunals could call witnesses to prove alleged customs, the African elders heading these tribunals were 'not obligated to require the custom to be proven through witnesses', since they were already familiar with the local customs.[60]

The principle that native customs need not be proven in native courts was reaffirmed in the Ugandan case of *Kigizi v Lukiko of Buganda*, where it was held that members of the native courts in Buganda 'generally speaking require no evidence to inform them what [their] customs are'.[61] In this case, the appellant had married the widowed mother of the King of Buganda, for which the Buganda parliament brought a criminal action against him in the native court. The mother of the King had consented to the marriage and, under English law, this would have been considered a normal marriage between two consenting adults. The Buganda parliament claimed that marrying the King's mother was against Buganda customary law, however, and amounted to a criminal offence under that law. In a ruling that surprised many observers, the British courts ruled that there was neither a requirement to prove the native law invoked by the Buganda parliament, nor any grounds for nullifying the ruling of the native court that criminalized the marriage.[62]

Judgments like these that upheld assertions of customary law even where they patently conflicted with statute law and English Common Law principles became more frequent in the later colonial period, as colonial authorities sought to preserve

[57] Acting Judge of Nyeri to Chief Registrar, Supreme Court of Nairobi, KNAN, DC/KSM/1/15/34.

[58] Criminal Records 1928, KNAN, SEC/2/4/26; Appeals by Natives on Criminal Charge 1910, KNAN, AP/1/619.

[59] *Ababio II v Nsemfoo* [1947] 12 WACA 127.

[60] *Ababio II v Nsemfoo*, 127.

[61] *Kigizi v Lukiko of Buganda* [1943] 6 ULR 113.

[62] 'West African Court of Appeal Cases' (1957) 1(1) *Journal of African Law* 55.

the traditional systems of dispute resolution, which were considered integral to the indirect native courts effectively strengthened the power and authority of African elders and senior men who dominated the native court system. These cases effectively illustrate the limits of the repugnancy doctrine. They show that even where African customary rule offended—or went contrary to—European values, European courts sometimes validated these rules in order to strengthen alliances with the Chiefs and groups in power. Both the doctrines of *repugnancy* and *ascertainment* were malleable enough for colonial courts to uphold claims of native difference, while affirming the imperial standards of justice.

The most important means by which colonial authorities sought to ascertain and validate customary law was by relying on 'native judicial assessors'. These were Africans who were presumed to be knowledgeable about local customs and traditions. They were chosen by colonial officials from the ranks of Chiefs, headmen, elderly men, or 'other natives suitably qualified to aid the courts'.[63] These assessors became exponents, interpreters, and sometimes 'inventors' of local customs, shaping the processes and outcomes of colonial law and justice.

Native Assessors and Colonial Justice

The tradition of electing assessors to serve in the courts was not unique to colonial Africa. The practice may date back to the medieval English manorial courts, as records refer to elected court assessors.[64] Judicial assessors were also present in English Admiralty Courts of the seventeenth century, where the assistance of nautical assessors in evaluating matters of nautical skill and seamanship was considered crucial. While most English courts retained the discretion of summoning assessors in civil proceedings, the practice became progressively rarer in non-nautical cases. By the early nineteenth century, the Admiralty Courts remained the only ones in England where judges were regularly assisted by assessors.[65]

Just as the institution of judicial assessors was weakening in England, however, circumstances gave it new life in India, where Britain sought to build English-style judicial structures after taking over from the East India Company. Until 1862, much of the colonial criminal law in India was based on Islamic law. A trial judge was required to obtain a *fatwa* (opinion) of a 'Mohammedan law officer' as to the law to be applied in each case.[66] Facing complaints from non-Muslims, however, the British authorities introduced legislation allowing colonial judges to appoint

[63] Swaziland High Court Proclamation 1938, [revised 1957], Section 8, reproduced in P. Mofokeng, *Criminal Law and Procedure through Cases* (Morija Sesuto Book Depot: Morija, Lesotho, 1997) 6.

[64] Zvi Razi, *Life, Marriage and Death in a Medieval Parish* (Cambridge: Cambridge University Press, 1980) 145.

[65] Anthony Dickey, 'The Province and Function of Assessors in English Courts' (1970) 33(5) *Modern Law Review* 494.

[66] G. Campbell, *Modern India and its Government* (London: John Murray, 1852) 472–3.

'respectable natives' in cases involving non-Muslims, to elicit their assistance in examining witnesses in court. Assessors were intended to serve more or less as native law experts, members of the court in an advisory capacity.[67]

The use of native assessors soon spread around the colonial world, for example in judicial systems in Fiji, Ceylon, and New Zealand.[68] For example, native assessors were used in the 1850s in the early Courts of Equity in the Niger Delta—courts that heard cases involving commercial transactions between Europeans and Africans.[69] In the Belgian Congo, judges heard disputes between 'natives' with the help of *assesseurs indigènes*.[70] In French West Africa, assessors assisted European courts; they were indispensable to the functioning of the native legal system and to French colonial rule. Far from being simple agents of colonial legal orders, they followed their own legal agendas, sometimes ignoring official rules and establishing spaces of their own—spaces the colonial administrators often found difficult to penetrate.[71] Still, like other local employees, they were crucial to the colonial enterprise because they played a central role in transmitting and interpreting knowledge and power in the Empire.

In the early twentieth century, specific colonial legislation began to provide the statutory framework for the institution of 'native assessors' in the judicial systems of British Africa. To avoid having 'alien courts' commit injustice through ignorance of local traditions, these laws required that all criminal trials without a jury in Superior Courts must employ local assessors. Employing African assessors to serve in native tribunals was a particularly prevalent practice in the colonies of eastern and southern Africa. They were used extensively in judicial proceedings in South Africa and in Kenya during the late colonial period, where they played an important role in the Mau Mau trials.[72]

The link between judicial assessors in India and Africa is clear. The Indian Evidence Act of 1872, applied as such or with modifications in East Africa, stated: 'When the court has to form an opinion as to the existence of any general custom or right, the opinion as to the existence of such custom or right, of persons who would

[67] J. H. Jearey, 'Trial by Jury and Trial with the Aid of Assessors in the Superior Courts of British African Territories' (1961) 5(2) *Journal of African Law* 95.

[68] P. Duff, 'The Evolution of Trial by Judge and Assessors in Fiji' (1997) 21 *Journal of Pacific Studies* 190–1; Charles Pridham, *An Historical, Political and Statistical Account of Ceylon and its Dependencies* (London: T. & W. Boone, 1849) 446; Danny Keenan, 'Aversion to Print? Maori Resistance to the Written Word' in Penelope Griffith, ed, *A Book in the Hand: Essays on the History of the Book in New Zealand* (Auckland: Auckland University Press, 2000) 24–7.

[69] A. E. Afigbo, *The Warrant Chiefs: Indirect Rule in South Eastern Nigeria 1891–1929* (New York: Humanities Press, 1972) 38–9.

[70] Marie-Bénédict Dembour, *Recalling the Belgian Congo: Conversations and Introspection* (New York: Berghahn Books, 2000) 28.

[71] Ruth Ginio, 'Negotiating Legal Authority in French West Africa: the Colonial Administration and African Assessors 1903–1918', Benjamin N. Lawrence et al, eds, *Intermediaries, Interpreters, and Clerks: African Employees in the Making of Colonial Africa* (Madison: University of Wisconsin Press, 2006) 132.

[72] David G. Anderson, *Histories of the Hanged: The Dirty War in Kenya and the End of Empire* (New York: W. W. Norton & Company, 2005) 158.

be likely to know of its existence, if it existed, are relevant'.[73] Similarly, the Swaziland High Court Proclamation of 1938 stated that a court could '[c]all to its assistance one or more native assessors, who shall be chosen by the paramount Chief of Swaziland from counsellors and headmen or other natives suitably qualified to aid the court'.[74] The courts were required to consider the assessor's opinion; however, final judicial decision was vested exclusively in the judge. Although these and similar laws gave colonial judges the discretion of whether to sit with assessors or not, most did in cases involving Africans.

As a general rule, assessors were of the same 'race' (tribe in the case of Africans) as the litigants, and were selected by the trial judge from among suitable persons summoned to attend the trial. Judges could also call to their assistance two administrative officers chosen by the senior colonial administrators. Some colonies further required that Africans selected as assessors had to be government employees with at least ten years of service in the Native Department.[75] Africans selected as assessors were almost always senior men, usually Chiefs or headmen. Older men were seen as the repositories of customary law, conceived as a set of rules that existed in the changeless pre-colonial past even though by the 1930s most of these men had little adult experience with the pre-colonial era.[76] While younger men were sometimes chosen, women were rarely appointed as assessors, even in cases involving them. Gender and generational imbalances sometimes became issues of contention when the evidence of assessors was reviewed in colonial appellate courts.

Colonial administrators attached considerable importance to the process of recruiting native assessors. Potential assessors were nominated by administrative officers and were appointed by judicial officers. In British East African colonies, yearly lists of eligible assessors were compiled by registrars of High Courts and published in official gazettes as 'Annual Rolls of Jurors and Assessors'. These Annual Rolls, some dating back to 1897, provide some biographical information, including the name, race, tribe, gender, residence, occupation and, in some cases, age and religion. In some territories, notably South Africa and Kenya, great attention was paid to categorizing jurors and assessors according to race, ethnicity, and religion. The Annual Roll of Jurors and Assessors in Kenya and Uganda typically included the following categories, in order: Europeans (jurors only), Arabs, Swahili and Beluchis, Memons, Sidhis and other Mohammedans, Isma'ili Khojas and Bohoras, Ithanasheri Khojas, Hindus, Parsis, Goans, and 'Natives of African extraction'.[77] The last category comprised local Africans, often senior men, nominated by Resident Commissioners from their districts to serve in cases involving natives (see Figure 3.1).[78]

[73] Indian Evidence Act 1872, Section 48, quoted in M. P. Jain, 'Custom as Source of Law in India' in Alan Dundes and Alison Dundes Renteln, eds, *Folk Law: Essays in the Theory and Practice of Lex non Scripta,* (Madison: University of Wisconsin Press, 1995) 80.

[74] Swaziland High Court Proclamation 1938, [revised 1957], Section 8.

[75] Criminal Procedure Act of Northern Rhodesia, [Revised Laws 1939] 28, Section 222.

[76] Martin Chanock, *Law, Custom, and Social Order: The Colonial Experience in Malawi and Zambia* (Cambridge: Cambridge University Press, 1985) 138.

[77] 'Jurors and Assessors', KNAN, AP/89.

[78] 'Magisterial Powers of Administrative Officers', KNAN, SEC/2/1/22.

Figure 3.1: Officials of the High Court of East Africa, 1902

Winterton Collection of East African Photographs, Melville J. Herskovits Library of African Studies, Northwestern University

The ostensible objective of using African assessors was, in the words of one judge, to 'guarantee to the native population that their own customs and habits of life are not misunderstood'.[79] The use of native assessors in the courts was equally driven by a hope for administrative expediency. African assessors were crucial to British 'pacification' agendas and to guaranteeing social order. The aim of the system was both practical and moral. It was practical in the sense that European judges often could not understand the language and customs of people in the dock, and moral in terms of legitimizing 'alien' courts in the eyes of Africans.[80] A commission of enquiry, set up in 1933 to review the administration of justice in British East Africa, stated that the central goal of employing African assessors in the courts was to prevent the appearance of injustice that could have a 'bad effect on native minds'.[81]

[79] Judgment in the case of *Mahlikilili Dhalamini and ors v The King* [1942] AC 583 at 589ff. (hereinafter, *Dhalamini v R*). For a discussion of this case, see Joseph Jaconelli, *Open Justice: A Critique of the Public* (Oxford: Oxford University Press, 2002) 104ff.

[80] L. A. A. Kyando and C. M. Peter, 'Lay people in the Administration of Criminal Justice: The Law and Practice in Tanzania' (1993) 5 *African Journal of International and Comparative Law* 669.

[81] Commission of Enquiry into the Administration of Justice in Kenya, Uganda and Tanganyika 1933, KNAN, AP/1/1659.

Most African assessors appear to have been ambivalent about their roles in the colonial courts. Although assessors were entitled to a modest stipend, Africans rarely sought these assignments. Attending lengthy trials in remote and unfamiliar court settings created perils. Moreover, African assessors were sometimes the target of intimidation, physical attacks, and even murder, because of opinions given in court trials.[82] Recruiting African assessors was particularly difficult in urban centres, where they were needed for criminal trials involving Africans. In 1942, one judge in Nairobi complained about the 'poor quality of urbanised assessors' who dressed in European clothes, spoke English and knew little about tribal customs that were recruited to his courts.[83] Colonial judges and administrators preferred 'traditional' men thought to be well versed in customary law, over 'modern' Africans, whom they believed to be more inclined to being 'corrupted in modern ways'.[84] With the widespread acceptance of the policy of indirect rule in administrative circles in East Africa in the inter-war period, colonial officials became enthusiastic about tribal institutions. Traditional authorities were not only to be preserved and strengthened, but were to be rescued from near-oblivion. Some were created as well. Even with the inevitable shift in the 1940s from reliance on 'traditional elders' to a programme favouring the appointment of African 'modernizers and progressives', colonial officials still searched for the 'right kind of elder' to serve in the courts.[85]

Inventors of Customary Law

When suitable Africans were found to serve as judicial assessors, defining their role in the courts raised problematic legal questions. Even though colonial statutes spelt out the role of native assessors, judicial and administrative officials continually grappled with how to precisely define that role in court trials. Like many imperial institutions, the challenge was how to adapt a legal institution originating in England—reinvented in a colonial context—to meet the specific legal and administrative needs.

One question that arose was how much weight colonial courts could place on the testimonies of African assessors with respect to the 'validity' of native customary law. Concerns were voiced within the colonial legal and judicial establishment that the customary law, on which African assessors were expected to give opinions, was being continually modified. Opinions by native assessors might, therefore, not always reflect the evolving and fluid nature of African customs. The dominant

[82] Acting Judge of Nyeri to Chief Registrar, KNAN, DC/KSM/1/15/34.

[83] Criminal Session Cases: List of African Assessors Roll and Letters to the Chief Justice, KNA DC/KSM/1/15/34.

[84] Ginio, 'Negotiating Legal Authority in French West Africa', 120.

[85] Brett L. Shadle, 'African Court Elders in Nyanza Province, Kenya, ca. 1930–1960: From "Traditional" to "Modern"' in Benjamin N. Lawrence et al, eds, *Intermediaries, Interpreters, and Clerks: African Employees in the Making of Colonial Africa* (Madison: University of Wisconsin Press, 2006) 182–3.

opinion was against granting permanent judicial recognition to the testimonies of native assessors on questions of customary law, out of concern that this would freeze the law at one stage of its development.[86] Similar arguments were made in opposition to codifying customary law in English-style statute books.

Several historical and anthropological studies have shown that the so-called customary law of the colonial period was forged in particular historical struggles between the colonial power and the colonized groups.[87] The customary law implemented in native tribunals was not a relic of the distant pre-colonial past, but instead an historical construct of the colonial period.[88] Both traditional and modernizing African elites took a central role in defining customary law in the native tribunals.[89] The unfamiliarity of British officials with local property, gender, and power relations sometimes created opportunities for litigants in colonial courts to present local customs as they wanted them to be.[90] African assessors who were seen as 'experts' in native customs were well positioned to do this, particularly in the early colonial period when European officials tended to readily accept their opinions on African customs. The process therefore was characterized as the 'invention of tradition', rather than the ascertaining of tradition.[91] Customary law was made, not found, and was forged in the struggles over land, labour, and property in the colonial era combining British law and a range of chiefly and tribal forms of law.

Being largely unscripted, African customary law was historically flexible and adaptable. As it intersected with British law and the demands of colonial administration, however, it fossilized into a fixed and rigid system. Customary law became a political resource, useful in continuing renegotiations of status and access to resources.[92] It emerged in the context of a colonial need for administration and control; it was an amalgam of the technical legalism of British forms of justice—a remote and authoritarian legal order and the vision of a 'strict and moral golden age'.[93] One of the more striking examples of this is the case of the Buganda Chiefs who entrenched their own wealth and positions largely at the expense of the under-represented traditional clan authorities during the negotiations with British representatives leading to the Uganda Agreement of 1900. The latter would discover later that their traditional rights of control over clan lands had been abrogated under the newly entranced customary law regimes.[94]

The historian Terence Ranger, an early exponent of the 'invention of tradition' thesis, argued that ethnic identities, like other 'traditions' in Africa, were essentially

[86] A. N. Allott, 'The Judicial Ascertainment of Customary Law in British Africa' (1957) 20 *Modern Law Review* 262.

[87] For a review of some of these studies, see Sally Engle Merry, 'Law and Colonialism' (1991) 25(6) *Law and Society Review* 889–992.

[88] Kristin Mann and Richard Roberts, eds, *Law in Colonial Africa* (Portsmouth: Heinemann, 1991) 4.

[89] Merry, 'Law and Colonialism', 897.

[90] Chanock, 'Laws and Contexts' (1989) 7(2) *Law in Context* 72.

[91] Terence Ranger, 'The Invention of Tradition in Colonial Africa' in Eric Hobsbawm and Terence Ranger, eds, *The Invention of Tradition* (Cambridge: Cambridge University Press, 1983) 211.

[92] See Chanock, *Law, Custom, and Social Order*.

[93] Chanock, *Law, Custom, and Social Order*, 136.

[94] Morris and Read, *Indirect Rule*, 188.

'inventions' of colonial intervention—the result of the divisive activities of European officials and missionaries working in concert with African elites. European colonial administrators, Ranger argued, set about inventing African traditions for Africans because few connections could be made between British and African political, social, and other legal systems. Their own respect for tradition disposed colonial authorities to look favourably upon what they understood as 'tradition' in Africa. European colonists in Africa drew on European-invented traditions both to define and justify their roles, and to provide models of subservience into which it was sometimes possible to draw Africans.[95] Colonial-invented traditions accentuated hitherto latent 'tribal consciousness among African peoples, making fluid ethnic boundaries and identities more rigid and making ethnic rivalries more pronounced'.[96] As one historian put it: 'Europeans believed that Africans belonged to tribes; Africans built tribes to belong to.'[97] More recent studies have exposed the limits of the 'invention of tradition'.[98] However, its basic assumptions are still relevant to understanding the role of African assessors in the colonial judicial system.

In civil cases, colonial courts sought the opinion of African assessors mainly in matters involving domestic and familial issues, such as divorce, inheritance, and disputes over property. In criminal cases, assessors were central to trials for murder and manslaughter. These were capital offences, in which the customs of those involved were considered crucial for achieving justice.[99] Judicial officers stressed the importance of the assessors' opinions when an African accused of a capital offence pled insanity. This was the process any time the mental state of a person accused of a criminal offence might mitigate culpability and result in a lighter sentence. The opinions of African assessors were also frequently sought where the defence of provocation was advanced in murder cases, to determine what constituted provocation in local culture—such that might provoke fits of rage and violence.

Indeed, it is a well-established principle of Common Law that, in examining the nature of the effect of provocation, the standard to be applied is determined by the effect upon an ordinary person of the community to which the accused belongs. Courts often noted that an ordinary person in Africa may react differently to particular acts or insults than an ordinary person in England.[100] As one colonial magistrate stated, 'circumstances that may compel a native to rise and strike a fatal

[95] Ranger, 'The Invention of Tradition in Colonial Africa', 211.

[96] Terrence Ranger, 'Missionaries Migrants and the Mayinka: The Invention of Ethnicity in Zimbabwe' in Leroy Vail, ed, *Creation of Tribalism in Southern Africa* (Berkeley: University of California Press, 1991) 120.

[97] John Iliffe, *A Modern History of Tanganyika* (Cambridge: Cambridge University Press, 1979) 324.

[98] Sally Falk Moore, *Social Facts and Fabrications: 'Customary' Law on Kilimanjaro 1880–1980* (Cambridge: Cambridge University Press, 1986); Thomas Spear, 'Neo-traditionalism and the Limits of Invention in British Colonial Africa' (2003) 44(1) *Journal of African History* 3–27.

[99] Criminal Records 1928, KNAN, SEC/2/6/54'; Magisterial Powers of Administrative Officers, KNAN, SEC/2/1/22.

[100] James S. Read, 'Criminal Law in the Africa of Today and Tomorrow' (1963) 7(1) *Journal of African Law* 10.

blow may cause no more than discomfiture elsewhere'.[101] As in other aspects of the colonial enterprise, underlying assumptions about African difference and exceptionality underscored the place of native assessors in the colonial judicial system. In most colonial jurisdictions customary law was not recognized as affording a general source of defences to criminal charges under the Penal Code. However, the definition of particular offences involved reference to customary law in certain circumstances. In several criminal appeals where the accused pleaded provocation or self-defence, the regional Courts of Appeal found it necessary to consider local customs and the accepted patterns of behaviour in the accused's community.[102]

Perhaps the most contentious debate over the use of native assessors was whether they should be treated as jurors or as 'expert witnesses' integral to the judicial process, or as outsiders invited to provide evidence before the courts.[103] This would determine how much weight judges could place on the testimony of assessors. At both practical and theoretical levels, the answer was not clear. In colonial Africa, as in England, a trial judge was not bound by the opinion of an assessor appointed to aid the court, because the final decision was vested solely in the judge. While in England assessors served more or less as expert witnesses, however, assessors in Africa and India were required to deliver an opinion on the general issues involved in a case and were often not confined by judges to answering questions on specific points.[104] Even so, native assessors were never intended to be jurors in the sense of directly determining the outcome of trials and colonial judges often overruled their opinion. In *Habiab Kara Vesta and Ors v R*, the East African Court of Appeal overruled the unanimous opinion of assessors, upholding the 'absolute power of the judge to give effect to his own views'.[105] Moreover, unlike jurors, native assessors were not required to reach a consensus; each gave his or her personal opinion. In criminal trials involving Africans, it was unclear whether assessors should simply aid colonial judges, or whether they should also protect the interests of African litigants by ensuring that their customs were properly articulated and duly considered.

Native Assessors and Criminal Procedure—The *Dhalamini* Case

Nowhere were the vexed questions raised in the forgoing section addressed more extensively than in the landmark Swaziland case of *Mahlikilili Dhalamini and Ors v The King*, which came before the JCPC in 1941. The process of appeal from the High Court of Swaziland provides unique insight into the contested role of African assessors in colonial courts and the interpretation of these roles by imperial appeal courts. The main legal question in the *Dhalamini* case was whether the opinion of a 'native assessor' needed to comply with strict rules of evidence in colonial statutes,

[101] *Rex v Egbe Nafe* [1936] WACA, Session, NANI, CSO 33115, Vol 2.

[102] See for example, *R v Nunguyashi* (1941) 8 EACA 55; *R v Mukye and Others* [1941] 8 EACA 96.

[103] John Gray, 'Opinion of Assessors in Criminal Trials in East Africa as to Native Custom' (1958) 2(1) *Journal of African Law* 8.

[104] Jearey, 'Trial by Jury and Trial', 85.

[105] Jearey, 'Trial by Jury and Trial', 85.

and whether such opinion could be mitigated by local exigencies. The *Dhalamini* case provided an opportunity for the JCPC to wade into longstanding debates among colonial administrators and judges over the role of native assessors in criminal trials. The central tension was between the position of colonial officials 'on the spot' who had to contend with the challenges of local administration, and the detached perspectives of appellate judges in metropolitan centres who were concerned more with upholding universalist standards of British justice throughout the Empire.

This case dealt with the sensitive matter of ritual or 'medicine' murder, which was of great concern to colonial authorities who feared a growing incidence of ritual murders in its African colonies. The three convicted murderers in the *Dhalamini* case were natives of Swaziland who allegedly conspired to kill their victims—also natives—in order to use parts of their body to make 'medicine' to increase their crops. An alleged conspirator, called on as a witness by the Crown, testified to the conspiracy and the actual killing. The original trial took place before a British judge, Judge Haggard. He was aided by two administrative officers and a native assessor as stipulated in the Swaziland High Court Proclamation of 1938, which required that all proceedings must take place in 'open court'.[106] When the case came before the JCPC, the main legal question for determination was a procedural one—whether the opinions of the said officers and the native assessor had been properly obtained.

It was not evident from the trial records whether the original trial judge had consulted native assessors in accordance with the law. To clarify this issue, the JCPC had a telegram sent to the Resident Commissioner in Swaziland. The latter replied that the trial had been conducted with the aid of a native assessor, but his opinions had been given to the judge in private rather than in open court. He explained that, although the Swaziland High Court Proclamation specified that such opinions be given in open court, such had not been the general practice due to 'local circumstances'. Instead, experience had shown that Africans were unlikely to give their honest opinion before an open court and, in the Commissioner's words, 'Insofar as the native is concerned, if his opinion had been given in public, he might feel constrained to decide in favour of a native accused, whereas in the privacy of the judge's room and in the company of the judge and the administrative officers, he could be more likely to give honest independent opinions.'[107] In many ways, this explanation typifies the workings of colonial native policies. Local officials often found it expedient, even necessary, to depart from statutory provisions on the administration of justice on the grounds that, in a colony, law had to serve more as a means to an end than being an end in itself. To these 'men on the spot', the end of British-style justice took precedence over strict adherence to procedural technicalities.

[106] Jaconelli, *Open Justice*, 104.

[107] Quoted in Barnett Hollander, *Colonial Justice: The Unique Achievements of the Privy Council's Committee of Judges* (London: Bowes and Bowes, 1961) 87.

The judges of the JCPC were not persuaded by the argument of the Resident Commissioner. They held that an assumption about the native's disinclination to give his opinion in open court was insufficient reason for the trial judge to have disregarded the statutory regulation on the use of native assessors in criminal trials. Indeed, they rejected the argument that natives in Swaziland would be less likely to give an honest opinion if they had to give it in open court. Their rationale was that in other British colonial jurisdictions similar laws requiring native assessors to give their opinions in open court had not resulted in difficulties in obtaining honest opinions. Their Lordships stated that, in at least three legal codes with which they were familiar (India, Gold Coast, and Nigeria), native assessors were required to give their opinion orally in open court. Furthermore, they claimed there had been no fear that a dishonest public statement by a native assessor would make it desirable to be given privately.[108] If the natives of India and West Africa could be trusted to give their free opinion in open court in accordance with local statutes and the general principles of English law, why not the natives of Swaziland? The JCPC also thought that there were 'grave questions' about the credibility of the accomplice testimonies which constituted the grounds for conviction.[109]

Given that the trial judge in Swaziland had not followed the statutory provision, the question before the JCPC was whether this procedural error amounted to a fatal flaw warranting the nullification of the earlier judgment convicting the accused. Delivering the judgment, Lord Atkin stated:

> It must be remembered that the provision for giving the judge, at his request, the assistance of native assessors cannot be regarded solely from the point of view of aid given to the judge. It operates, and is no doubt intended to operate, as a safeguard to natives accused of crime, and a guarantee to the native population that their own customs and habits of life are not misunderstood. From this point of view the importance of publicity is manifest.[110]

In this case, the opinion of the native assessor was not given in open court as required by law; furthermore, the presiding judge did not subsequently inform the public whether any such opinion had been given during the trial. Only the High Commissioner had been informed of the assessor's testimony in the judge's confidential report. It was not until the appeal case was opened at the JCPC in London that the facts about the role of native assessors in the trial were made public. To the JCPC, the entire trial lacked transparency and procedural fairness, and it had the makings of a secret trial. The Board easily reached the conclusion that the trial had been irregular.

On the question of what should be the result of a failure to hold the entire proceedings in public, Lord Atkin drew comparisons with the judicial system in England, stating: 'In this country the omission would be a fatal flaw entitling a convicted criminal to have the conviction set aside.... The failure to hold the

[108] Hollander, *Colonial Justice*, 87. [109] *Dhalamini v R*, 583.

[110] *Dhalamini v R*, 589. See also R. Vogler, 'The International Development of the Jury: the Role of the British Empire' (2001) 72 *Revue Internationale de Droit Pénal* 525–52.

whole of the proceedings in public must amount to such a disregard of the forms of justice as to lead to substantial and grave injustice within the rule adopted by this Board in dealing with criminal appeals.'[111] On these grounds, the JCPC recommended to the Crown that the appeal be allowed and the conviction set aside.

It is instructive that in a later Swaziland case, the JCPC (not bound by its decisions in previous cases based on similar considerations) took the view that the statutory provision requiring the public expression of the assessors' opinion in an open court was a purely ministerial obligation of Court officials, and that an omission to do so did not invalidate a conviction.[112] Nonetheless, the decision in the *Dhalamini* case had broader implications for the administration of justice in the colonies. In Swaziland and Basutoland, colonial officials seeking more flexibility in the use of native assessors amended local laws to dispense with the requirement that the opinion of assessors must be heard in open court.[113] The Swazi Proclamation of 1938 was itself amended in 1942, in response to *Dhalamini*; it stipulated that the judge only had to note the agreement or disagreement of the assessors on the record.[114]

Dhalamini reaffirmed the JCPC concern with procedural correctness and scepticism of deviation from procedure on grounds of native difference. The frequent excuse that the exigencies of administering justice among natives in the colonies required tweaking procedural law was roundly rejected. In his judgment, Lord Atkin cited the 1933 Nigerian appeal of *Lawrence v The King*, where the JCPC similarly overturned a conviction where a judge altered the sentence recorded, in the absence of the accused.[115] There was, however, no consistency in the JCPC's insistence on procedural correctness. In another case involving the interpretation of customary law heard two years after *Dhalamini*, the JCPC held that procedural irregularities in the initial trial were not enough to justify altering the decision of the lower court.[116] In another case, the Board stated that in reviewing native court proceedings 'too much importance could not be attached to the failure to observe a point of practice'.[117]

The *Dhalamini* case was frequently cited as applicable judicial precedent in subsequent cases involving the use of native and non-native assessors in criminal trials.[118] In a Basutoland case of *Tumahole Bereng v The King*,[119] a British administrative officer charged with assisting a judge in adjudicating a murder case, proceeded to inspect the site of the crime in the absence of one the disputing parties. Even though the officer justified his actions as the normal course of the local

111 *Dhalamini v R*, 589.

112 *Gideon Nkambule v The King* [1950] AC 379.

113 One such statutory amendment was introduced in Basutoland in 1947. See *Tumahole Bereng and Ors v The King* [1949] LJR 1607.

114 'Swaziland Criminal Procedure and Evidence Proclamation' in Arthur P. Stone, *The Law Reports of the Incorporated Council of Law Reporting* (London: William Clowes and Sons, 1950) 393.

115 *Lawrence v The King* [1933] AC 699.

116 *Fakisandhla Nkambule v The King* [1940] AC 760 at 767.

117 *Kwame Mensah v Kojo Abrokwa* [1961] UKPC 40 at 43.

118 See, for example, *Banyamini Pande v R* [1951] 18 EACA 263.

119 *Tumahole Bereng and Others v The King* [1949] LJR 1603.

adjudicatory process, the JCPC held that the officer's participation in the trial was 'highly irregular' and created a perception of bias. Citing *Dhalamini*, the JCPC invalidated the trial, stating that, 'Justice must not only be done but must manifestly be seen to be done'.[120] *Dhalamini* also became an important reference point for addressing legal questions concerning the admissibility of procedurally flawed evidence in criminal trials in other British jurisdictions. Four full decades later, it would be cited as applicable precedent in a landmark judgment of the Supreme Court of Canada.[121]

Custom and Gender in an 'Alien Court'—*Rex v Ndembera*

British colonial legal culture differed in various parts of Africa and varied according to social and political circumstances: criminal procedures in each jurisdiction reflected distinctive local concerns about administrative control and the maintenance of social order. However, the doctrine of precedent in English Common Law, by which courts were bound by prior decisions of superior courts (within prescribed limits), ensured that judicial decisions in one colony could influence decisions in another part of the Empire. This was evident in the case of *Rex v Ndembera*, in which the East African Court of Appeal (EACA) in 1947 reversed the conviction of an African for murder, on the grounds that the original trial judge in the High Court of Uganda should not have convicted the accused based solely on the uncontested opinion of native assessors. Beyond the role of assessors in criminal trials, the judgment also addressed important questions concerning gender and patriarchy in customary law. As several studies have shown, colonial courts were often sites of intense gender and generational struggles over the interpretation of customary law.[122] The *Ndembera* case provides a clear example of how forms of colonial difference—specifically gender and generational, in addition to the overriding otherness of race—were constructed and contested in the courts. It also shows how Africans in the lower ranks of colonial bureaucracy shaped these processes and raises questions about the dominance of male perspectives in the testimonies of African assessors that had implications for the rights of women in court trials.

The *Ndembera* case emerged within a transitioning socio-political context. The imposition of colonial law in East Africa in the late nineteenth century led to a reallocation of power among various elements and groups in traditional societies. Some of the main beneficiaries were young, educated women who resorted to the colonial courts for protection against the discriminatory and patriarchal justice of

120 *Tumahole Bereng v The King*, 1608.

121 *Morris v The Queen* [1979] 2 SCR 1041.

122 Cheryl Johnson, 'Class and Gender: A Consideration of Yoruba Women during the Colonial Period', eds. Claire Robertson and Iris Berger, *Women and Class in Africa* (New York: Africana Publishing Company, 1986) 237–54; Jane L. Parpart, '"Where is your mother?": Gender, Urban Marriage, and Colonial Discourse on the Zambian Copperbelt, 1924–1945' (1994) 27(2) *International Journal of African Historical Studies* 241–71.

traditional tribunals in matters of physical and sexual abuse and forced marriage. Among the greatest losers were practitioners of forms of ritual specialization who were looked upon indiscriminately by colonial authorities as practitioners of 'witchcraft' and as threats to civilized practices.[123] African Chiefs and senior men whose overall powers had been severely truncated by the imposition of the colonial court system and derived power from their symbiotic associations with ritual specialists also suffered further diminution of power.[124]

The 'facts' of the *Ndembera* case, as presented at trial, were that the accused was found eloping with another man's wife. An uncle of the woman's husband subsequently attempted to 'arrest' the accused and prevent him from leaving with the woman. In the struggle that ensued, the accused killed the uncle with his spear. During the original trial, the main issue before the court was whether, under local custom, the deceased uncle of the woman's husband was entitled to arrest the accused while eloping with his nephew's wife. Two male assessors stated their opinion that, according to local custom, the deceased was fully justified in attempting to restrain and arrest the accused. They stated that male family members such as brothers, uncles, and nephews had a customary right to prevent a relative's wife from eloping. This custom, they opined, was based on the notion that in marriage a woman became attached both to her husband and to her husband's extended family.[125]

Contradicting this opinion, however, Mosho, the 'woman in question,' as she was described throughout the proceedings and in the court records, gave the following testimony: 'Our custom about divorce is that a woman will run away with a man and then the husband will divorce her... I did not seek my husband's consent to a divorce. It is not in our custom to do so. I could please myself. I did not need my husband's consent.'[126] The concerned woman's own statement held significant legal implications in the criminal proceedings. It suggested that she was not simply eloping with the accused, as the prosecution had alleged, but was in the process of divorcing her husband. This claim, if established, would clearly mitigate the severity of any sentence passed on the accused. The European trial judge disregarded the woman's evidence on the customary law on divorce and upheld instead the opinion of the male assessors on the applicable native custom. On these grounds, the accused was convicted of murder.[127] The trial judge advanced several legal and evidentiary reasons for his judgment. For our purposes, it suffices to focus on those relating to the evidence of the 'woman in question'. One of the reasons for preferring the opinion of the male assessors over Mosho's testimony was the assumption that her views were more likely merely 'a progressive

[123] Alan R. Booth, '"European Courts Protect Women and Witches": Colonial Law Courts as Redistributors of Power in Swaziland 1920–1950' (1992) 18(2) *Journal of Southern African Studies* 253.

[124] Booth, 'European Courts Protect Women and Witches', 253.

[125] *Rex v Ndembera* [1947] EACA 83–5.

[126] *Rex v Ndembera*, 85. See also Gray, 'Opinion of Assessors in Criminal Trials in East Africa', 10.

[127] *Rex v Ndembera*, 85.

woman's conception of what a woman's right ought to be', rather than the proper native custom on divorce.[128]

This assumption, and the judgment arising therefrom, was in many ways typical of the attitudes of colonial courts towards evidence presented by African women, particularly on matters relating to marriage and divorce. Women's identities and status were constantly being questioned, with emphasis particularly on the identity of the woman's husband. The questions about a woman's marital identity were complicated by the contested interpretations of customary law. Queries regarding the marital identity of women in the courtroom highlight the role of colonialism in both the production and amplification of gender differences. They lend credence to the argument that, beyond racial and ethnic differentiation, colonial rule in Africa was a gendered project, shaped in many ways by the intersection of European and African patriarchies.

Upon appeal at the EACA, the *Ndembera* case focused on two main questions. The first was whether the original trial judge had erred by making a judgment adverse to the appellant based solely on the opinion of assessors, which the accused had no opportunity to challenge or rebut. On this question, the EACA noted that no evidence of the custom that the accused was alleged to have contravened was tendered during the original trial. The second and perhaps more crucial question was how to resolve the seeming contradiction between the opinion of the male assessors and the evidence of the 'woman in question', as to the correct local custom on divorce. Unlike the original trial judge, the judges of the EACA were reluctant simply to accept the opinion of two court-appointed male assessors over the evidence of the woman at the centre of the case. These European men who sat on the EACA bench seemed keenly aware of the possibility of patriarchal and generational biases in the opinions of the male assessors. They were also aware that such gender biases, both on the part of African assessors and European judges, could subvert much vaunted ideals of British justice in the colonies. Commenting on the dismissive attitude of the original trial judge towards Mosho's evidence, the judges of the EACA stated:

> If this [woman's evidence] is to be regarded merely as a progressive woman's conception of what a woman's right ought to be, it is surprising that it elicited no re-examination and no question by either assessors. It may well be that the trial Judge who has had a long African experience, was himself conversant with the native custom on the point, but if that was the case, we respectfully suggest that it would have been better had he attempted to elicit evidence of it by questioning either Mosho or her husband who was also a prosecution witness. Had such evidence been forthcoming, whether *pro or contra,* or both, the opinion of the assessors would have been pertinent and could rightly have been acted upon by the learned trial Judge. As it is, we feel bound to leave out of account this part of the judgment and treat this case as if the deceased had no business to interfere with the person of the appellant by physical force.[129]

[128] *Rex v Ndembera*, 86. [129] *Rex v Ndembera*, 85–6.

Accordingly, the EACA altered the conviction of the appellant from murder to manslaughter, guided by the principle enunciated by the JCPC in the *Dhalamini* case that the role of assessors in trials involving natives cannot simply be seen from the point of view of aid given to the trial judge. The institution of judicial assessors was also intended as a safeguard to natives accused of crimes, and to guarantee that the courts properly understood and applied their customs. Achieving this objective meant that accused natives must be given ample opportunity to challenge the opinions of court-appointed assessors on native customs, particularly in trials for capital offences. In the *Ndembera* case, the EACA was particularly critical of the dismissive approach of the lower court toward evidence of native customs that contradicted that of court-appointed assessors. The court noted that such uncritical approach to the use of native assessors threatened to 'hamper the institution of assessors in achieving its basic object to prevent an alien court doing justice through ignorance'.[130]

The reference to an 'alien court' in the judgment of the EACA is telling also. It is a term that appears frequently in JCPC judgments but hardly in the judgments of local courts. While local administrators mostly saw the courts as definitive institutions for colonial social re-ordering, appellate judges at the JCPC and the regional Courts of Appeal tended to be more cognizant of the foreign character of English-style courts in the colonies. Since these were 'alien courts' with procedures and conventions unfamiliar to Africans, the statutory provisions put in place were to ensure that native customs were properly represented in court trials and strictly observed. Unlike the colonial court hierarchy beneath them, the Imperial Appeal Courts were less preoccupied with maintaining social order. Their focus was on fashioning a centripetal jurisprudence in the Empire. This task revolved around the promotion of consistent standards of British imperial justice and the homogenization of local legal cultures, through the application of precedents from communities and contexts across the Empire. Imperial appellate judges were therefore less inclined than local colonial judges to accommodate arguments for local exigencies and administrative discretion in adjudicating native disputes.

Adjudicating Colonial Difference

The *Dhalamini* and *Ndembera* cases typify a trend in the 1940s, whereby colonial judges and magistrates became stricter in their application of legal rules of evidence and criminal procedures in cases involving Africans. Apart from the legal precedents, which appellate cases like these provided, the growing involvement of an emergent African intelligentsia in colonial politics meant that greater attention had to be paid to the role of Africans in the colonial legal system. Courts became increasingly reluctant to accept the opinions of assessors that were unsupported by other evidence, particularly in trials for capital offences, in which such opinions

130 *Rex v Ndembera*, 87.

were deemed unfavourable to accused natives. The significance of both the *Dhalamini* and *Ndembera* cases lies in the possibilities for new historical interpretations that they offer. One aspect of this relates to the discourse on imperial universalism and the historicization of globalization outlined in the introductory chapter of this book.

The *Dhalamini* case in particular reflects a central paradox in colonial legal systems in Africa—that between imperial universalism and local exceptionalism. There was a conflict between upholding the fundamental principles of British justice—principles that became the basis for legitimizing imperialism—and recognizing local African customs that were indispensable to achieving that justice. On the one hand, there was an aspiration toward maintaining a standard of law and justice in the colonies that was consistent with, or at least comparable to, what was obtained in the metropole. British courts in the colonies were expected to serve no lesser function than the courts in England. Their purpose was to deal with cases of conflicts with clear-cut rights and duties established by objective investigation of only those events deemed relevant to each case. Strict rules of evidence were to restrict the content of testimony that the courts could hear. Cases were to be treated as according to a shared understanding of 'right' and 'wrong', with judges and magistrates making final decisions—sometimes after consultation with local 'experts'.[131] On the other hand, there was some recognition that these principles, on which European-style colonial courts operated, differed from existing African notions of law and justice.

The contrasts were amplified by colonial officials and legal scholars who argued that the goal of dispute resolution under traditional African systems was not to uphold strict legal rights of the parties, but rather to achieve the amicable resolution of a dispute.[132] The duty of chiefly authorities administering the law in settling native disputes was to 'assuage injured feelings, to restore peace, to reach a compromise acceptable to both disputants'.[133] Writing in 1930, the colonial anthropologist Margery Perham stated:

> [My] impression from studying cases in the court-books of a dozen or more Districts bears witness to the African sense not only, or so much, of justice in our conception but also of something for which it is difficult to find a name—fairness, or equality; of a capacity to balance up the claims of individuals in relation to those of the group, and to come to a decision that satisfies even the party penalized.[134]

A government memorandum, issued in 1957 to regulate the activities of local courts in Tanganyika, stated that, whereas amongst Europeans the stress is on the

[131] Magisterial Powers of Administrative Officers, KNAN, SEC 2/1/22.

[132] Max Gluckman, *The Judicial Process among the Barotse of Northern Rhodesia* (Manchester: Manchester University Press, 1955); W. C. E. Daniels, *The Common Law in West Africa* (London: Butterworth, 1964); A. N. Allott, *Essays in African Law* (London: Butterworth, 1960); 'The Laws and Customs of the Yoruba County', NANI CSO 1/19 XVIA.

[133] J. N. Matson, 'The Supreme Court and the Customary Judicial Process in the Gold Coast' (1953) 2(1) *International and Comparative Law Quarterly* 48.

[134] Margery Perham, 'Tribal Rule in Africa: The Native Courts', *The Times* (27 November 1930) 15.

individual and his rights, 'amongst the Bantu it was upon the community, upon the family or clan, and its continuing solidarity'.[135]

To be sure, some scholars have questioned these representations of customary law, as they tended to elide ample evidence of inner struggles within indigenous communities in the colonial and pre-colonial periods. As several studies have shown, the 'social equilibrium' representation of African disputational logic was a mixture of African self-idealization and colonial and anthropological political theory.[136] Although the 'social equilibrium' depiction of traditional justice is not entirely without foundation, it is a well-edited version of the facts. Idealized notions of custom stood at the core of colonial assumptions about native difference in the realm of law and justice. Colonial legal re-ordering, particularly in relation to native tribunals, was founded on the idea that maintaining social harmony was the core objective of African legal proceedings.

The legitimacy of the British legal system introduced in the colonies rested on a certain imperial universalist idealism. This was evident in the establishment and regulation of the institution of native assessors, which drew on an imperial law-making template. Just as the law providing for native assessors in British East Africa derived from the Indian Evidence Act, so were the East African Criminal Procedure Codes taken directly from the Indian Code of Criminal Procedure.[137] Hence, in terms of legal procedure, Indian legal codes—rather than extant English laws from which these codes may have derived—provided the required imperial standards. Imperial legal and judicial standardization was also facilitated through the unification of the Colonial Administrative Service on the eve of the Second World War, and the creation of a unified Colonial Legal service in 1933.[138]

Still, colonial authorities sought to moderate the impact of colonial laws imported from England or India by recognizing pre-existing local customs, which were seen as traditionally regulating the lives of Africans. Imperial legal culture could accommodate such customs to the extent that they were not patently incompatible with English law, universal justice, equity, or 'good conscience'. The logic was self-evident: desirable as it was to extend British justice to natives in the colonies, local extenuating circumstances made wholesale imposition of English legal culture impractical. What colonial courts were therefore expected to enforce was not law exactly as it applied in England or even in India, but a curious blend of English Common Law and local African customary law. Such a justice system conformed to a framework of supposedly universal notions of morality and natural justice. As one colonial judge stated, 'it is not *law* that is required to be applied in Africa but *Equity*: the complex laws of England are unsuited to the primitive conditions under which people live in Africa.'[139]

135 *Tanganyika Local Government Memoranda No 2 (Local Courts)* (Dar es Salam: Government Printer) 2. Quoted in Moore, 'Treating Law as Knowledge', 18.

136 Moore, 'Treating Law as Knowledge', 32.

137 Criminal Procedure Code, Criminal Records 1928, KNAN, SEC/2/6/54.

138 Jerry Dupont, *The Common Law Abroad: Constitutional and Legal Legacy of the British Empire* (London: F. B. Rothman Publications, 2001) xvii.

139 *The Lagos Weekly Record* (21 April 1906).

The paradox of accommodating native difference while upholding imperial standards of justice was not easily resolved. Colonial legal systems may have sought to accommodate African difference, but imperial universalism required the containment of that difference. The *Dhalamini* and *Ndembera* cases epitomize the tension between upholding imperial justice and adjudicating colonial difference. In *Dhalamini*, the JCPC maintained that colonial law requiring that the opinion of African assessors be given in open court could not be dispensed with on grounds of African difference or exceptionality. To do so would compromise the transparency and due procedure considered to be the bedrock of British justice. Even more significant was the JCPC's strict interpretation of legal codes relating to native assessors and native customs, issues on which official attitudes were typically laissez-faire. On the question of due process, the JCPC came down quite firmly on the side of imperial universalism.

The *Dhalamini* case did not concern solely the issue of procedural correctness; it also revolved around a contest over who gets to define African 'custom'. Could a British judge with long African experience and knowledge of local customs make assumptions about customary law in judicial proceedings, or was the province of customary law the exclusive prerogative of the native assessors themselves? *Dhalamini* reaffirmed the principle that African customary law was something extraneous that had to be proved, unlike Common Law, which 'always resided in the bosom of the Judge'.[140] The JCPC's position was that the role of native assessors in trials involving Africans could not be construed simply as aid given to the judge. It had to be construed as a 'safeguard to natives' and a guarantee to them that their customs and traditions were not misunderstood or misapplied by an 'alien court'.

The view that safeguarding native customs in the courts was crucial to administering justice among natives was widely held. As other scholars have noted, the legal philosophies of British judges on the JCPC, including Lord Haldane, were influenced by early twentieth-century beliefs in the existence of a 'natural' African community. This notion arose from a complex web of radical liberal, neo-Hegelian, and Fabian socialist thought.[141] Writing in 1928, Lord Haldane argued that different nations had different experiences and, therefore, their laws embodied different 'stories of development'. When these distinct nations become grouped together under a common imperial Crown, new institutions naturally evolve to account for the difference. The role of the JCPC and other imperial appeal courts, as Haldane saw it, was a continually evolving one that had to meet the legal needs of the complex and expanding Empire.[142]

Although he made a strong case for the JCPC's role as the principal upholder of imperial judicial standards throughout his career, Haldane also acknowledged the real difficulties of adjudicating cases from varied and unfamiliar jurisdictions across

[140] Geoffrey Bing, *Reap the Whirlwind: An Account of Kwame Nkrumah's Ghana from 1950 to 1966* (London: MacGibbon & Kee, 1968) 201.

[141] Michael P. Cowen and Robert W. Shenton, 'British neo-Hegelian Idealism and Official Colonial Practice in Africa: The Oluwa Land Case of 1921' (1994) 22(2) *Journal of Imperial and Commonwealth History* 217.

[142] Haldane, *Selected Addresses and Essays*, 224.

the Empire.[143] For imperial judges, the tasks of upholding imperial justice and accommodating local customs were not contradictory or conflicted, but were complementary and even mutually reinforcing. By insisting on a strict interpretation of the law requiring openness in the testimony of native assessors in the *Dhalamini* case, the JCPC upheld universalist ideals of British justice and due process. By interpreting the philosophy behind that law in a way that safeguarded the exceptionality of native customs, the JCPC recognized and sought to accommodate native difference.

Contesting Native Difference

The cases examined in this chapter show how imperial belonging and colonial difference were constructed and contested in judicial discourses and the administration of justice. Native assessors, like other African employees of the colonial state, were crucial to these processes. They served as intermediaries in the interactions between Europeans and Africans, and created key intersections of power, authority, and knowledge.[144] Their role as intermediaries blurred colonial dichotomies, creating hybrid legal and judicial cultures and institutions.[145] Judicial discourses on native assessors exemplify this process of legal hybridization that tended to complicate the constriction of naive difference in colonial courts.

Originally a creation of European colonialism with roots in English legal culture, the institution of native assessors was re-invented, first in India and later in Africa, where it further evolved. Ultimately, it bore little resemblance to the original 'nautical assessors' of the English Admiralty Courts on which colonial judicial assessors were modelled.[146] The institution that emerged in Africa in the early twentieth century was largely shaped by the exigencies of colonial rule and by the peculiar attributes that the African employed assessors brought to their roles. This process of adaptation and creolization is evident, for example, in colonial legal debates over the institutional equivalents of native assessors in English courts. Were native assessors in Africa more akin to expert witnesses or juries in the courts of England? Ascertaining these institutional equivalents was crucial to standardizing imperial justice.

While it was clear that the role of assessors in English courts was that of expert witnesses, the same assumption did not apply to assessors in African courts. In Africa, the time-honoured English institution of judicial assessors morphed into something different. It became an entirely new institution that did not conform to a traditional definition or classification, even by colonial officials and legal experts.

143 Haldane, *Selected Addresses and Essays*, 225.

144 Benjamin N. Lawrence, Emily Lynn Osborn, and Richard L. Roberts, 'African Intermediaries and the "Bargain" of Collaboration' in Lawrence et al, eds, *Intermediaries, Interpreters, and Clerks*, 4.

145 D. A. Westbrook, 'Colonial Discourse Theory' in Robin W. Winks, ed, *The Oxford History of the British Empire Vol 5* (Oxford: Oxford University Press, 1999) 609.

146 Anthony Dickey, 'The Province and Function of Assessors in English Courts' (1970) 33(5) *Modern Law Review* 494–507.

A leading contemporary scholar of colonial law in Africa, A.N. Allott, sought to define the role of African assessors, comparing them to both a traditional jury and expert witnesses in English courts. He argued that the native assessors in Africa were unique, because they had the duty to assess (as did juries) and also the duty to advise, similar to expert witnesses. He stated:

> The functions of assessors can be collected under two heads—their duty to assess and their duty to advise. In the light of their special knowledge of African habits, customs and modes of thought and language, they are peculiarly qualified to judge the probability of a story told by a witness, and they may detect in his demeanour what may escape the presiding judge. In this role the assessor's task is similar to that of a juror's though he gives no verdict, but only his opinion on the evidence. Secondly, the assessor's duty is to advise the judge or magistrate on matters of which they have special knowledge, and to give their view, in the abstract, of what the custom or law is in the circumstances postulated ... The assessor though serving as an expert witness is not, therefore, an expert witness in the ordinary sense.[147]

What Allot describes, albeit in different words, was a process of hybridization that was typical of the operation of colonial legal institutions in Africa. Beyond being devices of colonial hegemony (as they may have been originally intended), ultimately they also became hybridized, shaped by local initiatives and responses. This process of hybridization was the outcome of the colonial administrators' attempts to tweak policies and institutions to meet local exigencies. It was a result of the complex ways in which Africans engaged with colonial law and judicial institutions.

In the *Dhalamini* case, for example, the official concern that Africans were less likely to give their honest opinions before an open court became one of the arguments for flexibility in interpreting colonial law. In the same way, the difficulty of recruiting elderly natives—presumed to be more knowledgeable in local customs—to serve as court assessors made it necessary for colonial officials to draw from the ranks of urbanised men. This led to unexpected outcomes. Conversely, the JCPC's insistence on due process in *Dhalamini* challenged assumptions about African difference that lay at the roots of colonial native policies. The result was a judgment that implicitly acknowledged the role of African assessors as the purveyors of customary law and justice within the colonial courtroom, yet insisted that the framework for dispensing such customary justice had to be grounded firmly in the universalist principles of British justice.

This process of hybridization is also evident in *Rex v Ndembera*.[148] Long before the 'invention of tradition' paradigm for explaining colonial constructions of indigenous traditions gained currency among scholars of Empire, colonial officials themselves were keenly aware of the possibility of distortion and idealization resulting from gender, class, and generational prejudices in the representation of African customs in the courts. In the *Ndembera* case, the question was whether native assessors—almost always senior men—brought patriarchal and generational

[147] A. N. Allott, 'The Judicial Ascertainment of Customary Law in British Africa' (1957) 20(3) *Modern Law Review* 250.

[148] *Rex v Ndembera* [1947] 14 EACA 83–5.

biases to their interpretations of customary law. A related question was whether the contradictory evidence of a woman had to be given more weight by a trial judge or be regarded merely as 'a progressive woman's conception of what her rights ought to be'.[149] Concerns about gender biases in the opinions of native assessors underscored the tensions between local officials and appellate judges, as they debated over the place of African customary law in the colonial legal system. Such tensions and contestations, mediated as they were by colonial power, were, however, not limited to interpretations of customary law. As the next chapter shows, they were also evident in the adjudication of criminal appeals at the Imperial Courts and to related judicial discourses on native crime and punishment.

149 *Rex v Ndembera*, 85.

4

Medicine Murders and Blood Money

Crime and punishment highlight a key tension in colonial justice. Officials understood that administering criminal justice among natives required recognizing African difference and accommodating native customary laws. Yet, they also believed that such accommodation had to be carefully reconciled with the goal of maintaining common standards of imperial law and justice. The bifurcated nature of the colonial criminal justice system underscored these dual agendas. In most parts of British Africa, colonial officials preferred to keep criminal trials within the jurisdiction of the British courts rather than the native tribunals. While there was relative consensus within the British colonial establishment that native customs could be accommodated to the extent of their non-repugnancy in civil matters, there were always doubts about extending such flexibility to critical matters of criminal justice. Regarding crime and punishment, colonial officials insisted, the sanctity and ascendancy of English law could not be compromised. The adjudication of capital offences in particular could not be subject to the vagaries of diverse, imprecise, and uncodified African customary laws. At stake were the very essence of British imperial liberalism and its civilizing agenda.

Colonial laws reflected this type of thinking. The Gold Coast Native Jurisdiction Ordinance of 1910 delineated spheres of criminal and civil jurisdiction. The Chiefs' role in the adjudication of serious criminal matters consisted only of 'apprehending, detaining, and sending to the Commissioner of the district' those people who were suspected of such crimes.[1] The jurisdiction of native tribunals in criminal matters was limited to offences criminalized under customary law, such as 'seduction', 'slander', 'fetishism', and 'witchcraft'. Similarly, the Kenyan Native Tribunal Ordinance of 1930 empowered the Governor or Provincial Commissioner to establish native tribunals with jurisdiction limited to civil matters and certain categories of criminal matters relating to natives and consenting Arabs.[2] Explicitly excluded from the tribunal's jurisdiction were criminal cases in which the sentence of death or life imprisonment may be imposed.[3]

The fault lines in the ideological and jurisprudential debate over the scope of customary law in criminal trials were clear. Officials within the colonial judicial

[1] An Ordinance to Facilitate and Regulate the Exercise of Certain Powers and Jurisdiction by Native Authorities (Accra, Ghana: Government Printer, 1910) Chapter 26.

[2] Native Tribunal Ordinance of 1930, *Gazette of the Colony and Protectorate of Kenya* Nairobi (20 June 1930), s 4.

[3] Native Tribunal Ordinance of 1930, s 8.

establishment, notably judges, magistrates, and law officers in the metropole, insisted on the strict application of colonial penal law in criminal trials. They believed that the attributes of the native tribunals that made them well-suited for administering civil and private law disputes among the natives also made them inappropriate for serious criminal trials. The African Chiefs and senior men who headed the tribunals were not qualified lawyers, even if they were versed in local customary law; as a result, legal practitioners were excluded from appearing before them, and the law they applied was flexible and imprecise.

On the other hand, local administrative officers who were more concerned with the maintenance of social order objected to a slavish adherence to the procedural technicalities of penal law in adjudicating crimes among natives. They argued for flexibility and a 'tweaking of rules' to reflect local exigencies and accommodate native sensibilities. Only then, they argued, could the ultimate goal of extending the civilizing influences of British justice to the natives be attained.[4] The administration of criminal justice was therefore one legal arena where tensions within the colonial legal and judicial establishment most evidently shaped the construction of native difference. This chapter examines these tensions through the lens of both official discourse in the colonies and the jurisprudence of the Imperial Appeal Courts.

Colonial criminal law defined the African as an individual with inalienable rights, but also as subject to the 'civilizing' and disciplinary apparatus of the state. Although colonial states tended to think of African subjects within tribal collectivities and stereotypes, criminal proceedings before the courts individualized the accused Africans.[5] The colonial criminal justice system operated on the principle that the native subject in Africa was entitled to the same standards of British criminal justice as availed the British citizen in England. Appeals were possible from the lowest rungs of the colonial court hierarchy through the Supreme Courts and regional Courts of Appeals, all the way to the Privy Council in London. Every convicted person had, in principle, the right to petition the JCPC for Special Leave to appeal a decision of local courts or tribunals. In reality, the JCPC did not primarily concern itself with criminal appeals, and fewer criminal cases than civil cases from colonies were fully adjudicated by the JCPC.

Generally, the Lords of the JCPC were reluctant to intervene in criminal matters, save in exceptional cases. The limitation of the JCPC in reviewing criminal cases from the colonies was laid down in its judgment of a case in 1887 that stated: 'Her Majesty will not review or interfere with the cause of criminal proceedings, unless it is shown that, by a disregard of the forms of legal process, or by some violations of the principles of natural justice, or otherwise, *substantial and grave injustice* has been done... There must be something so irregular, or so outrageous, as to shake the

[4] Annual Report of the Gold Coast 1938, Public Records and Archives Administration Department, Accra (hereinafter PRAADA), ADM/5/1/70; Palaver Book (Kumasi District Office 1922), PRAADA, ADM/45/5/4.

[5] Stacey Hynd, 'The Extreme Penalty of the Law: Mercy and the Death Penalty as aspects of State Power in Colonial Nyasaland' (2010) 4(3) *Journal of Eastern African Studies* 542.

vary basis of justice.'[6] Rejecting a Nyasaland murder conviction appeal, the JCPC restated its disinclination to intervene in colonial criminal appeals. Lord Donovan emphasized that the Board was not a court of criminal appeal. It was not guided by its own doubts of the appellant's innocence or suspicion of his guilt, and would not interfere with the course of criminal law unless there had been a 'violation of the natural principles of justice so demonstrably manifest as to convince their Lordships . . . that the courts would have reached an opposite outcome if the defect in the trial had been avoided'.[7]

The instructions issued to lawyers appearing before the JCPC in 1930 similarly stressed that the Board was not a 'reversing court of criminal appeal'. It would only interfere where there has been proven infringement of the 'essential principles of Justice'.[8] Lawyers representing parties were cautioned not to expect the JCPC to re-try a criminal case or concern itself with the weight of evidence, the conflict of evidence, the interferences drawn from evidence, or whether there was sufficient evidence to satisfy the burden of proof. Appeals on such grounds were considered 'futile' and 'an abuse of the process of the court'.[9]

The requirement that appellants establish 'substantial and grave injustice' to merit JCPC's intervention, makes the criminal cases appealed to the Board all the more significant from a historical standpoint. Primarily, such cases provide us with insights into what was considered, in the view of the Law Lords of the JCPC, 'substantial and grave injustice'. They indicate how important these cases were to the colonial authorities and tell us something about how African appellants navigated through the highest levels of the colonial criminal justice system.

My analysis of the reported 'native' African appeals to the JCPC in the first half of the twentieth century reveals certain important trends. First, the cost and stringent procedural requirements involved in taking criminal appeals to the JCPC suggest that both the native litigant and the particular case were of a unique nature. Most African appeals to the JCPC concerned what I term 'high-stakes matters' involving individual litigants or 'high-impact matters' involving entire communities or community interests. By the time a case reached the JCPC, it typically would have undergone previous adjudication in at least two courts of judicial review in the colony of its origin. This process took considerable time and often involved great expense. Appellants in criminal cases were therefore almost always men, and were usually senior men of means and influence who could afford the cost of lengthy legal proceedings in the regional Courts of Appeal and at the JCPC in London. Where the stakes were high enough, people of modest means pooled resources to lodge appeals to the JCPC. Indigent appellants convicted of capital offences could also appeal to the Privy Council *in forma pauperis*. But even this course of action required an approval from the JCPC and the ability of the appellant to find a qualified lawyer in London willing to take on the case *pro bono*.

[6] Lord Watsons in *Re Dillet* [1887] AC 12 at 467. My emphasis.
[7] *Tadeyo Kwalira v The Queen* [1964] UKPC 12.
[8] 'Practice Notes of the Judicial Committee of the Privy Council' (1942) 44 *Bombay Law Review* 8.
[9] 'Practice Notes of the Judicial Committee of the Privy Council', 8.

Either way, a criminal appeal to the JCPC did not come cheap; it took resources, influence, and some sophistication.

The Strange Case of Dr Knowles

One early high-stakes criminal appeal from Africa that would have far-reaching impact on the colonial criminal justice system was *Benjamin Knowles v The King*, which came before the JCPC from the British West African colony of Ashanti in 1930. The case marked the first time that the JCPC agreed to hear an appeal from a criminal conviction originating in West Africa.[10] The case involved a European medical officer, Dr Benjamin Knowles, who was tried and convicted for the murder of his wife without the benefit of a jury trial or the assistance of a legal counsel.[11] The Ashanti Administration Ordinance of 1902, under which Knowles was tried, provided that 'in no cause or matter, criminal or civil, shall the employment of a barrister or solicitor be allowed'.[12] Dr Knowles was convicted of murdering his wife and sentenced to death, despite the fact that Mrs Knowles, who did not die until some days after she was shot, had told everyone with whom she spoke that the revolver from which the shot was fired had gone off accidentally. Since it was established at trial that she used to fire this weapon from time to time, and had once previously shot at her husband in anger, her testimony appeared to be a reasonable possibility.[13] The case was complicated by the relationship between the couple. It turned out that, while living with Dr Knowles in Ashanti, Mrs Knowles who was a 'popular music comedienne' was still legally married to an English actor in London with whom she regularly corresponded. Throughout this time, she had led her husband and relatives in England to believe that she was on a music tour of South Africa and China.[14]

Upon his conviction in the Gold Coast, Dr Knowles applied for special leave to appeal to the Privy Council. The JCPC granted leave to appeal on the grounds that it was against the law for a judge to try a capital case without a jury.[15] However, on appeal, their Lordships refused to consider that the absence of a jury or defence lawyer was grounds for setting aside the conviction. It accepted the respondent claim that it was not practical, given the local circumstances in Ashanti, for Knowles to be tried by a jury of his peers. 'Practicability and the state of local circumstances,' Viscount Dunedin stated, 'are questions which can only be determined in Ashanti

[10] Roger Gocking, 'The Adjudication of Homicide in Colonial Ghana: The Impact of the Knowles Murder Case' (2011) 52 *Journal of African History* 90; 'Knowles, Benjamin Convicted at Ashanti, Gold Coast on 23 November 1928 for murder and sentenced to death', NAUK, HO 144/17804.

[11] The *Knowles* case is well documented in Albert Lieck, ed, *Trial of Benjamin Knowles* (Edinburgh: William Hodge & Co., 1933).

[12] 'Ashanti Administration Ordinance of 1902', cited in Geoffrey Bing, *Reap the Whirlwind: An Account of Kwame Nkrumah's Ghana from 1950 to 1966* (London: MacGibbon and Kee, 1968) 82.

[13] Gocking, 'The Adjudication of Homicide in Colonial Ghana', 90; 'Case of Dr Knowles: Proceedings of Trial', CO 96/686/3.

[14] Author, 'Shot Reveals Double Life', *The New York Times* (17 November 1928) 12.

[15] Lieck, *Trial of Benjamin Knowles*, 2.

on the spot. It is impossible for their Lordships of this Board to form a conclusion on such matters, and it is not for them to turn themselves into a local tribunal.'[16] Nevertheless, the JCPC quashed the murder conviction on the grounds that there was enough indication that the case might have been one of manslaughter. While the case was still at the JCPC, the Governor of the Gold Coast bowed to official and public pressure and commuted Knowles' sentence to imprisonment for life. Knowles was subsequently repatriated to England for imprisonment and was eventually released.[17]

Knowles' trial and initial death sentence created outrage in Britain and West Africa, and placed a spotlight on the adjudication of capital crimes in the colony.[18] The scandalous circumstances of the *Knowles* case and the unusual spectacle of a white colonial official in tropical Africa facing trial for murdering his wife attracted international media attention.[19] In London, many were concerned about the draconian nature of a justice system that denied an 'Englishman' something as basic as 'the right to trial by jury'.[20] In West Africa, the case underscored a longstanding demand of the educated elites that the same standards of criminal justice applicable to English citizens in England should be extended to African subjects in the colonies. One of the resolutions passed at the meeting of the National Congress of British West Africa in Accra in 1920 called for the right of citizens to trial by jury in criminal cases, which should be 'regulated in accordance with English Common and Statute Laws'.[21] The Congress was also critical of the appellate system 'in which Judges [sat] on their Judgments' and called for an appellate court with 'experienced judges from outside the British West African Judiciary'.[22] The call here was clearly for privileging universalist British standards of criminal justice over notions of African difference and exceptionality.

The West African intelligentsia who controlled the nascent indigenous press seized on the *Knowles* case to highlight what they considered the sub-standard justice to which Africans were subjected in the colonies. The *Gold Cost Times* stated that the *Knowles* case posed a difficulty for colonial officials because 'the judicial system in Ashanti was intended solely for the natives, and the possibility of white people being entangled in its mashes never entered into the calculations of those who designed it'.[23] The newspaper noted that the reason for the 'travesty of justice' was the nature and limitations of the judicial system in Ashanti under which the Circuit Judge was required to sit as both judge and jury. It called for urgent reform of the colonial criminal law and judicial system.[24]

[16] *Benjamin Knowles v The King* [1930] AC 366 at 378; 'Dr B Knowles: Appeal to Privy Council', CO 96/694/2.

[17] 'Dr Benjamin Knowles: West African Case Recalled', *The Times* (30 October 1933) 17.

[18] The *Knowles* case was extensively reported by *Gold Coast Times* from December 1929 to April 1930.

[19] 'Shot Reveals Double Life', 12; 'Dr Benjamin Knowles', 17.

[20] Lieck, *Trial of Benjamin Knowles*, 2.

[21] *Resolutions of the Conference of Africans of British West Africa held at Accra, Gold Coast, from 11th to 29th March, 1920* (Accra, n.p., 1920) 86, PRAADA, ADM/11/1/1427.

[22] Gocking, 'The Adjudication of Homicide in Colonial Ghana', 89.

[23] *Gold Coast Times* (26 April 1930) 7.

[24] *Gold Coast Times* (26 April 1930) 7.

Similarly, the Nigerian *Daily Times* editorialized that the case, though unfortunate, had been hailed by all West Africa as God sent in making the British public acquainted for the first time with the existence in a British territory of a court which can, without a jury, try even an Englishman for capital offence without the right of legal representation.[25] 'Dr Knowles' trial,' the newspaper stated, had

> exposed to the British public, as nothing else would have done, the legal disabilities under which we suffer in these parts. The prompt commutation of the death sentence by the Governor of the Gold Coast did not escape the watchful eye and careful notice of the African who knows very well that he or his brother in similar circumstance might have died in the gallows before anything was heard of his fate.[26]

Following the Knowles trial and the public indignation it generated within and beyond West Africa, the colonial government opened up Ashanti courts to lawyers, and introduced other changes in the administration of criminal justice.[27] The high-stakes case of Dr Knowles effectively opened up possibilities for other high-impact native criminal appeals to the JCPC. Among these were the so-called African 'medicine murder' appeals that dominated the criminal appeals docket of the JCPC and the regional Courts of Appeal in the 1930s and 1940s.

Medicine Murder Appeals

Medicine murder cases typically involved traditional African men of means and influence. A Chief, medicine man, or 'witch-doctor' who, having been tried and convicted in a local court for premeditated murder, subsequently lodged legal appeals before the Privy Council. For example, out of thirty-eight randomly selected African criminal appeals that came before the JCPC between 1930 and 1945, nineteen involved ritual or medicine murders. Typical of these medicine murder cases was the Basutoland case of *Tumahole Bereng v The King*, which came before the JCPC in 1947. The seven appellants were convicted of murder and sentenced to death. The case against the accused was that they had conspired to murder their victim for the purpose of obtaining human blood to be used by a witch-doctor in connection with a dispute over land. Among those convicted for the crime was the witch-doctor who had allegedly orchestrated the crime. The key question that arose at trial was whether the conviction of the accused—based solely on the implicating evidence of two accomplices—was in accordance with Basutoland Criminal Procedure law. The JCPC determined that the evidence presented against the accused did not establish proof of murder as required by the relevant statute law, and proceeded to set aside the conviction.[28]

[25] *Daily Times* (Nigeria) (3 December 1929) 5.
[26] *Daily Times* (Nigeria) (3 December 1929) 5.
[27] Gocking, 'The Adjudication of Homicide in Colonial Ghana', 85.
[28] *Tumahole Bereng v The King* [1949] AC 253. Also see *Fakisandhla Nkambule v The King* [1940] AC 760.

The earlier case of *R v Nwaoke*, heard by the WACA in 1939, exemplifies the attitudinal gaps in the adjudication of witchcraft and medicine murder trials. Here, the appellant was charged with murder, convicted of manslaughter, and sentenced to ten years' imprisonment with 'hard labour'. He appealed to the WACA against this conviction. It was explained that the deceased was at one time the wife of the accused. Following the breakdown of their marriage and refusal of the deceased to continue living with him, the accused asked her family for the repayment of his bride wealth as was the customary practice. Dissatisfied with assurances that his money would be repaid, the accused brought a 'Juju' (fetish amulet), pointed it to the wife and stated: 'since you refuse to pay me my money, this *Juju* will kill you; since you refuse to pay me you shall no more eat or drink'. It was established at trial that the woman was psychologically affected by this *Juju* threat. She subsequently became depressed, although there was no evidence that she actually stopped eating or drinking or that her physical health was in any way affected. Six days after the *Juju* curse, she committed suicide by hanging.

At trial, the central question was whether the suicide was a reasonably foreseeable consequence of the threat made by the accused. The case raised questions about interpretation of the Criminal Code provisions relating to the offence of causing death by threats. At the initial trial, the court held that a case of manslaughter had been established against the accused. At the WACA, however, the presiding judge, who evidently did not believe in the causal powers of witchcraft, allowed the appeal and nullified the conviction. He stated: 'There is no evidence whatever that the invoking of this Juju, to the knowledge of the accused at the time he invoked it would be reasonably likely to cause the deceased to take her own life, and in our opinion that element of reasonable likelihood must be present.'[29]

Why did so many medicine murder appeals from Africa come before the JCPC in the mid-twentieth century? Two explanations are apparent. First, Europeans in Africa, from the earliest visitors to later colonial administrators, were both fascinated and repulsed by the custom of human sacrifices and ritual murders in Africa. As one British official remarked, such killings represented 'the grossest forms of superstition and savagery'.[30] Officials in the colony and in the metropole saw the eradication of these practices as a cardinal object of the civilizing mission. In 1933, the Colonial Office set up the 'Bushe Commission', headed by the Colonial Office Legal Adviser H. G. Bushe, to address the problem of administrating criminal law in the Empire. While the Commission covered a variety of legal topics, witchcraft beliefs and practices, particularly as they precipitated murders and assault, constituted its central focus.[31]

[29] *R v Nwaoke* [1939] 5 WACA 120 at 126; Also see J. D. Ojo, 'Supernatural Powers and Criminal Law: A Study with Particular Reference to Nigeria' (1981) 11(3) *Journal of Black Studies* 327–48; and Kharisu Sufiyan Chukkol, *Supernatural Beliefs and the Criminal Law in Nigeria: A Critical Appraisal* (Zaria: Ahmadu Bello University, 1981) 32.

[30] A. Burns, *Colonial Civil Servant* (London: Allen & Unwin, 1949) 179.

[31] *Report of the Bushe Commission of Inquiry into the Administration of Justice* (Nairobi: Government Press, 1933) in Colonial Legal Service and Cognate Matters, KHAN, AP 1/1693.

Faced with similar concerns in 1949, the British government asked the Cambridge anthropologist G. I. Jones to investigate the notorious ritual murders in Basutoland. His task was to unravel the underlying causes of the apparent increase in ritual murders, and to suggest steps that could be taken to remedy the situation.[32] Public fascination with this subject and his study of what he described as 'diretlo' murders earned him the sobriquet 'Sherlock Jones' in the popular press.[33] However, Sotho Chiefs and nationalists rejected the whole idea of medicine murder as a British invention, imposed through a series of show trials and intended to destroy the chieftainship in order that the country could be handed over to South Africa.[34]

The disproportionate number of medicine murder cases that came before the courts reflects the preoccupation of the colonial state with what were considered irrational and intolerable crimes. Conflicts between state authorities and Africans over witchcraft-related crimes provided an important space in which the meanings of justice, law, and order in the Empire were debated. Several studies have traced the emergence of imperial networks of knowledge about witchcraft, showing how colonial concerns about witchcraft produced an elaborate body of law and jurisprudence about capital crimes.[35] Twentieth-century interest in unravelling and prosecuting these 'crimes of superstition' in Africa mirrored what has been described as the 'Jewish ritual murder lie' of the eighteenth and nineteenth centuries.[36] Between 1887 and 1891, no less than twenty-two cases occurred in which charges of ritual murder were levelled against British Jews; these led to elaborate show trials and to convictions in some cases. Ritual murder trials elsewhere were keenly followed by the British press. One such case was the celebrated 1911 trial of the Russian Jew Mendel Bayliss for murdering a 'Christian boy' and using his blood for Jewish ritual ceremonies. Bayliss was eventually acquitted, but not before an outraged British press had presented Russia as 'the most backward and superstitious country in Europe'.[37] By the twentieth century, the mechanisms for prosecuting, adjudicating, and reporting on ritual murders in the British legal system were well honed.

Another explanation for the number of African medicine murder appeals lodged before the JCPC may be sought in the changes made by colonial rule on traditional

[32] G. I. Jones, *Basutoland Medicine Murder: A Report on the Recent Outbreak of 'Diretlo' Murders in Basutoland* (London: HMSO, 1958); Colin Murray and Peter Sanders, 'Medicine Murder in Basutoland: Colonial Rule and Moral Crisis' (2000) 70(1) *Africa: Journal of the International African Institute* 49–78.

[33] Alicia Fentiman, 'Obituary: G. I. Jones', *The Independent* (27 February 1995) 15. For a more recent study of medicine murders in Southern Africa, see J. Evans, 'Where Can We Get a Beast without Hair? Medicine Murder in Swaziland from 1970 to 1988' (1993) 52 *African Studies* 27–42.

[34] Colin Murray and Peter Sanders, *Medicine Murder in Colonial Lesotho: The Anatomy of a Moral Crisis* (Edinburgh: Edinburgh University Press, 2005).

[35] See, for example, Katherine Luongo, *Witchcraft and Colonial Rule in Kenya, 1900–1955* (Cambridge: Cambridge University Press, 2011); E. E. Evans-Pritchard, *Witchcraft, Oracles and Magic Among the Azande* (London: Oxford University Press, 1937); John Parker, 'Witchcraft, Anti-Witchcraft and Trans-Regional Ritual Innovation in Early Colonial Ghana: Sakrabundi and Aberewa, 1889–1910' (2004) 45(3) *The Journal of African History* 393–420.

[36] Sidney Solomon, *The Jews of Britain* (London: Jarrolds, 1938) 99.

[37] Josephine Bacon and Martin Gilbert, *The Illustrated Atlas of Jewish Civilization: 4000 Years of History* (New York: Quantum Books, 2007) 153.

African political and social institutions. The late-nineteenth century imposition of colonial law in Africa led to significant re-allocation of power among various elements and groups in traditional societies. Some crimes previously regarded as befitting death—such as adultery, theft, and witchcraft—were no longer capital offences. Others, on the other hand, which had been accepted as legitimate mechanisms of social defence—for example the killing of suspected witches—now resulted in a capital sentence. These changes created significant tensions. Capital punishment for these offences became a political penalty as much as a judicial punishment, with both didactic and deterrent functions operating through executions as well as mercy and the sparing of condemned lives.[38]

Among the greatest losers of colonial legal and social re-ordering were the practitioners of forms of ritual specialization who were looked upon indiscriminately by the colonial authorities as practitioners of 'witchcraft' and as threats to civilized practices.[39] Ritual practitioners in particular suffered further diminution of power. Their powers over life and death, once sacrosanct and valued in the community, were criminalized under colonial law. Ancient practices of trial by ordeal became aggravated assault, and ritual execution once rationalized as the verdict of the gods, became premeditated murder. Ritual practitioners who previously offered prized services to their communities suddenly became outlaws. In Kenya, for example, the Witchcraft Ordinance of 1909 held criminally liable 'any person who in the opinion of the elders of the Native Councils, with evil intent, holds himself out as a witch-doctor or pretends to exercise or use any kind of supernatural power, witchcraft, sorcery or enchantment'.[40] Such laws produced what has been described as a 'legal and an anthro-administrative complex' leading to unprecedented state-sponsored cleansings of witches and Mau Mau adherents during the late 1940s and 1950s.[41]

Despite the official hostility towards ritual practitioners, however, some colonial officials acknowledged the socio-political disruptions wrought by these transformations, and urged caution and toleration in dealing with African 'witch-doctors'. In a letter to *The Times* of London in 1933, Frank Worthington, the Secretary for Native Affairs in Northern Rhodesia, called for tolerance in colonial attitudes towards African witchcraft, since the English, too, had gone through a 'phase of witchcraft' they outgrew through education and science. Worthington reminded his British readers: 'We no longer vent our spleen upon an unfortunate individual but upon a microbe, thanks to science.'[42] Colonial response to African witchcraft,

[38] Hynd, 'The Extreme Penalty of the Law', 543.

[39] Alan R. Booth, '"European Courts Protect Women and Witches": Colonial Law Courts as Redistributors of Power in Swaziland 1920–1950' (1992) 18(2) *Journal of Southern African Studies* 253.

[40] Witchcraft Ordinance 1909, KNAN, AP/1/1009.

[41] Luongo, *Witchcraft and Colonial Rule in Kenya*, 13.

[42] Frank Worthington, 'Witchcraft in Africa', *The Times* (3 February 1933) 6. These views are expressed in greater detail in F. V. Worthington, *Chiromo the Witch Doctor and Other Rhodesian Studies* (London: The Field Press, 1922).

Worthington argued, should take the 'slow path of education and enlightenment', rather than condemnation and criminalization. He stated:

We should assist the witch-doctor by education, not drive him underground by persecution; for all the persecution we can bring to bear upon him will not eradicate the natives' belief in him but will cause them to lose faith in us if we persist in our course. The witch-doctor is a power in Africa and does his best according to his lights to help his fellows. We should be his ally, not his enemy.[43]

While these sentiments may have resonated well among some colonial officials, there is little evidence to suggest that they actually shaped local policies. The wave of ritual murders that came before the courts in the 1940s and 1950s particularly from West Africa and Southern Africa are telling signs of a deeply eroded traditional authority.[44] They also tell of the tension between the legal and cultural ethos of the colonizers and the colonized. Many of the ritual murder appeals that came before the JCPC, the WACA, and the EACA, emerged in the context of drastic colonial socio-legal and political re-ordering of African societies. Although the colonial state was keen to prosecute and punish ritual practitioners accused of such crimes, many of these men retained considerable influence and power within their communities. They were sometimes able to mobilize communal support and resources to sustain lengthy legal appeals all the way to the Privy Council. This was certainly the case in the celebrated *Kibi* murder case from the Gold Coast, which came before the JCPC between 1944 and 1947 respectively.

The *Kibi* Murder Case

On 3 March 1947, the Secretary of State for Colonies Arthur Creech Jones sent a telegram marked 'Secret' and 'Most Immediate' to Governor Alan Burns in the Gold Coast. It read:

Parliament informed by Private Member today of the execution tomorrow of men condemned for the Apedwa Murder. Speaker ruled question out of order but discussion pursued in great excitement and efforts in all quarters of the House to compel my intervention to overrule your decision that the men should be executed. Whole House deeply moved and demonstrated hostility to your decision. Attack was led by Winston Churchill and supported by Sir John Anderson and Liberal Leader as well as by Labour Leaders. House in uproar for forty minutes demanding that death sentence should be stayed.[45]

The case that elicited this frantic telegram from the Secretary of State was *Abontendomhene Asare Apietu v The King*, which became known as the *Kibi* murder case. As one of the most celebrated murder cases in colonial Africa, the case had

[43] Worthington, 'Witchcraft in Africa', 6.

[44] Richard Roberts, 'Review of *Murder and Politics in Colonial Ghana*, by Richard Rathbone' (1994) 35(2) *The Journal of African History* 328.

[45] Creech Jones to Alan Burns, Confidential Dispatch, 3 March 1947, NAUK, CO 96/783/5.

significant implications for the administration of justice in the Gold Coast colony and for nationalist politics and de-colonization in this part of Africa. Previous studies of this case have focused on exploring its repercussions for those involved, and on providing understanding of the texture of post-Second World War politics in the Gold Coast.[46] The concern here is with the role of the JCPC in adjudicating high-profile criminal appeals and the insights this case offers for understanding the tensions between assertions of imperial universalism and the realities of native 'otherness' in the administration of criminal justice.

In the *Kibi* case, officials in the palace of a recently deceased king were alleged to have conspired to kill one of his Chiefs as part of the funeral rites believed to facilitate the deceased king's transition into the afterlife.[47] The deceased king in this case was Nana Ofori Ata, the paramount ruler of the Akyem Abuakwa in the south eastern region of the Gold Coast. During police investigations that followed in *Kibi*, the traditional capital of Akyem Abuakwa, two men were found who stated they had witnessed the murder. Their account indicated that the missing Chief had been the victim of a ritual murder and that his blood was used as part of the funeral rites.[48] Eight relatives of the deceased king were subsequently arrested and charged with murder. The claim was that the 'eight insecure, grief-stricken men' murdered the victim to commemorate the passing of a great King who they felt was destined to join his ancestors accompanied by rituals.[49] The nature of the charge carried with it an imputation of barbarism at a significant moment in the nationalist history of the Gold Coast.[50] The sensationalist press coverage of the murder and the trials that followed ensured that the case reverberated throughout British West Africa.

At the initial trial in Accra Assizes in November 1944, the accused men were all found guilty by a jury of six Africans and one European, and were sentenced to death.[51] Complicating the case from the beginning, however, was the fact that the body of the victim was not immediately found, and when a body was uncovered later, poorly developed forensic science in the colonies provided no definitive proof that it was that of the allegedly murdered Chief.[52] There were also concerns that some of the convicted men should have been tried as accomplices and accessories to the crime, rather than as principal offenders. At an early stage, Governor Alan Burns exercised his prerogative of mercy and commuted the sentences of two of the accused who were considered less involved in the crime than the others. What followed was a long sequence of legally technical appeals by the accused men against the convictions. Following the failure of the initial appeals to the Supreme Court of

[46] Richard Rathbone, *Murder and Politics in Colonial Ghana* (New Haven: Yale University Press, 1993) and H. A. Nuamah, *Murder in the Palace at Kibi: An Account of the Kibi Ritual Murder Case* (Accra: Educational Press, 1985).

[47] C. F. H. Benjamin, Internal Memorandum, 23 September 1944, NAUK, CO 96/783/2.

[48] Gold Coast: Ritual murder of the Odikro of Apedwa 1951–1952, NAUK, CO 554/531.

[49] *Abontendomhene Asare Apietu and others v The King* (Appeal to the WACA Gold Coast Session), WACA Judgment in CO 96/783/3.

[50] Rathbone, 'A Murder in the Colonial Gold Coast', 458.

[51] Trial for alleged murder of Odikro of Apedwa 1946, NAUK, CO 96/783/2.

[52] A. L. Bryden, Sworn Affidavit, 3 November 1945, NAUK CO 96/783/3; *Rex v Abontendomhene Asare Apietu* [1943] Selected Judgments of the WACA 9 at 24.

the Gold Coast and the West African Court of Appeal, the accused men lodged the first in a series of appeals to the Privy Council in 1945. The protracted litigation was due partly to the wealth and influence of the accused men, which enabled them to retain lawyers in the Gold Coast and England to prosecute their appeals.

The trials created deep fissures along clan and political lines. One faction aligned with the colonial government; it was resolved to enforce capital sentences in what was considered an abhorrent and barbaric crime. Senior officials were convinced of the need to send a strong message that ritual crimes would not be tolerated in the colony, irrespective of how highly placed the offenders were. Governor Alan Burns was of the opinion that the men should be executed, and that granting reprieve would mean 'surrendering of the principles of justice to powers of money and influence'.[53] The majority of the members of the Executive Council also voted against commutation and wanted the law to take its course in order to 'satisfy public vengeance for the crime'.[54]

Allied with the state were sections of the Akyem community that wanted to see justice in the murder of one of their Chiefs. The 'Council of Akyem Abuakwa' sent a petition to the Secretary of State for the Colonies in hopes of persuading him that freeing the accused men would amount to a 'perversion of British justice and would have untold ramifications for the Gold Coast'.[55] Other petitioners appealed to the Secretary of State to uphold British standards of justice in the colony by stating:

> It has always been a cardinal point in the assumption of English justice that an accused is entitled to be tried strictly in accordance with law and that his guilt shall only be found by the jury according to the procedure and standards laid down by statute and the Common Law of England as appropriate to criminal trials. We beg that this standard be not departed from in the case of Africans in a colony when it would certainly not be departed from in England. . . . What price British justice is, if it can be unduly influenced in such a premeditated cold blooded murder of a Chief of an important constitutional section of the Gold Coast. Such injustice would be unprecedented in the annals of British justice in Gold Coast . . . If British justice fails to atone for the innocent blood of Akyea Mensah, surely we can avenge this death of our chief.[56]

The tone of this and other petitions seeking justice for the allegedly murdered Chief caused colonial officials to worry that the outcome of the case might threaten peace and order in the Gold Coast.

Gold Coast elites were divided on this case. In the opposing faction were some influential members of the Akyem royal family and the Western-educated intelligentsia who remained firmly supportive of the accused men. They saw their conviction and sentence as part of a longstanding vendetta by the government against their faction of the traditional political establishment. The high politics that played out behind these scenes made for a particularly knotty trial. Despite the

53 Alan Burns to George Hall, 20 November 1945, NAUK, CO 96/783/3.

54 Alan Burns to George Hall, 20 November 1945, NAUK, CO 96/783/3.

55 Amantoommiensa Council Akin Abuaka to Creech Jones, Inward Telegram, 8 March 1947, NAUK, CO 96/802/5.

56 Kwadjo Asante to Creech Jones, 8 March 1947, NAUK, CO 96/783/5.

availability of copious transcripts and reports of the trial in the archives, it is difficult for the historian looking from a distance to come to firm conclusions on some of the crucial facts of the case.[57] What is significant for our purpose is how the accused men used the imperial legal appeal process to challenge their criminal conviction, the colonial state, and its justice system. The successive appeals lodged on their behalf at the JCPC became more than simply a quest for judicial review of a criminal conviction—they also became opportunities to put the colonial justice system on trial at the centre of Empire.

The accused men first sought leave to appeal to the JCPC in October 1945. The question of not having an established victim—there being no evidence that the disappeared Chief was actually dead—was the main focus of the first round of appeals. Leave to appeal was denied on the grounds that the appellants had not shown that substantial injustice was done at the initial trial. A subsequent appeal to the Supreme Court of the Gold Coast to quash the judgment on legally technical grounds was also rejected, with the presiding judge stating that the applicants had exhausted their right of appeal.[58] He was to be proven wrong. Lawyers for the accused men lodged a new petition with the JCPC in January 1946, which was also rejected. At this point, the case was beginning to cause concern beyond the JCPC chambers. Supporters of the convicted men petitioned King George VI under the auspices of the 'Enlightened sons and daughters of Akim Abuakwa', accusing the government of the Gold Coast of malice in the prosecution of the case and demanding further investigation. The petitioners, including prominent Akan elites such as the vocal nationalist politician and government critic J. B. Danquah, helped to fund the costly appeals of the accused men.[59]

Amidst growing interest in the case from the British press, Secretary of State for the Colonies, Creech Jones, asked for an extended minute from the Gold Coast government on the background of the case and the subsequent appeals. In his response, Governor Alan Burns remarked that there was a concerted effort on the part of a section of the Gold Coast elite to 'delay the course of justice . . . [and] bring our judicial system into contempt'.[60] He feared that British colonial authority and Africans' respect for British rule of law was being eroded by the incessant legal appeals launched by the defendants' well-paid lawyers. Governor Burns was also piqued by pressures from London to commute the sentences and the Secretary of State's vacillations on the rule of law and the extent of administrative authority.[61]

The accused men lodged a third application for Special Leave to Appeal to the Privy Council in June 1946. The JCPC bench, which included two Indian judges, rejected this again.[62] It is not clear whether the inclusion of the two Indian judges had anything to do with the peculiar challenges that the *Kibi* murder case posed to

[57] Rathbone, 'A Murder in the Colonial Gold Coast', 458.

[58] Quoted in Rathbone, 'A Murder in the Colonial Gold Coast', 451.

[59] Margaret Joyce Field, 'Field Notes on the Kibi murder trial', Cambridge University Library: Royal Commonwealth Society Library, 'The Kibi Murder Trial', RCMS 138.

[60] Memorandum from Governor Burns to Secretary of State for Colonies, NAUK, CO 96/783/3.

[61] Alan Burns to Creech Jones, 4 March 1947, NAUK, CO 96/783/5.

[62] A. W. Burchell to S. Abrahams, 18 September 1946, NAUK, CO 96/783/5.

the JCPC. At this stage the accused men's lawyer, the solicitor A. L. Bryden, took the case beyond the JCPC to the court of British public opinion. He circulated a memorandum about the case to all British parliamentarians who were lawyers, with the intent of bringing further public attention to what was already a widely publicized case. His letter echoed accusations of political vendetta raised in the petition by the 'Enlightened sons and daughters of Akim Abuakwa'. Bryden also questioned the competence and impartiality of the Gold Coast government in prosecuting the case.[63]

A. L. Bryden had a long history of representing appellants before the Privy Council from all over the British Empire. At the time of the *Kibi* murder appeal, he was also the Privy Council agent in two other high-profile murder cases from Africa at the JCPC. In one of these cases he successfully got the JCPC to change a conviction for murder to manslaughter.[64] Somewhat of an iconoclast in the conservative circles of elite solicitors qualified to practise at the JCPC, Bryden often took his advocacy beyond the courtroom. His letters to British MPs on the *Kibi* murder case had immediate impact. The Secretary of State was inundated with letters from MPs who saw the protracted trial and the delay in dispensing justice as a humanitarian cause. Nine MPs submitted a petition for clemency addressed to the King on legal and humanitarian grounds. They demanded that the question of the legality of the accused men's conviction be referred to the Law Officers of the Crown for proper investigation.[65]

MPs also accused Governor Burns of playing 'cat and mouse' with the accused, and questioned the propriety of hanging men after a long lapse of time.[66] One petitioner expressed concern that the convicted men had been subjected to the 'dreadful process of being taken, on five separate occasions, to the place of execution and that on more than one occasion, to the execution scaffold'.[67] There were comparisons with the scandalous American case of Sacco and Vanzetti of the late 1920s, in which two Italian immigrants accused of murder were convicted and hanged after highly publicized trials and legal appeals dogged by controversy and contradictory evidence.[68]

As a direct result of Bryden's letter, the group of MPs sent a petition to the Secretary of State for Colonies, stating that they believed it would be contrary to public policy and 'an offence to the spirit of British legal institutions, if the condemned men were executed'. They questioned whether the trials in the colony conformed to the minimum British standards of justice:

> It can never be a satisfactory trial where the Judge, Jury, Accused and Witness speak different languages; where in particular the Jury is exclusively composed of persons who

[63] A. L. Bryden, Sworn Affidavit, 3 November 1945, NAUK, CO 96/783/3.

[64] *Kwaku Mensah v The King* [1946] AC 83. For a discussion of this case see Gocking, 'A Chieftaincy Dispute and Ritual Murder', 215.

[65] Alan Burns to Creech Jones, 4 March 1947, NAUK, CO 96/783/5.

[66] Trial for alleged murder of Odikro of Apedwa, NAUK, CO 96/783/4.

[67] Leslie Hale to R. T. Lennox-Boyd, 14 March 1952, NAUK, CO 554/531.

[68] For a history of this trial see Paul Avrich, *Sacco and Vanzetti: The Anarchist Background* (Princeton, NJ: Princeton University Press, 1996).

understand neither the language nor the customs of the accused persons or of the witnesses; where the Judge understands the language and custom of neither. All these are of even greater significance where the whole background and circumstance of the alleged offence cannot be understood except in relation to the tribal religious customs.[69]

The petition hinged mainly on what the petitioners saw as a flawed adjudicatory process that neither recognized nor adequately accommodated native difference. Questions were also raised about judicial standardization in the colonies, given that in a similar and contemporaneous case of ritual murder in Northern Rhodesia the imposed sentences only ranged from twelve to eighteen months of imprisonment.[70]

In reply to the flood of petitions about the case, Colonial Secretary of State Creech Jones insisted that he had no constitutional power to intervene unless a miscarriage of justice had occurred. After the numerous appeals, no such miscarriage had come to light. He stressed that the prolonged delay in bringing the convicted men to justice was due to no fault of the colonial authorities, but had been occasioned by the fact that the appellant had sufficient funds to enable their lawyers to raise technical legal points in courts.[71] Officials in the Gold Coast blamed the delays and the complications of the case specifically on the 'indefatigable and pertinacious solicitor for the convicts in London, Mr Bryden'.[72]

Just when officials in London thought the publicity generated by the *Kibi* murder case was fizzling out, lawyers for the accused men lodged a fourth appeal to the JCPC in February 1947.[73] The comments of Lord Thankerton in turning down this final appeal conveyed the displeasure of the judges of the JCPC at what they considered an abuse of the appeal process. He stated:

Their Lordships viewed with grave concern and disapproval the unusual procedure adopted in this case *in the multiplication of applications to the Board*. Their Lordships found it difficult to avoid the conclusion that the course was either adopted deliberately which would constitute an abuse of the due administration of justice or arose from an inexcusable ignorance or disregard of the laws, procedural or otherwise, involved.[74]

Evidently, Bryden and other lawyers for the accused men were able to marshal complex and arcane legal technicalities in the appeal process to slow down what appeared to be a rapid rush to the gallows. Bryden's tactics of taking the prosecution of the appeal beyond the JCPC into the court of British public opinion opened fissures within the colonial establishment, and contributed to a crisis of confidence in the administration of criminal justice and in British colonial policy more generally. In Accra (capital of the Gold Coast) and in London, the case took a heavy toll on officials. There were frantic and tense correspondences over the case between Governor Burns and senior officials in Whitehall. The Colonial Secretary repeatedly sought the counsel of Privy Council officials to address questions raised

69 J. Silverman to Creech Jones, 24 January 1947, CO 96/783/5.
70 Leslie Hale to R. T. Lennox-Boyd, 14 March 1952, NAUK, CO 554/531.
71 A. Creech Jones to C. W. Dumpleton, 3 July 1946, NAUK, CO 96/783/4.
72 O. G. R. Williams, Internal Memorandum, 18 June 1946, NAUK, CO 96/783/4.
73 *Daily Times* (28 August 1947) 7.
74 *The Crown Colonist* [1947] Vol 17, 7–12, 468.

by the MPs in parliamentary debates, petitions, and in official letters. At some point, Governor Burns even tendered his resignation partly because of the perceived challenge to his authority and imputations on his character. In the end, something of an uneasy compromise was struck. Two of the accused men died in prison before the execution of the sentence; two had their sentences commuted to life imprisonment, while the remaining three believed to be the ringleaders of the murders were hanged.

The *Kibi* case was only one of several highly politicized African medicine murder cases that came before the Imperial Courts of Appeal in the 1940s and 1950s.[75] One of the other cases was the Bridge House murder, so called after the name of the house in Elmina in the Gold Coast where the crime took place in 1946.[76] The case was connected with bitter factional disputes over chieftainship succession. The Regent of the Edina State, Kweku Ewusie, and four of the town's *mpanyimfo* (influential men) were charged with murdering a young girl of ten, in order to use her blood and body parts to make 'medicine' to help them win a court case in which they were defendants.[77] After exhausting their legal options in the colony, the accused men—supported by sections of the Edina aristocracy—appealed to the Privy Council that promptly rejected their appeal. As in the *Kibi* case, A. L. Bryden who was also the lawyer for the accused men in this case, took his advocacy beyond the courtroom. Having failed to get reprieve for his clients at the JCPC, he sent multiple petitions to the Colonial Office, challenging the trial and official handing of the case.[78] His efforts were unsuccessful and the accused men were executed.

Criminal Justice and the Politics of Difference

The *Kibi* and *Bridge House* medicine murder cases offer important insights into the judicial and extra-judicial discourse of native difference in colonial criminal justice. First, they show that legal debates about native difference in colonial adjudicatory processes were not confined to the courtroom. In the administration of criminal justice, colonial 'otherness' was constructed and invoked as much outside the courts as it was within the courts. For colonial subjects in the outposts of the Empire, an appeal to the Privy Council in London—even when unsuccessful—sometimes opened up opportunities to appeal directly to the metropolitan court of public opinion. There, the colonial justice system could be put on trial in ways that it could not be done in the colonies.

The metropolitan discourse on the *Kibi* case also underscores salient paradoxes in the ways in which native difference was invoked. The petitioning MPs in England wanted universalist standards of British justice extended to the accused men who, they thought, had been improperly tried and sentenced in the colonies. What was

[75] For example, *Nkau Majara v R* [1954] AC 235.
[76] Gocking, 'A Chieftaincy Dispute and Ritual Murder in Elmina', 216.
[77] *West Africa* (22 October 1988) 366.
[78] Bryden to the Legal Adviser, Colonial Office, 15 January 1946, PRAADA, CSO 15/3/213.

at stake wasn't simply the liberty of six Africans wrongly convicted and sentenced to death, but the integrity of British justice. As one MP put it, executing the convicted men would 'shock the conscience of civilised society wherever the facts are known', given the irregularities and delays in their trial.[79] The petitioners claimed that there had been a miscarriage of justice partly because the criminal justice system under which the accused men were tried was not attuned to native customs and circumstances. Implicit in this claim was the notion that universal British justice could only truly be guaranteed by countenancing native otherness.

The African petitioners who opposed clemency for the accused men invoked British justice and imperial universalism quite differently. They too wanted to see British standards of justice upheld; not by accommodating African difference but by discounting it. The 'Council of Akym Abuakwa' considered reprieve for the accused men as 'perversion of British justice'.[80] It urged colonial authorities not to depart from 'cardinal principles' of the Common Law and British justice in dealing with Africans in the colonies.[81] A crime considered severely punishable in England could not be allowed to go unpunished in Africa, for reasons of native custom and circumstance. The *Kibi* case highlights how imperial universalism and native difference were constructed in both the metropole and colony to serve competing agendas.

The *Kibi* and *Bridge House* murder cases also provide insights into the contested political life in the colony at the time when colonial rule drew to a close. As anthropologist David Pratten argued in his study of the so-called 'man-leopard' murders in Southern Nigeria, colonial officials and the British press were keen to portray these killings as medicine, witchcraft, or ritual murders. In fact, most cases concerned more mundane matters, including the resistance to British rule, the need to contest European domination of local knowledge, competition over land, labour, and intra-community rivalries. The so-called 'medicine murders' also arose from tensions in everyday colonial life and involved husbands engaged in polygamous marriages, Chiefs eager to collect tributes, nationalists seeking to inherit power from the British, and deviants who wanted to challenge the police.[82]

The *Kibi* murder case in particular showed the fragility of traditional rule at a time when the British were beginning to despair over the 'indirect rule' system that had formed the basis of colonial administration in this part of Africa.[83] The indirect rule system had optimistically envisioned incorporating traditional chiefly authorities into colonial administration as an integral part of the machinery of governance. The competition for office that indirect rule unleashed, however, greatly undermined what officials hoped would be a smoothly-functioning native customary

[79] J. Silverman to Creech Jones, 15 February 1947, NAUK, CO 96/783/5.

[80] Amantoommiensa Council Akin Abuaka to Creech Jones, Inward Telegram, 8 March 1947, NAUK, CO 96/802/5.

[81] Amantoommiensa Council Akin Abuaka to Creech Jones, Inward Telegram, 8 March 1947, NAUK, CO 96/802/5.

[82] David Pratten, *The Man-Leopard Murders: History and Society in Colonial Nigeria* (Edinburgh: Edinburgh University Press, 2007).

[83] Rathbone, *Murder and Politics in Colonial Ghana*, 202.

order. By the 1940s, endless chieftainship succession disputes, disagreements over the limits of native political authority and challenges from Western-educated African elites who thought themselves the rightful heirs of colonial government, had destabilized indirect rule.

Medicine murder trials and the legal appeals that followed provided opportunities for increasingly marginalized traditional elites to confront the colonial state and its justice system. Access to cash and the legal appeal process in London meant that otherwise routine criminal trials assumed unusual salience. In the *Kibi* murder appeals, for example, the wealth of the Akyem royal family whose close kin stood in the dock accused of a foul murder provided the defence with apparently unlimited funding for what was an extremely expensive legal struggle in both the Gold Coast and Britain. The case involved five of the most prominent lawyers in the Gold Coast, including J. B. Danquah, reputed to be one of the first continental Africans to receive a doctorate degree in Law.

This group of Western-educated African elites saw these murder trials as opportunities to challenge colonial authority in the arena that they had mastered. The legal powers of the state and the state's use of those powers were called into question on appeal before the Imperial Appeal Courts. The imperial legal arena was one in which African litigants could challenge the legitimacy of the colonial legal order and defy colonial power even if the judicial outcomes were not always favourable.[84] According to one contemporary observer of the *Kibi* murder trials: 'No one had seriously doubted the guilt of the accused and no one had realized, until Dr Danquah and his colleagues found them, that so many loopholes existed in British law. It was said that the law was brought into contempt by the murder case.'[85]

Legal challenges inevitably had political overtones. For nationalist elites like J. B. Danquah, who played active roles in the *Kibi* and *Bridge House* trials, highlighting the weaknesses of the colonial justice system was part of a broader political agenda. In the *Kibi* case, close kinsmen of the accused—the vanguard of moderate nationalism—became radicalized by their extended confrontation with the colonial justice system. Their political initiatives accelerated the formation of the Gold Coast's first national political party, the United Gold Coast Convention (UGGC) in the late 1940s. It would come to play a key role in the struggle for independence. In his biography, Kwame Nkrumah who later became the first Prime Minister of independent Ghana, states that some of the most prominent members of the independence movement were 'affected in one way and another by the result of the *Kibi* murder trial and this was what influenced them to join the UGGC'.[86]

[84] Rathbone, 'A Murder in the Colonial Gold Coast', 459.

[85] Elspath Joscelin Grant Huxley, *Four Guineas: A Journey Through West Africa* (London: Chatto & Windus, 1957) 92.

[86] Kwame Nkrumah, *Ghana: The Autobiography of Kwame Nkrumah* (New York: International Publishers) 86.

The resolve of the colonial state to prosecute and punish ritual murders and the ways in which African litigants used the legal appeal processes to challenge their convictions reflect a central tension in the colonial criminal justice: the maintenance of native otherness within a legal framework premised on normative universality and imperial standardization. Inside and outside of the courts, these cases forced open fissures within the colonial establishment, and contributed to a crisis of confidence in the administration of criminal justice and in British colonial policy more generally. These fractures would be exacerbated by the conflict between administrative justice and due process—ie, justice administered by colonial administrators premised mainly on customary law versus justice administered in formal court settings by judges adhering to statute law and proper criminal procedures.

Colonial administrators were generally more inclined to condone and promote administrative adjudication because it made their work easier. Though saddled with magisterial responsibilities at the district and provincial levels of the colonial legal system, few of these local administrators had formal legal training. They were weary of being bogged down with legal technicalities in adjudicating cases that involved natives, and preferred flexibility and discretion in the administration of justice. To them, justice among the natives was best measured by the outcomes rather than by the processes of judicial governance. This position sometimes brought administrative officers on the spot in direct conflict with colonial legal officers and metropolitan judges who were more inclined to uphold the principles of English common law and the strict application of colonial penal law. The arguments marshalled on both sides of the divide would define and challenge the meaning of native difference and imperial universalism in the administration of justice. Nowhere was this tension more evident than in the debates over the place of blood money customs in the colonial criminal justice system.

Blood Money

The influence of the JCPC on imperial law and justice was not limited to the adjudication of colonial appeals, the finality of its judgments, or the high precedential value of its judgments in colonial courts. Outside the courtroom, JCPC decisions or assumptions about its position on particular legal questions shaped the administration of justice in the colonies. Guided by the JCPC's decisions in previous and similar cases, officials in the colonies speculated on the proper course of action in questions of law and justice. Even where they did not directly intervene in the administration of justice, the shadow of the Imperial Appeal Courts hung over judicial governance in the colonies. This was particularly true for questions of native customary law and its place in the administration of criminal justice.

The custom requiring an offender to pay a monetary penalty to a victim or the family of a victim generated some of the most impassioned debates about native otherness in colonial criminal justice in Africa. Traditionally, blood money fines imposed in cases of murder protected the offender and his kinsfolk from the vengeance of the victim's family. Colonial ethnographers and anthropologists recognized this system as essential to settling feuds and maintaining social order in the communities where the custom was practised.[87] In British Somaliland, for example, the killing of a member of a 'tribal group' or clan by a member of another clan often disrupted the peace between the two groups, and resulted in protracted tribal vendettas. Unless appropriate compensation was obtained, the injured clan would take retaliatory action against the killer's clan. In pre-colonial times, the injured group sometimes exacted the life of the offender, who was then turned over to that group and executed according to the *lex talionis*.[88] By the late nineteenth century, the more common means to fend off reprisals was for the offender's group to pay blood money (*dia*) to the group of the deceased as ransom in lieu of the offender's life.[89]

In the community's view, the murder of a relative constituted the loss of a working unit of the family. Whether a homicide was premeditated, voluntary, or accidental, the damage was the same for the group—it meant the loss of one of its members. In some cases, this loss was made good by a relative of the murderer who pledged to work for free, for a given period every year, for the victim's family. The payment of blood money, therefore, primarily represented communal remediation of economic loss. Blood money was not solely for economic compensation, however, but held deeper cultural and religious significance as well. In the Akamba communities of Kenya, blood money fines for murder consisted of a bull, a cow, and a goat. While the bull and the cow were given to the spouse of the deceased as compensation for economic loss, the goat was used for sacrificial purposes and ceremonial purification. It was believed that unless this ritual was observed to cleanse the land and appease the spirit of the deceased, a blood curse remained on both the families of the offender and victim.[90]

With the spread of English-style legal systems in British East Africa in the early twentieth century, colonial officials confronted well-established customary rules on criminal homicide. Under the indirect rule system, officials sought to build on these customs in administering criminal justice among the natives. The challenge they faced was determining how to distinguish between three categories of African customary laws. The first were 'innocuous' customs that could be easily accommodated within the legal system without compromising British standards of justice. The second were customs considered undesirable but tolerable in the legal system, for the purpose of maintaining social order in tribal communities undergoing a social transition. The third were customs considered fundamentally repugnant to British justice and to its idea of 'justice, equity and good conscience'. These had to be abrogated completely. Blood money customs were problematic because it was

87 See, for example, John Middleton, *The Ethnographic Survey of Africa: East Central Africa, Vol V* (London: International African Institute, 1950).

88 The law of retaliation founded on the premise that a punishment inflicted should correspond in degree and kind to the offence of the wrongdoer, as an eye for an eye.

89 Arthur Bonham-Carter, Internal Memorandum, 9 March 1911, KNAN, AP/1/923.

90 Gerhard Lindblom, *The Akamba in British East Africa: An Ethnological Monograph* (Uppsala: Appelberg, 1920) 155–7.

uncertain how they fitted in these categories of African customs and whether they were tolerable or outright objectionable.

The custom of blood money represented a classic conflict of the laws. Under native customary law blood money was considered a matter of criminal justice. On the contrary, under English law compensation for 'assault against the person' could only be brought to court as a civil claim. In cases of homicide, the customary law in some African communities prescribed the payment of blood money as restitution. With the introduction of English-style codes of criminal law and procedure, offences such as murder and manslaughter fell under the exclusive jurisdiction of the British courts applying the codes. Certain legal questions inevitably arose. The first was whether a 'British court' guided by customary law could award blood money as compensation, given that no such claim could be entertained under English law.[91] In many colonial jurisdictions, the obstacle to blood money being awarded was that 'British courts' could only be guided by native law, and native tribunals could only apply customary laws that did not conflict with statute laws—the latter mostly framed after English laws. The legal question that engendered much debate was whether—in the case of blood money—there was irreconcilable conflict between English law and native customary law.

The conflict of laws was evident in *Bornu Native Authority v Magudama Abatcha* heard in 1946, which involved a disagreement among the judges of the WACA. The question was whether the customary Islamic law of homicide should prevail over the provisions of the Northern Nigeria Criminal Code, when adjudicating criminal cases involving natives who were subject to Islamic law.[92] Under the Sharia-based customary Islamic law of Northern Nigeria, homicide was regarded as a civil or 'private wrong', and provocation was legally irrelevant. If 'accidental', homicide gave rise to a claim for blood money. If 'deliberate', it allowed the heirs of the deceased to demand blood money or another person's life (for the life taken) at their discretion. In either case, the heirs of the victim had the prerogative to forgo their right to blood money or retribution.[93] This custom conflicted with colonial statute law, under which murder constituted an offence against the state, and where clear distinctions existed between intentional murder and accidental manslaughter. In the *Magudama Abatcha* case, the WACA ruled that Islamic *Maliki* law of homicide and of evidence was applicable, and that blood money could be awarded—the provisions of the Criminal Code notwithstanding. The dissenting Judge Cecil Ames took a markedly different view, however. He argued that where native customary law conflicted with the Criminal Code, the latter must be applied. 'Can it be the law of this large British Protectorate,' Judge Ames queried, 'that in many parts of it, a man can be sentenced to death for what is shown by evidence to

[91] H. F. Morris, 'The Award of Blood Money in East African Manslaughter Cases' (1974) 18(1) *Journal of African Law* 104.

[92] For a full discussion of the problem of conflicting laws of homicide, see J. N. D. Anderson, *Islamic Law in Africa* (London: HMSO, 1954).

[93] Colonial Office, *Native Courts and Native Customary Law in Africa* (London: HMSO, 1957) 18; J. N. Matson, 'The Common Law Abroad: English and Indigenous Laws in the British Commonwealth' (1993) 42 *International and Comparative Law Quarterly* 775.

have been at the most manslaughter and not murder?... Mohamedan law has no privileged position; it prevails, where it does prevail, because it is there the local law and custom.'[94]

Colonial judges expressed concern about the impact of 'uncivilized' natives on the quality of criminal justice administered in the colonies. In a memorandum to the Commission of Inquiry, established in 1933 to oversee the administration of justice in East Africa, Judge S. J. Thomas of the EACA called for reforms in the criminal justice system in Kenya, hoping to maintain uniformity across the Empire. 'Native customs,' Judge Thomas argued, 'should not be allowed to disturb the basic apparatus and principles of British justice administered in African territories.' He noted that, having previously served as a judge in the colonies of St Vincent and Trinidad, he saw the benefits of maintaining a standardized system of justice in the Empire.[95]

Some judicial and administrative officials also believed that the custom of paying blood money stood at variance with the fundamental principles of English criminal justice. 'The view that civilization takes of homicide being an offence against the state,' wrote Judge J. W. Barth of Kenya in 1909, 'can never be reconciled with the view of primitive men that it is a private loss to the family which may be compensated by payment.'[96] The custom of paying blood money as a recompense for murder had no place in the English-style legal system being introduced in East Africa. Homicide, he insisted, must be punished as an offence against the state; the 'primitive ideas of the savage' had to give way to ordered rule, as it was impossible to expect the two systems to co-exist.[97] Judge Barth, however, acknowledged that before the 'savage system' disappeared entirely, there would inevitably be a period of legal transition that would have to be carefully managed (see Figure 4.1).

Many local administrators did not share Judge Barth's views, however. John Ainsworth, a Native Commissioner and one of the more experienced officers in the Kenyan government, led the chorus of disagreement. A pioneer of British rule in East Africa, he epitomized the pragmatism of the colonial 'man on the spot'. Starting out as a trading agent with the Imperial British East Africa Company in the late nineteenth century, he oversaw a number of 'punitive expeditions' and, after three decades as a field administrator, rose to become the Chief Native Commissioner in Kenya.[98] Ainsworth's official writings convey an inclination toward supple pragmatism in the administration of native affairs. He had little patience for legal dogmatism and technicalities in judicial governance.

Responding to Judge Barth's memorandum denouncing the payment of blood money, Ainsworth argued that the custom, objectionable as it was to British

[94] *Bornu Native Authority v Magudama Abatcha* [1946], reported in *Selected Judgments of the West African Court of Appeal, Vol 12* (Lagos: Government Print Department, 1946) 141.

[95] S. J. Thomas, Memorandum to the Commission of Inquiry into the Administration of Justice, 3 April 1933, KNAN, AP 1/1659.

[96] J. W. Barth to C. W. Hobley, 13 March 1911, KNAN, AP/1/923.

[97] J. W. Barth to C. W. Hobley, 13 March 1911, KNAN, AP/1/923.

[98] Robert M. Maxon, *John Ainsworth and the Making of Kenya* (New York: University Press of America, 1980) 7.

Figure 4.1: Judge J. W. Barth, Mombasa, *circa* 1910
Winterton Collection of East African Photographs, Melville J. Herskovits Library of African Studies, Northwestern University

officials, was integral to the native's sense of justice. He stated that the payment of blood money was an acknowledgement of a time-honoured custom prevalent throughout Africa, and that he saw nothing in it that was repugnant.[99] It was, in his view, unreasonable to force the technicalities of English penal laws on Africans who had just been brought under colonial influence. Ainsworth premised his position on the essential difference between the native individual and his circumstances on the one hand, and British notions of law and justice on the other. 'You will pardon me,' he wrote to Judge Barth,

> . . . for saying that in my opinion, while law and justice are supposed to be one and indivisible, among savages, and considering the class of evidence we have to rely upon, it may often happen that law and justice are as district and as apart as the poles . . . Is it justice for us to suddenly impose a law upon a people of whom we pose as their protectors, by which we upset their ideas of justice before preparing them for change?[100]

Ainsworth also argued the practicality of accommodating African blood money customs in the colonial law. Cold-blooded and premeditated murders, he noted,

[99] John Ainsworth to J. W. Barth, 18 March 1909, KNAN, AP/1/923.
[100] John Ainsworth to J. W. Barth, 18 March 1909, KNAN, AP/1/923.

were rare among the natives. Many of the killings resulting in criminal proceedings in Kenya were the result of faction fights and stock theft that were best resolved through native laws and customs. Ainsworth warned that insisting on the strict application of statute law and English Common Law principles in such cases would almost certainly result in the proliferation of inter-tribal blood feuds and vendettas that could disrupt order in the colony.[101] Rejecting African blood money customs, he insisted, would alienate native opinion, lead to concealment of crimes, and foster a feeling of injustice and unfairness among the natives. Indeed, disagreement over the payment of blood money led to deterioration of the otherwise cordial relationship between the Giriama and British officials in Kenya in 1913.[102]

Other local administrators shared Ainsworth's concerns as well. One official wrote: '[blood money] is one of those native customs, which not being repugnant to morality, should be retained. It has a restraining influence on crimes of violence and helps to stabilize the equilibrium of social life in primitive communities.'[103] Others stressed the sheer impracticality of abolishing centuries-old blood money traditions that were so deeply entrenched in native lifestyles. Writing in 1915, one local administrator posed the classic dilemma that confronted colonial officials in adjudicating blood money cases.

> A native (A) murdered another native (B). By native law this is a private matter and is settled by A's relations paying blood money to B's. The government however insists on hanging (A) or imprisoning him for a long term of years. The natives have asked me whether under these circumstances B's family can still get their blood-money. If it is ruled that they cannot do so then there is the greatest incentive to B's relatives to assist in hiding the murderer. If they say he has run away and cannot be found they can exact their blood money, whereas if they catch him they lose their blood money and run a good chance of being made to pay for him by his relative if he is sentenced and hanged.[104]

This dilemma reflects a key challenge that confronted local officials in the administration of criminal justice throughout Africa: maintaining British standards of justice when the normative assumptions underpinning those standards were fundamentally inconsistent with local customs and practices.

Senior officials responded to this quandary by reiterating that punishment for murders could no longer be treated as a question of compensation to a private family that had been weakened by the loss of one of its members, but as a question of the 'Government making life and property secure and maintaining the King's peace'.[105] Chief Native Commissioner G. V. Maxwell stated in a memorandum to the magistrates: 'Any native community failing to take all possible steps to arrest a murderer and deliver him to justice is liable to collective punishment under the

[101] John Ainsworth to J. W. Barth, 18 March 1909, KNAN, AP/1/923.

[102] Cynthia Brantley, *The Giriama and Colonial Resistance in Kenya, 1800–1920* (California: University of California Press, 1981) 84.

[103] Provincial Commissioner, Eastern Province to Chief Secretary, 5 March 1936, cited in Morris, 'The Award of Blood Money', 109.

[104] C. M. Dobbs to District Commissioner Kisumu, 29 June 1915, KNAN, AP/1/923.

[105] R. W. Hamilton, Circular to Magistrates No 4 1907, KNAN, AP/1/923.

Collective Punishment Ordinance.'[106] He added that the acceptance of blood money accompanied by a deliberate refraining from prosecution also constituted an offence under the Indian Penal Code applicable in the colony at the time.[107]

The difficulties of adjudicating blood money cases could not simply be resolved by asserting the supremacy of colonial statute law. Under the Indian Penal Code of 1860, extended to most of British East Africa in the early twentieth century, murder was punishable by hanging or by 'transportation for life' (later changed to 'life imprisonment'). Manslaughter was mostly punished by imprisonment. These changes marked a significant departure from prevailing African customary laws on crime and punishment. As other studies have shown, penal incarceration was largely unknown to sub-Saharan African societies prior to European incursion, when colonial regimes built prisons as a means of imposing taxes, extracting labour, and ensuring European domination.[108] In many parts of Africa, the abrupt and intrusive spread of prisons systemically destroyed indigenous social control mechanisms such as offender reparations, temporary or permanent banishment, tribal networks, and the sanctions of chiefly authorities.[109]

In the early colonial period, many Africans could not understand the rationale behind hanging or imprisoning a convicted offender who could be compelled to make restitution to the family of the deceased. During a 1911 provincial tour in Kenya, Commissioner C. W. Hobley was inundated with queries about the question of blood money from several African elders and heads of the Native Councils. The natives he encountered stated that they were satisfied with compensation being awarded for murder, and regarded any imprisonment inflicted by the government as a purely governmental matter. They particularly resented the fact that the government had, without consulting them, introduced a new practice of putting a murderer to death and thereby depriving the victims' relatives of compensation.[110] One puzzled councillor wondered why the government would choose to have a murderer idle away in captivity, instead of involving him in work to compensate the victim's family for their loss.[111] Evidently, the problem lay in a fundamental difference between the British and African perceptions of justice. British officials thought in terms of state retribution and detached punishment; the African elders charged with judicial governance in the native tribunals thought of criminal justice in terms of communal restitution and reparation. Here, the reality of native otherness was inescapable.

[106] G. V. Maxwell, Internal Memorandum, 31 March 1927, KNAN, AP/1/923.

[107] G. V. Maxwell, Internal Memorandum, 31 March 1927, KNAN, AP/1/923.

[108] Although some African societies such as the Dahomey Kingdom and Fulani Emirate used prison-like facilities before the coming of Europeans, imprisonment was mostly used for detention by Europeans. For a detailed discussion of imprisonment and confinement in pre-colonial and colonial Africa, see Florence Bernault, *A History of Prison and Confinement in Africa* (Portsmouth: Heinemann, 2003).

[109] Florence Bernault, 'The Politics of Enclosure in Colonial and Postcolonial Africa', in Bernault, *A History of Prison and Confinement in Africa*, 11.

[110] C. W. Hobley to Provincial Judge, Mombasa, 23 February 1911, KNAN, AP/1/923.

[111] C. W. Hobley to Provincial Judge, Mombasa, 23 February 1911, KNAN, AP/1/923.

Retribution versus Restitution

The case of *Nguniu v Ngarange*, which came before the Magistrate Court in Kyambu, Kenya in 1916, exemplifies the ideological tension between the restitutive and retributive justice paradigms in the debate over blood money.[112] The 'facts' of the case, as presented at trial, were that the defendant had, in a fit of anger, cut the plaintiff so severely in the leg that amputation became necessary. The defendant was subsequently tried by a native tribunal and sentenced to eighteen months' imprisonment. Under prevailing local customs, the loss of a leg had to be paid for with fifty goats, which the victim demanded. At trial, the central issue was whether blood money could be claimed in criminal proceedings after the crime has been expiated by imprisonment. The court held that it could not. It ruled that since—under native customary law—blood money was intended primarily to 'compose a quarrel' and prevent revenge, it could be said that the quarrel had been composed by the offender's imprisonment. In the view of the presiding Judge G. A. S. Northcote, imprisonment was full interpretation of the *lex talonis* (a leg for a leg). If *lex talionis* had been fulfilled, albeit allegorically, the claim for blood money failed.[113]

The case unleashed a spirited debate within the colonial legal establishment in Kenya over the legality of blood money claims in situations where the claimant was the direct victim of an offence. The main legal question was whether blood money could be awarded by British courts to a victim in a civil action, if not in criminal cases. Under these circumstances, the payment of blood money related mostly to the so-called 'trespass to the person' cases in tort law, which included murder, assault, battery, and other offences against the person. Under the English Common Law, two distinct liabilities arose upon such a trespass. The first liability was to punishment by the state; the other to civil claims of damages by the injured persons. The judgment in the *Nguniu v Ngarange* case apparently privileged the former liability over the latter.

Some officials, including Judge R. W. Hamilton, disagreed with the ruling in *Nguniu*. He thought that it should be possible for natives to demand and receive compensation for personal injury, and for the state to exert punishment. The fact that the serving of the tribunal's sentence purged the offence against the state should not deprive the sufferer of his right to damages for the criminal wrong committed. In England, Hamilton argued, it was possible to bring a private claim for damages before the court even when a defendant had been criminally convicted. Under the Fatal Accidents Act in England, a widow whose husband has been killed could sue the murderer for damages. Why, then, should the native in Africa be denied similar legal remedies, Hamilton queried (see Figure 4.2).[114]

112 *Kamau Wa Nguniu v Kinyanjui wa Ngarange*, [1916] KNAN, AP/1/923.

113 R. W. Hamilton to G. A. S. Northolt, 3 October 1916, KNAN, AP/1/923.

114 R. W. Hamilton to G. A. S. Northolt, 3 October 1916, KNAN, AP/1/923.

Figure 4.2: Judge R. W. Hamilton, Mombasa, *circa* 1910
Winterton Collection of East African Photographs, Melville J. Herskovits Library of African Studies, Northwestern University

Blood money remained a contentious legal issue well into the 1930s, dominating deliberations of the Bushe Commission of Inquiry set up by the Colonial Office in 1933 to investigate the administration of criminal justice in East Africa.[115] In its report, the Commission acknowledged that discovering and accommodating—to the extent possible—African blood money customs was crucial to the effective administration of criminal justice in the colonies. Given the socio-cultural significance of blood money customs, it was clear to members of the Commission that some compromise was inevitable. They stated:

> We cannot accept the thesis that part of the punishment for so serious a crime as murder should under any system of modern jurisprudence take the form of the award of compensation; but we see no reason why, if the death sentence is not carried out, native courts in their civil jurisdiction should not take cognisance of such a claim, provided always that the criminal proceedings in the matter from which such civil claim flows must first be completed according to law.[116]

[115] *Report of the Bushe Commission of Inquiry into Justice* (Nairobi: Government Press, 1933) Colonial Legal Service and Cognate Matters, KHAN, AP 1/1693.
[116] *Report of the Bushe Commission of Inquiry into Justice*, 16.

The position of the Bushe Commission represented an attempt at a compromise solution to the conflict of laws. The premise was self-evident: ancient African customs based on the notion that the killing of a person was a private and kinship matter could not be maintained wholesale under the modernizing agenda of the colonial legal system. Yet, homicide could not be viewed solely as an offence against the state without any regard for the socioeconomic loss to the victim's family. Confronted with these realities, colonial officials trod a middle path between abrogation and toleration. They created a hybrid system that combined English Common Law principles with African blood money customs. A new rule provided that in the event of a murder, the family of the offender could be required to pay a 'collective fine' in lieu of blood money to the family of the deceased, even after the offender had been convicted in a 'British Court' and sentenced to imprisonment or execution.[117] Under this 'overlapping system', both punishments would be reduced in order to match the whole punishment that would fit the offence. It was also stressed that what the court imposed in such circumstances was a 'collective fine' rather than a blood money fine.[118]

Even this attempt at a middle-of-the-road solution proved contentious, however. It alienated some Africans within the traditional elite class, who thought it was a perversion of the very essence of blood money, meant to protect the offender and his kinsfolk from the vengeance of society. If the government insisted on extracting its own 'vengeance' on the offender through imprisonment or execution, what justification was there in demanding blood money from an offender's family? The family of an offender would be doubly burdened with the loss of a working member under British law, and paying compensation under native law.[119] Other Africans questioned the scope of blood money enforcement. In the Kingdom of Bunyoro, the *Mukama* (King) and his government wanted civil claims for blood money to be allowed in cases of accidental death, but not in cases of murder where imprisonment or the death penalty had been imposed. In contrast, the Ministers of Buganda insisted that, whether a murderer was hanged or not, the relatives of the victim should have the right to sue against his estate for blood money compensation. They argued this was the customary tradition in Buganda.[120]

These divergent positions on blood money customs offer insight into the process of how colonial customary laws were forged in particular historical struggles within the colonial establishments and among colonized groups. Traditional elites took a central role in defining 'indigenous law' on blood money, both in the courts and in official discourse.[121] The unfamiliarity of British officials with these traditions and the prevarications resulting from their attempts to accommodate African customary law within colonial law, created opportunities for traditional elites to present local customs as they wanted them to be.[122]

[117] Arthur Bonham-Carter, Internal Memorandum, 9 March 1911, KNAN, AP/1/923.
[118] Arthur Bonham-Carter, Internal Memorandum, 9 March 1911, KNAN, AP/1/923.
[119] H. R. Jates to Chief Justice, Mombasa, 5 January 1916, KNAN, AP/1/923.
[120] Quoted in Morris, 'The Award of Blood Money', 110.
[121] Sally Merry, 'Law and Colonialism' (1991) 25(4) *Law and Society Review* 897.
[122] Martin Chanock, 'Laws and Contexts' (1989) 7(2) *Law in Context* 72.

Officials opposed the overlapping system of combining blood money penalties with state sanctions for different reasons. E. H. Pickering, the Chief Justice of Kenya, described such a hybrid model as 'fundamentally repugnant to British ideas'. Native customs relating to blood money, he argued, should be treated simply as superseded by the provisions of the Indian Penal Code applicable in the territory.[123] Other officials thought that the combination of British and native penalties for murder amounted to punishing offenders twice for the same offence.[124] They argued that the defence of 'double jeopardy' would benefit those natives subjected to these punishments if an appeal was made to the Privy Council.[125] Chief Justice G. H. Pickering was convinced that the only way to obtain judicial clarity on the matter was to reach a decision in a superior court—preferably the Privy Council—through a test case involving blood money. The kind of case he thought suitable was the case of *Malau wa Nyawa*.[126]

In 1939, Malau wa Nyawa, a relative of a convicted murderer, petitioned the Chief Justice of the Supreme Court in Mombasa, Kenya, against an order to pay blood money to the family of the victim. Malau claimed that his brother had been sentenced by the Supreme Court in 1933 to life imprisonment for murder. Five years later, a brother of the murdered man claimed forty-five head of cattle as *Kore* (blood compensation) from Malau before a native tribunal. The claim was initially dismissed according to the prevailing judicial instructions. A month later, however, the same native tribunal reversed its verdict and sought to enforce a blood compensation claim against Malau. Malau initially petitioned the local District Commissioner, but he did not wish to interfere with the verdict of the native tribunal. He subsequently turned to the Chief Justice of the Supreme Court, claiming that he was not bound to pay blood money, since his brother had been properly convicted and sentenced for the offence by a British court.[127]

An investigation, ordered by the Chief Justice, considered local blood money customs and longstanding legal debates on the subject. In his report, District Commissioner K. W. Simmonds, who led the investigation, stated that he was 'very much in sympathy' with Malau's case and considered the payment of full blood money an injustice.[128] He went to great lengths to make a distinction between the two forms of blood compensation claims in Malau's case. One was the compensatory *Kore* paid to the relatives of the murdered man, which he thought should not be enforced against Malau. The other was *Kiruruma*, the sacrificial price of three cattle and three sheep, which was customary for the brother of the murderer to pay to the elders of the community. *Kiruruma*, which was the expiation of the shedding of blood, was distinct from the purely economic and

123 G. H. Pickering, Internal Memorandum, 10 May 1927, KNAN, AP/1/923.

124 'Double jeopardy' refers to the Common Law principle that prohibits a defendant from being tried again on the same or similar charges following a legitimate acquittal or conviction.

125 Minutes of Departmental Meeting, Supreme Court of Kenya, 15 January 1939, KNAN, AP/1/923; J. W. Barth to Chief Native Commissioner, 2 June 1922, KNAN, AP/1/923.

126 G. H. Pickering, Internal Memorandum, 5 February 1927, KNAN, AP/1/923.

127 Malau Wa Nyawa to His Majesty's Supreme Court of Kenya, 19 June 1938, KNAN, AP/1/923.

128 K. W. Simmonds to G. H. Boulderson, Mombasa, 30 January 1939, KNAN, AP/1/923.

compensatory *Kore*. Simmonds recommended that, while the *Kore* claim on Malau should be rejected as unjust, the customary *Kiruruma* should be allowed because of its social and religious significance to the natives involved.[129]

In the final analysis, Chief Justice Pickering of Kenya was thwarted in his attempts to have the case appealed to the JCPC. The views of their Lordships were not canvassed as a result, and a compromise between the competing systems was reached within the colony. By the 1930s, the consensus within the colonial legal establishment was that blood money should not be encouraged, even though many recognized that the practice could not simply be discounted. A memorandum clarifying the official position stated that natives who had suffered loss by reason of 'trespass to the person' could sue in the colony's courts for compensation. The relations of a murdered man would sue under the Fatal Accidents Act of 1846, and for damages under the Common Law.[130]

As dusk fell on the African Empire in the 1950s, enforcement of blood money claims in Britain's East African colonies was limited. The position of a compromise was laid down in a 1957 judgment of the Hargeisa Subordinate Court in British Somaliland. It delineated the respective roles of compensation under customary law and punishment in the territory: 'compensation, where no criminal action is taken, is a tribal responsibility. Where criminal proceedings are instituted, compensation may still be a tribal responsibility if the accused is acquitted. Where the accused is convicted, tribal responsibility lapses but compensation may be sued... this being payable by the defendant and his relatives.'[131]

Although the case of *Malau wa Nyawa* never reached the Privy Council, the legal debate it provoked is significant for our purpose for several reasons. Primarily, it illustrates the complex alliances that merged behind the scenes when administering criminal justice in the Empire. It shows that colonial judges and administrators were not always in agreement, as their divergent positions on the custom of blood money reveal. Rules of judicial governance were constantly modified to address local exigencies. The case of *Malau wa Nyawa* is also significant because it highlights the indirect influence of the Imperial Appeal Courts on judicial governance in the colonies. Considerations of how particular cases might be determined if appealed to the Privy Council influenced the positions of local officials on contentious questions of law and justice. The imperial influence of the JCPC and of the regional Courts of Appeal was not limited to the cases that came before them; instead, it extended to the official readings and interpretations of their jurisprudence that invariably shaped the ideas and actions of the men locally in charge. In the case of the regional Courts of Appeal, their influence extended to the extra-judicial writings and pronouncements of the colonial judges who staffed these courts.

Moreover, in addressing the legal issues arising from blood money cases, local administrative and judicial officers were guided by the JCPC's judgments in other

[129] K. W. Simmonds to G. H. Boulderson, Mombasa, 30 January 1939, KNAN, AP/1/923.

[130] G. H. Pickering, Internal Memorandum, 5 February 1927, KNAN, AP/1/923.

[131] Quoted in Paolo Contini, 'The Evolution of Blood-Money for Homicide in Somalia' (1971) 15 (1) *Journal of African Law* 80.

similar cases involving African customary law. One case that came up frequently in the blood money debates was the 1916 Gold Coast case, *Angu v Atta*. In this case the JCPC outlined the principle that (subject to the repugnancy doctrine) a court was obliged to take judicial notice of a custom that had been proven in court and had become 'notorious' by frequent proof in courts.[132] This 'doctrine of judicial ascertainment of customary law' served to progressively incorporate the rules of customary law into the fabric of colonial law throughout British Africa.[133] The key question in the blood money debates was whether the custom passed the repugnancy test, and whether it should be accorded judicial notice in British courts.

The legal and policy debates over blood money customs in East Africa also underscored the reciprocal relationship between the JCPC and local courts in adjudicating Empire. Local judges and officials looked up to the JCPC as the highest Court of Empire, to make definitive pronouncements on contentious questions of colonial law and justice. Still, the JCPC often had to rely on these 'men on the spot' for facts and evidence relating to customary law and justice. In the Gold Coast Case of *Amissah v Krabah*, the judges of the JCPC urged the courts in Africa to provide them with guidance on local customs deserving judicial recognition by the Board.[134] There was recognition that the JCPC, though the highest court in the Empire, was in no position to provide answers on factual questions of African customary law. Local officials and courts, which were in closer proximity to the natives, were better placed to make such decisions.

The symbiotic relationship between local and metropolitan apparatus of judicial governance was crucial to the synthesis of English and indigenous law in imperial legal culture. Customary law varied from colony to colony and from one ethnic group to another. Accordingly, it showed considerable capacity for adaptation amidst the far-reaching changes that occurred in Africa during the twentieth century. This process of adaptation was essential to resolving the tensions inherent in constructing and maintaining native otherness in judicial governance. It consisted of the gradual and often subtle assimilation (as well as transformation) of the principles of English law exported to the colonies. It also involved the emergence of new hybrid systems that underscored the resilience of native customary law and traditional notions of justice.

Conclusion

The political and ideological tensions evident in medicine murder cases and the debates over blood money provide further contexts for understanding the cosmopolitan nature of British imperial legal culture and the ideological hybridities that

[132] '*Angu v. Atta*, 1916', *Gold Coast Privy Council Judgments, 1874–1928*, 44.

[133] A. N. Allott, 'The Judicial Ascertainment of Customary Law in British Africa' (1957) 20(3) *The Modern Law Review* 257.

[134] *Effuah Amissah v Effuah Krabah* [1936] reported in *Privy Council Judgments: Opinions of the Judicial Committee of the Privy Council in Appeals from West Africa, 1841 to 1973*, ed, Olisa Chukura (London: Gilford, 1981) 280.

shaped it. They show that, even in the improbable realm of criminal justice, Britain's African colonies were laboratories for legal experimentation and the production of knowledge. For various groups within colonial society, including both traditional and modern African elites, colonial administrators, and metropolitan judges, these cases and the debates surrounding them provided opportunities to shape political power and social order. Challenges to the colonial criminal justice system typified in the medicine murder cases and the blood money debates also force us to re-think what has been described as one 'of the most persistent myths about the age of Empires'. This is the idea that a well-formed Euro-modernity exported itself to faraway places, to introduce its already well-refined, highly developed systems and structures to 'primitive' peoples, either as philanthropic moral missions or as calculating and violent acts of conquest.[135]

The tensions and compromises over medicine murders and blood money suggest that European modernity, as it was exported abroad, was in many respects a tentative set of cultural, social, and material practices. Colonialism was, in this sense, a regime of exception in that it was reliant on its ability to negotiate and break its own rules. The colonial criminal justice system was always a work in progress, uncertain and contested, clearly more an aspiration than an achievement. African blood money customs were deemed repugnant to British legal traditions, and yet the beliefs and practices behind those customs could, at certain moments, be accommodated in a convoluted process of legal hybridization. Such compromises were required to maintain the sinews of imperial power. Colonial judicial policy was less the product of careful planning than of what Thomas Richards has described as a process of 'collective improvisation'.[136] The Empire was sustained more by a 'fictive thought of an imperial control' than by any real and actual command. This was mainly because the Empire was too far away, and metropolitan bureaucrats had limited control over local men and over the ways they dealt with local exigencies.[137] It is impossible to interrogate colonial processes without taking into account these accidental and experimental dimensions.

More significantly, the political character of African challenges to the colonial criminal justice system underscores a central theme of this book: the paradox of imperial universalism and local exceptionalism in the making of colonial legal culture. Although the medicine murder appeals at the JCPC involved 'exotic crimes' on the fringes of the Empire, they provided opportunities for subjects on those fringes to put the colonial justice system on trial at the centre of Empire. In this regard, the *Kibi* murder case is particularly instructive. In the hallowed chambers of the JCPC in London, their Lordships were not persuaded that 'grave and substantial injustice' had been done in the initial trials held in the colony. They rejected the appellants' successive requests for judicial review. In spite

[135] John L. Comaroff, 'Colonialism, Culture, and the Law: A Foreword' (2001) 26(2) *Law & Social Inquiry* 305.

[136] Thomas Richards, *The Imperial Archive: Knowledge and the Fantasy of Empire* (London: Verso, 1993) 3.

[137] Thomas Richards, *The Imperial Archive: Knowledge and the Fantasy of Empire*, 3.

of these rejections, however, the JCPC appeals provided a platform for further appeals to the metropolitan court of public opinion. Outside the courtroom, the appellants' lawyers drummed up public interest in the case. The British MPs who petitioned to overturn the sentence in the *Kibi* case also became arbiters of imperial justice. Like the Lords of the JCPC, their main interest was upholding universalist standards of British imperial justice. As the British MP Enoch Powell enjoined his parliamentary colleagues in another case: 'We cannot say we will have African standards in Africa, Asian standards in Asia and perhaps British standards here at home . . . We cannot, we dare not, in Africa of all places, fall below our own highest standards.'[138] Similar concerns about maintaining imperial standards of justice informed the position of senior officials in Whitehall who, in the *Kibi* murder case, cautioned Governor Burns to tread cautiously in his handling of the case.

The universalist considerations of metropolitan judges and officials were sometimes at odds with the exigencies and expediencies of judicial governance in the colonies, however. The uneasy relationship between metropolitan officials and local administrators illustrates the disjuncture of managing the Empire from afar. The debates over blood money show the difficulties that colonial officials encountered in seeking to uphold British standards of justice, while accommodating conflicting African customs that were deemed indispensable to achieving justice. The conflict was not easily resolved. Colonial law may have sought to accommodate African difference, but imperial universalism required the containment of that difference. Evidently, the fault-lines were not only between colonizers and the colonized, but also within each of these categories. Judicial officers in East Africa insisted that capital offences such as murder should, in line with Common Law principles, be prosecuted strictly as offences against the state. Local administrators, on the other hand, advocated accommodating African blood money customs because they were more concerned with maintaining social order than with technicalities and imperial standardization. In between, Africans articulated and negotiated colonial enforcement of these customs in ways that best suited them.

What emerged at the end was a tenuous but functional compromise: a hybrid system aimed at both affirming imperial legal standards while accommodating local difference. Blood money remained a 'tribal responsibility' where the state did not or could not prosecute a crime, or where an accused had been acquitted. When an accused individual was convicted in a British court (as opposed to a native tribunal), however, tribal responsibility lapsed and the payment of blood money could not be enforced.[139] In practical terms, this meant that African blood money customs continued to be accommodated within the colonial legal system even in cases in which they had been deemed 'repugnant' and in conflict with statute law and British legal standards. The doctrine of repugnancy, used to subordinate customary law to colonial law, clearly had its limitations in the practical work of administering

[138] Enoch Powell MP, 'House of Commons Debate', HCD Vol 610, col 237, 27 July 1959. Quoted in Caroline Elkins, *Imperial Reckoning: The Untold Story of Britain's Gulag in Kenya* (New York: H. Holt, 2005) 325.

[139] *Omar Ismail v Askar Abdullahi*, cited in Contini, 'The Evolution of Blood-Money', 80.

criminal justice. Colonial power could neither fully subordinate African customary law to English law, nor subjugate customary forms of justice to the British standards of justice. Instead, imperial justice was underscored by a legal and juridical syncretism that was shaped as much by African contestations as it was by colonial power.

Like the institution of native assessors and the doctrine of repugnancy discussed in the preceding chapter, the medicine murder trials and the debates over blood money customs illustrate the tensions in the administration of imperial justice that produced new hybrid legal cultures. They show that, far from being a process of transporting well-defined European standards of law and justice to Africa, the evolution of colonial legal culture was more a dialogic and syncretic encounter. This was true even within the broader framework of the colonial state's hegemonic power. In the realms of colonial law and imperial justice, Euro-modernity framed in universalist terms was constantly mediated by African initiatives and local exigencies in ways that could not always be ordered by colonial authority. This process of contesting and mediating colonial power also characterized legal battles over native land rights, Crown title, and chiefly authority in the Imperial Appeal Courts, as the next chapter demonstrates.

5

Litigious Chiefs and Land Palavers

The solemn chamber of the JCPC was occasionally the venue of courtroom theatrics. One such occasion was during the winter session of 1901. The case before the JCPC was an appeal from Zanzibar in the east coast of Africa that required their Lordships to determine whether Islamic law or English law should apply in a land dispute between a British company and the colonial government.[1] As in most British African possessions, a dual legal system prevailed in Zanzibar, where customary Islamic law existed alongside imported English law. In this case, the government had leased a piece of land from a landowner and subsequently built on it a railway line without the landowner's assent. At the end of the lease, the landowner claimed not only his land but also the railway line on it, in accordance with English Common Law principles. The British Courts in Zanzibar had dismissed the landowner's claim over the railway line partly on the grounds that Islamic or 'Mohamedan law' should apply rather than English law. The landowner subsequently appealed to the Privy Council, and the case came before a powerful JCPC bench of seven of the most senior judges on the Board, with Lord Chancellor Halsbury presiding.

Representing the Zanzibar landowner, Lord Haldane—then a Queen's Counsel and practising barrister—argued before their Lordships that the applicable Islamic law in Zanzibar was not different from English law. Their Lordships, being unfamiliar with the Islamic land law in Zanzibar in this early period of British rule, countered that they could make no such assumption since Haldane had provided them with no supporting proofs of the Islamic law on the subject. 'My Lords,' Haldane replied, 'I am addressing your Lordships, not as seven English Judges who require to have foreign law proved to them, but as seven *Cadis* of the Mohammedan religion who are presumed to know the Koran.' At that point, presiding Lord Chancellor Halsbury picked up a copy of the Qur'an available nearby and searched it on the spot. He discovered a crucial text. As Haldane later recalled, the text stated: 'if anybody plants a plane tree on his neighbour's land, the neighbour shall not claim the plane tree without making proper compensation'.[2] It was proof, ascertained by the Lords of the JCPC themselves, that the Islamic land law on the subject of litigation was, indeed, different from English law.

[1] *The Secretary for State for Foreign Affairs v Charlesworth Pilling & Co.* [1901] AC 373.

[2] Lord Haldane, 'The Work for the Empire of the Judicial Committee of the Privy Council' (1922) 1(2) *Cambridge Law Journal* 152.

In its judgment, the JCPC established that English law was applicable because jurisdiction over the case resided with the British government under the provisions of treaty agreements between the British Crown and the Sultan of Zanzibar in 1886 and the subsequent Orders in Council. Their Lordships noted, however, that English law recognized the principle that 'the incidents of land are governed by the law of its site'.[3] They therefore held that 'Her Majesty would exercise her Zanzibar jurisdiction on the principle that Zanzibar law, which is Mahomedan law, applies to this case'.[4] On the question of ascertaining the applicable Islamic land law, their Lordships made it clear that, though the Board had limited experience with Islamic jurisprudence, this task posed no difficulty. They stated that they had been guided by the law laid down in authoritative textbooks on Islamic Law, notably the twelfth century text on Islamic jurisprudence, *The Hedaya*.[5]

This early colonial land case demonstrates the centrality of questions arising from the conflict of laws and ascertaining customary law in JCPC appeals even when disputes did not directly involve native litigants. The case shows the difficulties that JCPC judges confronted in trying to adjudicate appeals based on the local laws of the originating territory. More significantly, cases like these indicate that the ascertainment and production of native law and custom took place on two levels: first through official policies and judicial decisions in the colonies, and secondly through the jurisprudence of the Imperial Courts of Appeal.

British imperial doctrine on indigenous land rights was shaped largely by several high-profile land disputes that came to the JCPC from the colonies of Africa in the inter-war years. The key legal questions arising from these disputes reflect the difficulties and uncertainties of colonial social and economic re-ordering in Africa and elsewhere in the Empire. These cases also reflect the struggles for economic control and political ascendancy within transitioning colonial societies. The judgments of the JCPC and the regional Courts of Appeal concerning indigenous title and native land rights addressed a key tension in colonial society arising out of the effort to enable continuity in social and economic systems while simultaneously encouraging modernist evolution into commodification and capitalism.[6]

Land and chieftaincy appeals were at the crux of what I term 'high impact' cases—cases with broad ramifications for economic and political power in the colonies. Because they operated beyond the direct reach of the colonial establishment, the Imperial Appeal Courts were preferred sites for challenging the government's control over land and its exercise of political authority. Most land appeals that came before the JCPC from Africa were between Africans. The cases that had the most enduring legal and political impact, however, were land disputes involving the government, such as disputes over compulsory acquisition, inadequate compensation

[3] *Secretary for State for Foreign Affairs v Charlesworth Pilling & Co.* [1901] AC 373 at 379.

[4] *Secretary for State for Foreign Affairs v Charlesworth Pilling & Co.*, 376.

[5] The JCPC referenced Alī ibn Abī Bakr Marghīnānī, *The Hedaya, Or Guide: A Commentary on the Mussulman Laws* [Translated by Charles Hamilton] (London: W. H. Allen & Company, 1870). See *Secretary for State for Foreign Affairs v Charlesworth Pilling & Co.* [1901] AC 373 at 780.

[6] Ben Silverstein, 'The Rule of Native Title: A View of Mabo in the British Empire' (2007) 16(1) *Griffith Law Review* 62.

and restrictions on alienation rights. Whether it was a British company asserting land claims under a lease agreement or an African Chief seeking compensation for land expropriated by the government, the underlying question in many land appeals was the struggle for economic advantage at a moment of significant social and economic change. Disputes over chieftaincy authority often arose from struggles for ascendency among traditional and modern African elites, and amidst the political changes wrought by colonial administrative policies.

This chapter examines how the tensions between imperial universalism and colonial difference played out in the high-stakes legal battles over land and political authority in the Imperial Appeal Courts. Because land was so central to colonial material culture, disputes over land and property rights provide us with unique insights into the processes by which colonial difference was constructed, contested, and maintained within the imperial justice system. It also explores how assertions of imperial ideals of justice and equity, the notion of propertied personhood, and the commodification of land intersected with notions of native otherness in judicial discourse and adjudicatory processes. It investigates how colonial difference was invoked and negotiated within and outside of the courts in land and chieftaincy appeals. It also considers the impact of these appeals on imperial jurisprudence and the colonial political order.

The Colonial Land Question

Scholars of Empire have long drawn attention to the centrality of land and power over land in the colonial enterprise. Edward Said argued that, more than anything else, imperialism is an act of geographical violence, through which virtually every space in the world is explored, charted, and finally brought under control.[7] 'For the native,' Said wrote, the history of colonial servitude was inaugurated by 'the loss to an outsider of a local place, whose concrete geographical identity must thereafter be searched for and somehow restored.'[8] The great imperial land rush of the seventeenth to the twentieth century, which helped to frame modern property rights, involved moral and legal issues that marked turning points in the destinies of both colonizers and the colonized.[9] No less significant than the New World, the territories of Africa were defining sites for colonial reconstructions of land rights. The legal and land tenure regimes introduced by European colonists provided new opportunities for various groups within the colonial society to assert and contest land ownership claims.

For the colonizers, law and cartography were the two most important instruments of land control—in many ways more efficient than the coercive power of

[7] Edward Said, *Culture and Imperialism* (New York: Knopf, 1994) 225.

[8] Edward Said, 'Yates and Decolonization' in Terry Eagleton, Fredric Jameson, and Edward Said, eds, *Nationalism, Colonialism and Literature* (Minneapolis: University of Minnesota Press, 1988) 77.

[9] John Weaver, *The Great Land Rush and the Making of the Modern World, 1650–1900* (Montreal: McGill-Queen's University Press, 2003) 6.

guns and armies. Law and cartography were crucial because they rendered land and territory 'knowable, controllable, and ownable'.[10] The 'most important laws,' one colonial official proclaimed, 'were those that dealt with land'.[11] Land was also a key concern of indigenous people. Writing in 1946, the colonial anthropologist Charles Kingsley Meek stated that, among the natives, 'rights over land are more jealously treasured than any other form of rights'.[12] Meek also noted that the 'land question' provided a terrain like no other in the colonial period, where issues of rights entailments and obligations were realized and thoroughly contested.[13] For the natives, European law was not only an instrument of dispossession and state control; it was also a means of contesting colonial control over land and other resources.

Colonial land law centred primarily on three key ideas: the notion of propertied personhood, the 'commodification' of land, and customary communal land rights. While the colonial period opened with widespread acceptance of the evolutionary superiority of Western concepts of individual property rights, it closed with a general atmosphere of suspicion towards individual land rights and a persistent emphasis on 'customary communal rights'.[14] These shifts were shaped by both the expediencies of colonial administration and the nature of African engagements with colonial land policies.

The notion of a right to property as necessary to human nature, a just reward for labour, and as the very basis of proper political society, was deeply embedded in nineteenth-century British political theory. Across the spectrum of political and legal thought, property came to be defined as 'private property' and considered to be the foundation of a civilized society. These notions influenced the decisions of colonial officials about the types of land regimes and property rights that should be accorded legal protection. Land policies were largely informed by a belief in the superiority of European concepts of individual property rights over what were considered traditional African notions of communal land ownership. Possessive individualism was taken to be the foundation of civilized society, and the corollary idea was that private property was unknown in 'savage' Africa.[15]

Although policy documents such as the 1898 *Report on Land Tenure in West Africa* canvassed communal land rights and declared individual ownership of land foreign to 'native' ideas, colonial policy during this period promoted individual land claims. Colonial officials sought to re-orient a supposedly communal land tenure system towards a more European and egalitarian model.[16] The growing

[10] Silverstein, 'The Rule of Native Title', 61.

[11] William McGregor, 'Introduction', in J. H. P. Murray, ed, *Papua or British New Guinea* (London: T. Fisher Unwin, 1912) 25.

[12] Charles Kingsley Meek, *Land Law and Custom in the Colonies* (London: Frank Cass, 1946) 5.

[13] Meek, *Land Law and Custom in the Colonies*, 5.

[14] Martin Chanock, 'Paradigms, Policies and Property: A Review of Customary Law of Land Tenure' in Kristin Mann and Richard Roberts, eds, *Law in Colonial Africa* (Portsmouth: Heinemann, 1991) 62–3.

[15] Chanock, 'Paradigms, Policies and Property', 63.

[16] Bonny Ibhawoh, *Imperialism and Human Rights: Colonial Discourses of Rights and Liberties in African History* (Albany: State University of New York Press, 2007) 92.

demand for land titles freed from the restrictions of local customs and traditions, by both affluent Africans and European traders, was satisfied by English-style grants of land by the Crown.[17] In some parts of Africa, colonial authorities encouraged private ownership and sale of land as a way to promote urbanization, the development of a money economy, and private cultivation of commercial crops. These they considered to be the key tenets of the colonial project they envisioned.

By the 1920s, however, colonial officials confronted new circumstances that necessitated shifts in land policies. In West Africa, the main challenge became how to react to the widespread sale and alienation of land in the colonies, and the threat of agricultural land scarcity. This issue became a crucial source of conflict over land. Whereas in the past colonial officials had been eager to promote 'healthy individualism' among natives, new realities demanded a policy shift towards greater state control. The idea that individual and commercial dealing in land were contrary to African land tenure systems was reinforced.[18]

Colonial governments began to emphasize communalism and customary law, rather than individualism and contract law, as being more naturally African. Colonial regimes also began to position the state, not the community or the family, as the source and guarantor of whatever rights were deemed customary. It was the beginning of the process where the nation-state was gradually perceived as the ultimate guarantor of communal land rights in late colonial and post-colonial Africa. The 'land question' became part of a delicate political balance symbolizing the chasm—and sometimes contradiction—between imperial idealism and local realities. If the earlier discourse of radical individualism bore the promise of colonial land reform, the later discourse on 'customary' communal land rights reflected the hard realities of reform.

As colonial land policies shifted, administrative and judicial officers began to support a model of land tenure characterized by the oft-quoted saying that 'land belongs to a vast family of which many are dead, few are living and countless numbers are still unborn'.[19] Chiefs were seen, or at least presented, as the holders of land with rights of administration and allocation. Rights in land were seen as flowing downwards, deriving from traditional political authority, rather than residing in the peasantry. These ideas became the canons of academic and popular knowledge about indigenous land tenure systems in Africa, and served to reinforce colonial policy.[20] The right of Africans to use land came to be generally understood as being dependent on allegiance to traditional political authorities. Land allocation was seen as a means by which local Chiefs 'customarily' maintained the loyalty of their people and asserted control over them. It served the British officials' interest to

[17] T. O. Elias, *The Nigerian Legal System* (London: Routledge & Kegan Paul, 1963) 325.

[18] See H. L. Ward-Price, *Land Tenure in the Yoruba Provinces* (Lagos: Government Printer, 1939) *passim* and Philip Igbafe, *Benin under British Administration, 1897–1938: The Impact of Colonial Rule on an African Kingdom* (Atlantic Highlands, NJ: Humanities Press, 1978) 28–9.

[19] Meek, *Land Law and Custom in the Colonies*, 5.

[20] Max Gluckman, *Ideas and Procedures in African Customary Law* (London: Oxford University Press, 1969) 56–7.

maintain the authority of Chiefs as allocators of land, ensuring the allegiance of their subjects and sustaining the indirect rule system.

These shifts in colonial land policies certainly did not follow the same patterns or occur at the same pace throughout British Africa. Differences in the political and social landscapes of the non-settler societies of West Africa and settler societies of Eastern and Southern Africa ensured that there could be no uniformity in colonial land policies.[21] In West Africa, where agriculture was based primarily on peasant farming, colonial regimes discouraged large-scale land alienation and any attempts at plantation-type production.[22] This differed from land policies in British East Africa and French Equatorial Africa, where colonial regimes granted large-scale land concessions to European firms for plantation agriculture.

Notwithstanding these divergences in land policies, it is possible to identify certain commonalities in colonial legal and policy discourse on African customary land tenure. The dominant theme was that customary African land tenure systems were based on communal rather than individual land ownership.[23] There was also the view that African notions of property ownership differed fundamentally from European individualistic and egalitarian ideas about land and property rights. These assumptions about the nature of customary land law and its relationship with English law of real property lay at the centre of several land disputes that came before the Imperial Appeal Courts.

Crown Title versus Native Rights

The tension between enabling continuity in customary land tenure systems and encouraging an evolution into capitalism and the commodification of land was evident in several appeals that came before the Imperial Appeal Courts in the first half of the twentieth century. One of the earliest cases that addressed this question was *Angu v Attah*, heard by the JCPC in 1916. It became *locus classicus* on the ascertainment and proof of native customary law.[24] In this Gold Coast case, which concerned a dispute over land title and the payment of land tributes, the JCPC held that customary law had to be proved in the first instance by calling witnesses acquainted with the custom until the particular custom became so 'notorious' that

[21] Kofi Anyidoho, 'Custom Colonial Ideology and Privilege: The Land Question in Africa' in Helen Lauer and Kofi Anyidoho, eds, *Reclaiming the Human Sciences and Humanities through African Perspectives, Vol 1* (Accra: Sub-Saharan Publishers, 2012) 282. Samir Amin's pioneering study also identified three economic spheres that emerged under colonialism: Africa of the labour reserve, Africa of trade, and Africa of Concession Companies. Samir Amin, 'Underdevelopment and Dependence in Black Africa-Origins and Contemporary Forms' (1972) 10(4) *Journal of Modern African Studies* 503–24.

[22] Tekena Tamuno, *The Evolution of the Nigerian State: The Southern Phase, 1898–1914* (London: Longman, 1972) 310.

[23] Elias, *The Nigerian Legal System*, 325.

[24] *Kobina Angu v Cudjoe Attah* [1916] UKPC 53; OlisaChukura, ed, *Privy Council Judgments: Opinions of the Judicial Committee of the Privy Council in appeals from West Africa, 1841 to 1973* (London: Gilford, 1981) 117.

the courts took judicial notice of them. The Board noted that, although there was at that time little statutory law relating to land in the Gold Coast, the native customs on land tenure had crystallized to a point where the courts could recognize and apply them.

Their Lordships went further to outline what they understood to be the guiding principles of native land law in this part of Africa. They noted that, under native customary land law, lands were attached to the 'stools' (thrones) of Chiefs who were entitled to tribute from the occupants or users of that land. The Chiefs possessed some power of alienation that enabled them to transfer land; this authority could only be exercised with communal consent.[25] Apart from chiefly lands, there was also a class of lands known as 'family land' under collective family ownership. These general principles provided the framework for adjudicating *Angu v Attah*. Their Lordships cautioned, however, that such representation of the native custom should not be taken as the authoritative position of the JCPC. They urged that the JCPC had no first-hand knowledge of the customary law in the colony and had relied only on what had been earlier proved in the local courts in the colony.[26] The difficulty with ascertaining and interpreting applicable customary land law was a recurring theme in land appeals at the JCPC and the regional Courts of Appeal.

A related question that the JCPC was often called upon to address in land appeals was the legal scope of Crown 'radical title', that is, the underlying title of the British Crown acquired at the acquisition of sovereignty in the colonies. The central question concerned the limits of the native communal 'usufructuary' land rights imposed on the Crown's radical title. The imperial jurisprudence on this and other key questions surrounding indigenous land rights was crafted at the Privy Council in a series of cases arising from land disputes in the African colonies of Southern Rhodesia, Nigeria, the Gold Coast, and British East Africa.[27]

The defining case in the question of Crown title and the land rights of indigenous people was *Re Southern Rhodesia*, which came before the JCPC in 1919. The case dealt with the legal status of lands in Mashonaland and Matabeleland, consisting of 'native reserves', 'unsettled country', and land occupied by the British South African Company. In its judgment, the JCPC famously noted that determining the status of native land rights in Africa was 'inherently difficult' because of the peculiar and varied character of indigenous customary land tenure systems. Lord Summer stated:

> Some tribes are so low in the scale of social organization that their usages and conceptions of rights and duties are not to be reconciled with the institutions or the legal ideas of civilized society. Such a gulf cannot be bridged. It would be idle to impute to such people some shadow of the rights known to our law and then to transmute it into the substance of transferable rights of property as we know them. . . . On the other hand, there are indigenous people whose legal conceptions, though differently developed, are hardly less precise than our own. When once they have been studied and understood, they are no less foreseeable

[25] *Kobina Angu v Cudjoe Attah* [1916] UKPC 53.
[26] *Kobina Angu v Cudjoe Attah*, 53.
[27] Silverstein, 'The Rule of Native Title', 65.

than rights arising under English law. Between the two there is a wide tract of much ethnological interest, but the position of the natives of Southern Rhodesia within it is very uncertain; clearly they approximate rather to the lower than the higher limit.[28]

This statement conveys the view that some indigenous societies were too primitive at the time of first contact with the Europeans to develop a notion of tenure rights that could be sufficiently reconciled with British legal ideas and allow their members to successfully assert such rights in court action. The JCPC recognized, however, that land tenure 'primitiveness' was not a permanent and universal feature of indigenous societies. Native otherness was not monolithic; it could be differentiated hierarchically according to the level of reconcilability of indigenous tenure systems with English legal ideas. This hierarchy of native difference required the judge to evaluate in each instance whether a native community met the required standards of civilization and legal reconcilability to sustain a claim in court. Judges effectively needed to differentiate between indigenous cultures where these rights were recognized and those where they were not.[29] Lord Sumner's judgment in *Re Southern Rhodesia* epitomizes the conservative side of the docket in the JCPC's handling of native land rights which stands in contrast with the more liberal approach taken in African appeals by later judges such as Lord Haldane and Lord Atkin.

Colonial assumptions about the hierarchies of native difference provided grounds for accepting or disregarding indigenous land ownership and occupancy claims. Assumptions about native difference also provided jurisprudential validation to the theory that indigenous inhabitants of certain territories had no proprietary interests in the land that were separate from, or equivalent to, Crown interests. The rejection of native title rights in *Re Southern Rhodesia* was clearly premised on the essential and subordinate difference of the native. This difference was couched in social Darwinian terms: the relatively 'low stage of social organization' found among the natives of Southern Rhodesia, which stood in contrast to the colonial social and legal order that Britain sought to establish in the territory in the early twentieth century. As Lord Sumner stated, 'the old state of things, whatever its exact nature has passed away and . . . better has been established in lieu of it. Whoever now owns the unalienated lands, the natives do not.'[30]

The rigid articulation of native difference in *Re Southern Rhodesia* does not tell the whole story of the JCPC's interventions in the tensions between Crown title and indigenous customary land rights, however. Two years after its ruling in *Re Southern Rhodesia*, the JCPC took a markedly different position in the case of *Amodu Tijani v The Secretary of Southern Nigeria*, known locally as the 'Apapa Land Case'.[31] The *Amodu Tijani* case concerned the disputed ownership of certain lands in the Apapa community of Lagos that had been compulsorily acquired by the

[28] *Re Southern Rhodesia* [1919] AC 211 at 233–4, per Lord Summer.

[29] Catherine Bell and Michael Asch, 'Challenging Assumptions: The Impact of Precedent in Aboriginal Rights Litigation' in Michael Asch, ed, *Aboriginal and Treaty Rights in Canada* (Vancouver: UBC Press, 1997) 57.

[30] *Re Southern Rhodesia* [1919] AC 211 at 235, per Lord Sumner.

[31] *Amodu Tijani v The Secretary of Southern Nigeria* [1921] AC 309. My emphasis.

government in Nigeria in 1913, under the Public Lands Ordinance for the purpose of providing land for European merchants. The government offered a token compensation to the occupants for their eviction from the land, but had no intention to pay full compensation for the land.

Chief Oluwa, a Yoruba Chief, applied for full compensation, claiming that the land constituted a portion of his personal estate. The claim was rejected by the court in Nigeria, however, because the Chief's claims supposedly did not reflect the customary norms. The problem lay in determining the applicable customary law and the effects of nineteenth-century treaty agreements between the British Crown and African rulers on native land rights. The position of the colonial government was that the acquired lands were part of the territory ceded in 1861 to the British Crown in a treaty with King Docemo of Lagos.

Rejecting Chief Oluwa's claims of absolute ownership rights, the Chief Justice of Nigeria, Edwin Speed, restated the standard position of the government. He asserted that native customary rights to land belonged to the community, rather than the individual. He argued that Chief Oluwa's interest in the land in Lagos was 'merely a seigneurial right, giving the holder the ordinary rights of control and management of the land in accordance with the well-known principles of native law and custom'.[32] In what seemed like a reversal of roles, the colonial state invoked 'native law and custom' to challenge an African Chief's claim for compensation based on individual land rights. To the end, this invocation of 'native law and custom' was of no practical value, because the Supreme Court gave to Chief Oluwa no more than administrative rights over the land in question.[33]

In 1921, Chief Oluwa appealed the Supreme Court's decision in the Privy Council. His appeal rested on the claim that the land in question constituted the land of the community, of which Chief Oluwa was the elected head and trustee. Compensation was demanded on the basis of trusteeship over customary land, rather than absolute right. For the JCPC, the central concern was ascertaining the applicable Yoruba customary law through ethnographic accounts by European missionaries and official government reports.

The judgment of the JCPC reaffirmed the position that individual ownership of land was foreign to native ideas, and that land was vested in communities or families but not in individuals. While community members had right of use to land, the land was primarily vested in the Chief as the trustee. Lord Haldane in his judgment referenced the *Report on Land Tenure in West Africa*, written in 1898 by T. C. Rayner, a former Chief Justice of the Lagos Supreme Court. The Report outlined the official view that African land tenure systems centred on communal ownership, and were averse to individual possession. The JCPC rejected the nineteenth-century history of land alienation and individual land holding in Lagos as an aberration. Lord Haldane asserted that a 'pure native custom' of communal land tenure existed across communities along the entire length of the West African coast, and that the exceptional incidents of individual land ownership

[32] *Amodu Tijani v Secretary, Southern Provinces*, 3 NLR 24 at 31.
[33] Adewoye, *The Judicial System in Southern Nigeria,* 260.

in Lagos were due only to the introduction of 'English ideas'.[34] Despite the influence these English ideas had, Lord Haldane argued, the native idea that land belonged to the family rather than the individual still held firm among the people of Lagos.[35]

Addressing the question of the scope of Crown title, Lord Haldane stated that, since cession, the radical title to land in Lagos was vested in the Crown. Even so, native customary title could also be accommodated in the courts. He referred to the different forms of real property recognized around the Empire, from 'Indian title' in Canada, to 'life estates' in Scotland, to communal title in India. None of these forms of property could be likened to the English notions of land ownership, but they could still be recognized by British courts.[36] The custom of communal land ownership in Lagos—though different from the English system—was therefore no less valid. The JCPC resolved the tension between Crown title and native rights by upholding that, although the radical title to the land rested with the Crown, a Chief held a 'full *usufructuary* title' on behalf of his community. In Chief Oluwa's case, this usufructuary title thus was not affected by the cession of Lagos to the British Crown in 1861.[37] As Lord Haldane stated:

> The title to land occupied by a native community is *prima facie* based not on such individual ownership as English law has made familiar, but on a communal *usufructuary* occupation, which may be so complete as to reduce any radical rights in the Sovereign to one which only extends to comparatively limited rights of administrative interference.[38]

Based on this interpretation, Chief Oluwa won his claim to compensation from the government. Instead of the £500 offered by the government, Chief Oluwa was eventually paid £22,500.[39] The JCPC further ordered that the compensation should be distributed among the members of Chief Oluwa's community, according to the procedures provided in local statute law.

It is instructive that Chief Oluwa's appeal at the Privy Council succeeded mainly because it rested on colonial notions of what constituted native customary tenure, and on its essential difference from the English system. Earlier attempts to obtain compensation on grounds of personal property and absolute rights had been unsuccessful in local courts. In this regard, Chief Oluwa's appeal illustrates how colonial subjects invoked colonial notions of difference to assert legal claims and to challenge authority in the Imperial Appeal Courts.

The communal land tenure systems invoked in *Amodu Tijani* did not, of course, fully reflect the social and economic realities of early twentieth-century Lagos. Individual land ownership had, in fact, been known in Lagos since the 1850s, due mainly to the influence of the Sierra Leonean and Brazilian immigrants

[34] *Amodu Tijani v Secretary of Southern Nigeria* [1921] AC 399 at 402.
[35] *Amodu Tijani v Secretary of Southern Nigeria*, 404–5, per Lord Haldane.
[36] Silverstein, 'The Rule of Native Title', 68.
[37] *Amodu Tijani v Secretary of Southern Nigeria* [1921] AC 399 at 404, per Lord Haldane.
[38] *Amodu Tijani v Secretary of Southern Nigeria*, 404, per Lord Haldane.
[39] Omoniyi Adewoye, 'The Tijani Land Case 1915–1921: A Study in British Colonial Justice' (1976) 13 *Odu* 30.

following the abolition of the slave trade and the corresponding growth in 'legitimate' commerce.[40] With the establishment of British rule, the population of Lagos became increasingly cosmopolitan, similar to other major coastal cities of West Africa. The town became a crucial space for the intermingling of ideas that weakened traditional social ties, loosened the hold of traditional norms, and promoted new ideas and social ethos.[41] One result of this urban cosmopolitanism was the rapid evolution of traditional land tenure systems alongside the development of the colonial legal system.[42] Bustling commercial activities in Lagos provided fertile ground for civil suits, where individual ownership of land and property could be claimed and contested.

Despite these social and economic changes, the jurisprudence on native land rights throughout the colonial period was dominated by references to the customary, the tribal, and the communal. Even where the courts acknowledged the social transitions in native societies or the 'modernizing' influence of British ideas on indigenous tenure systems, these rarely affected judicial outcomes. The emphatic assertion of the universality of communal land ownership inhibited colonial and imperial judges from readily recognizing the natural evolution of customary law, so as to incorporate individual ownership and free alienability of land.[43] In the 1957 case of *Adeyinka Oyekan v Musendiku Adele*, for example, Lord Denning stated that the judges of the JCPC were well aware that in several parts of Lagos the native law had been superseded by English conceptions of individual ownership. These realities notwithstanding, their Lordships held that 'modern notions' of English law did not apply to this case, which was a dispute over the residence of the *Oba* (King) of Lagos. Such disputes over property in traditional settings, the JCPC held, remained subject to the native law and custom.[44]

The tendency of the courts to treat African customary land tenure systems as static and undifferentiated proved to be problematic in the case of *Awgu v Nezianya*, in which the WACA was called on to determine which of the several customary laws relating to the ownership of property title should apply in a land dispute.[45] Although the case originated from Eastern Nigeria, counsel for the appellant relied on Gold Coast precedents relating to customary land law. This raised questions about the relevance of customary law from one region of Africa to another region with potentially different customary laws. In his judgment, the presiding Judge John Verity suggested that the court could safely assume that the general principles of African customary law were the same unless the contrary was proven. He stated:

[40] Bonny Ibhawoh, 'Imperial Cosmopolitanism and the Making of an Indigenous Intelligentsia: African Lawyers in Colonial Urban Lagos' in Elizabeth Fay and Leonard von Morze, eds, *Urban Identity and the Atlantic World* (New York: Palgrave Macmillan, 2013) 125.

[41] Thomas Hodgkin, *Nationalism in Colonial Africa* (London: Frederick Muller, 1956) 63.

[42] A. O. Adewoye, 'Legal Practice in Ibadan 1904–1960' (1986) 24 *Journal of Legal Pluralism* 57.

[43] Adewoye, *The Judicial System in Southern Nigeria*, 273.

[44] *Adeyinka Oyekan v Musendiku Adele* [1957] 2 All ER 785 at 790.

[45] *Awgu v Nezianya* [1949] 12 WACA 450.

Although the principles of native law and custom to which we have referred are, in the specific instances cited, applicable expressly to the law and custom of the Gold Coast, they are nevertheless equally applicable as general principles to the law and custom of Nigeria, a departure from which can only be justified if it is established by evidence that the native law and custom in any particular area differs from the general principle.[46]

This ruling was widely criticized by legal scholars and practitioners who thought it established an erroneous precedent that could disrupt the proper administration of customary laws.[47] The ruling suggested that there was a single system of customary law applicable throughout West Africa; in reality the law systems were multiple and varied across the region. Critics of the ruling considered it unsatisfactory for the Appeal Court to rely on authorities drawn from a territory with its own customary laws, to ascertain the applicable customary laws in another territory. It was argued that there was inherent injustice in subjecting natives to 'alien and irrelevant customary rules'.[48] The decision in *Awgu v Nezianya* was seen as evidence of the flawed processes by which the colonial superior courts in Africa ascertained the applicable rules of customary land law.

The principle of native difference espoused in *Amodu Tijani* in the 1920s endured well into the late colonial period. In several land appeals heard in the 1940s and 1950s, the JCPC and the regional Courts of Appeal approvingly referenced the view in *Amodu Tijani* that individual ownership was foreign to Africa.[49] The reference to 'seigneurial' and 'usufructuary' rights in these cases underscores the tendency of colonial judges and lawyers to draw analogies between their understanding of African institutions and familiar concepts of English land tenure. But, as several historians of Africa have pointed out, these European institutions did not correspond to the African tenure systems. Omoniyi Adewoye has argued that the concept of 'seigneurial rights' conjuring up a picture of the Medieval European feudal system was 'completely unknown in Nigeria or indeed African land tenure system'.[50]

Chief Oluwa, like any other Chief in Lagos, was responsible for his family members' lands as a trustee. He did not usually own it the same way that a feudal lord owned his land. Even though individuals from outside the Chief's family circle were allowed to farm or use portions of the land, the bond between the Chief and his tenants was not one of feudal relationship also because the tenants were not liable to military or another type of obligatory service, as long as they recognized their status as tenants. Sometimes, the tenant was asked to pay an annual fee to the guarantor of the land he occupied. Such tributes were, however, usually no more than a token recognition of where the ultimate ownership of land lay.[51] Similarly, the description of African land tenure system as usufructuary or communal was

[46] *Awgu v Nezianya*, 455.

[47] 'West African Court of Appeal' (1957) 1(1) *Journal of African Law* 53.

[48] 'West African Court of Appeal', 53.

[49] See, for example, *Kwesi Enimil v Kwesi Tuakyi* [1952] UKPC 22; *Eze v Igiliegbe* [1952] 14 WACA 2.

[50] Adewoye, 'The Tijani Land Case', 32.

[51] Adewoye, 'The Tijani Land Case', 27.

mistaken. In most parts of Africa, communal land ownership was not merely usufructuary; the community's right to the land was for all practical purposes absolute, as nothing precluded the alienation of that right by the community.[52] Why then did the discourse of communal ownership and the rejection of native absolute rights become so dominant in imperial jurisprudence on indigenous land rights? The answer is not limited to the judicial processes of the Imperial Courts. It lies partly in the complex political process by which colonial difference was constructed and maintained within and beyond the courts.

Negotiating Difference: *Amondu Tijani* as Precedent

Amodu Tijani was perhaps the most important of the JCPC's decisions on native title, laying down the principle that native land rights pre-dating colonization were to be recognized by the British administration. The case served to dramatically bolster the legal merits of outstanding aboriginal claims elsewhere in the British Empire, particularly in Canada, where political authorities took several actions aimed at preventing similar claims by indigenous communities from reaching the judicial arena.[53] It has been suggested that *Amodu Tijani* had more far-reaching implications for the 'settled colonies' of Canada, Australia, and New Zealand than it did for the franchise colonies.[54]

Apart from its legal import, *Amodu Tijani* was also of great political and symbolic significance in West Africa, where it was celebrated as a victory against the injustice of local colonial regimes. Cases like these provided occasions for African elites to gain political advantage by calling governments' actions into question through the law and the courts. In the 1920s, African opposition was directed less against the idea of empire than against what many considered to be the subversion of imperial ideals by local colonial officials. Commenting in 1921 on the JCPC's ruling in *Amodu Tijani,* one contributor to the *Lagos Weekly Record* stated that the judgment was a 'confirmation that the British Empire is founded upon justice, righteousness and fair play notwithstanding that the policy of some of those entrusted with power in West Africa has usually indicated the contrary'.[55] The ruling was welcomed as assurance to the 'natives of West Africa that the Privy Council is a place of refuge from colonial oppressors'.[56] The *Gold Coast Independent* editorialized: 'Justice was denied Oluwa and his people in Nigeria but the Privy Council, the Tribunal dreaded by every administrator obsessed with autocratic predilections, granted it fully and freely.'[57] After the JCPC's judgment on 11 July 1921, Chief Oluwa was reported to have commented:

[52] Adewoye, 'The Tijani Land Case', 32.

[53] Robert M. Campbell, Leslie A. Pal, and Michael Howlett, *The Real Worlds of Canadian Politics: Cases in Process and Policy* (Peterborough: Broadview Press, 2004) 283.

[54] Silverstein, 'The Rule of Native Title', 58.

[55] Alfa Usman, 'Letter to the Editor', *Lagos Weekly Record* (10 September 1921) 6.

[56] Usman, 'Letter to the Editor', 6.

[57] *Gold Coast Independent* (21 October 1922) 476.

It is good to meet judges like these; they are straight and open to the King's subject... The Englishman in his own country, from the king downwards, makes no difference in race or colour. We get justice here in England.[58]

In prosecuting his appeal at the Supreme Court and the JCPC, Chief Oluwa received support from both traditional and 'modern' African elites. Prominent among them was the pioneer nationalist politician Herbert Macaulay. As Chief Oluwa was illiterate, he relied on educated supporters like Macaulay who could 'speak the white man language with poise and authority'.[59] Macaulay served as Chief Oluwa's interpreter and private secretary, travelling with him to London to witness the JCPC appeal. He was the first indigenous civil engineer in Nigeria, and worked with the colonial government as a surveyor of Crown lands before he resigned following disagreements with the local colonial officials.[60] He subsequently established a newspaper and became an ardent critic of the government. One British official described him as a 'public agitator for the people's so-called rights—a man who posed as a loyal subject of the King on one hand and a protector of the liberties of the subject from what he calls the tyrannies of local Government on the other'.[61] Another official described him as 'a dangerous man—as likely as anybody in Nigeria to be leader of anti-European movements on the American negro lines'.[62] Along with Macaulay, two leading African lawyers, Joseph Egerton-Shyngle and Montacute Thomson, litigated Chief Oluwa's case at the Supreme Court in Nigeria. They also worked closely with Sir William Finlay who litigated the JCPC appeal in London.[63]

Chief Oluwa, in London to witness his JCPC appeal in the summer of 1920, used the occasion as an opportunity to generate metropolitan public interest in his case. With Hebert Macaulay as his interpreter, Chief Oluwa granted interviews to British reporters covering the proceedings at the JCPC.[64] This resulted in news reports on the case in newspapers both in England and West Africa that stirred up popular interest.[65] One correspondent reported on the hearings:

To the end of the hearing, the case has been followed with intense interest by many West Africans. All roads for them have led to Downing Street during the days the case has been before the Privy Council and the little Courtroom has always been crowded with the fellow countrymen of the Oluwa.[66]

While in London, Chief Oluwa and his entourage also met with members of the English nobility, including King George V, at a 'royal outing' at the Botanical

[58] *West Africa* (16 July 1921). [59] *Lagos Weekly Record* (10 September 1921) 8.

[60] H. Macaulay to Lord Passfield, 13 January 1930, NAUK, CO 583/173/10.

[61] W. Birrell Gray to Chief Secretary of the Government of Nigeria, 28 February 1930, NAUK, CO 583/173/10.

[62] W. Birrell Gray to Secretary to the Government, 28 February 1930, NANI, CSO 33115 Vol 1.

[63] H. Macaulay to Lord Passfield, 13 January 1930, NAUK, CO 583/173/10.

[64] Herbert Macaulay, *Justitia Fiat: The Moral Obligations of the British Government to the House of King Docemo of Lagos* (London: St Clements Press, 1921) 6.

[65] *Daily Mail* (13 July 1920); Herbert Macaulay to Lord Passfield, 13 January 1930, NAUK, CO 583/173/10.

[66] *West Africa* (25 June 1921).

Gardens. A photograph of Chief Oluwa shaking hands with the King soon appeared in newspapers and magazines in Britain and Africa, including *Drum*, which at the time was the widest-circulating magazine in English-speaking Africa.[67] The circumstances under which Chief Oluwa met with King George V are not clear. Some accounts suggest that Chief Oluwa was invited to the 'royal outing' following the press coverage of his visit to London.[68] Officials in Nigeria were convinced that Herbert Macaulay had 'contrived' to have Chief Oluwa presented to the King, in order to give an 'exaggerated idea' of the importance of Chief Oluwa and his Privy Council appeal to the British public.[69] Local officials were particularly riled because Chief Oluwa's meeting with the King had taken place without their knowledge and did not follow the proper royal protocol.[70]

Figure 5.1: Chief Oluwa, London 1920

Bassano, *Amodu Tijani, Chief Oluwa of Lagos* © National Portrait Gallery, London

[67] 'Chief Oluwa received by His Majesty King George V', *Drum* (25 July 1920).
[68] T. O. Elias, *Makers of Nigerian Law* (London: Hazell Watson & Viney, 1955) 26.
[69] J. E. W. Flood, Official Minutes, 27 May 1930, NAUK, CO 583/173/10.
[70] J. A. Calder, Official Minutes, 25 September 1930, NAUK, CO 583/173/10.

Figure 5.2: Chief Oluwa with King George V
The Bronzeman (Chicago), May 1931

Chief Oluwa's activities in London drew even more public interest when the JCPC's judgment was delivered. When he returned to Lagos in August 1921, Oluwa was welcomed with wild celebration in the streets of Lagos. The local press reported enthusiastically about his victory against the government at the Privy Council as well as about his meeting with King George V and the English nobility.[71] Newspapers also published special editions to commemorate the legal victory.[72] The story was that Chief Oluwa, who had suffered injustice in the hands of local British officials, had sought and received justice from King George V himself. It was even rumoured that the King had personally apologized to Chief Oluwa for the indiscretions of his local representatives in Nigeria, and had ordered them to reverse their decision.[73] For the thousands of Lagosians who thronged the streets to welcome the victorious Chief Oluwa, there could be no better proof of this than the pictures of the Chief shaking hands with King George splashed over the newspapers. (See Figures 5.2 and 5.3).

[71] *Daily Telegraph* (1 August 1921).
[72] *Lagos Weekly Record* (10 September 1921). Chief Oluwa's Supplemental Edition.
[73] *Lagos Weekly Record* (10 September 1921). Chief Oluwa's Supplemental Edition.

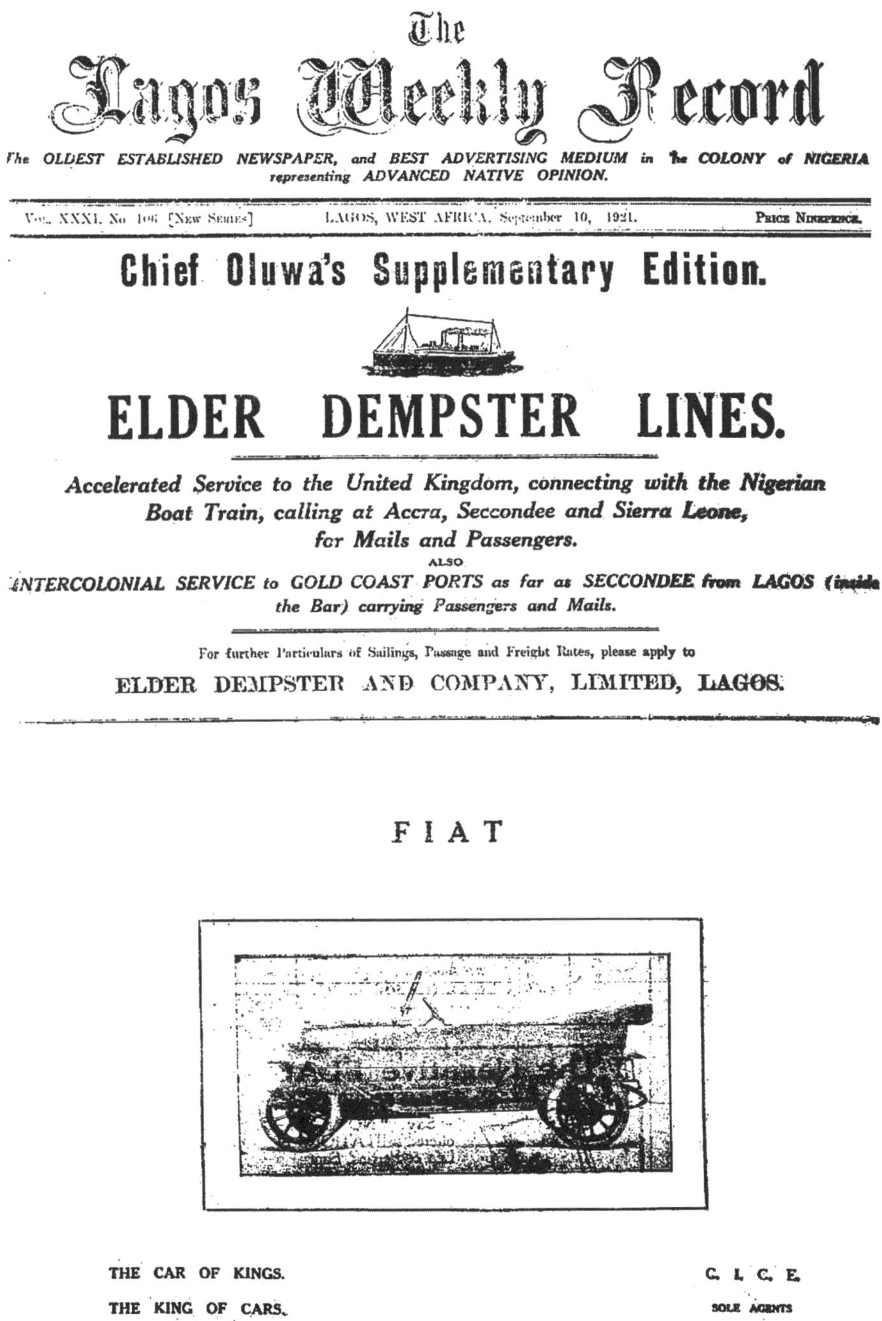

The

Lagos Weekly Record

The OLDEST ESTABLISHED NEWSPAPER, and BEST ADVERTISING MEDIUM in the COLONY of NIGERIA representing ADVANCED NATIVE OPINION.

VOL. XXXI. No 106 [New Series] LAGOS, WEST AFRICA, September 10, 1921. PRICE NINEPENCE.

Chief Oluwa's Supplementary Edition.

ELDER DEMPSTER LINES.

Accelerated Service to the United Kingdom, connecting with the Nigerian Boat Train, calling at Accra, Seccondee and Sierra Leone, for Mails and Passengers.

ALSO

INTERCOLONIAL SERVICE to GOLD COAST PORTS as far as SECCONDEE from LAGOS (inside the Bar) carrying Passengers and Mails.

For further Particulars of Sailings, Passage and Freight Rates, please apply to

ELDER DEMPSTER AND COMPANY, LIMITED, LAGOS.

FIAT

THE CAR OF KINGS.
THE KING OF CARS.

C. I. C. E.
SOLE AGENTS

Figure 5.3: *The Lagos Weekly Record*, 'Chief Oluwa's Supplementary Edition'
Lagos Weekly Record, 10 September 1921. Chief Oluwa's Supplemental Edition.

Prosecuting his appeal at the JCPC provided Chief Oluwa and his supporters with the opportunity to challenge colonial authorities in the ultimate Imperial Court. It also offered them a chance to put the colonial legal and administrative system on trial in the court of metropolitan public opinion. Apart from the public interest it generated, Chief Oluwa's victory in *Amodu Tijani* was precedent-setting in the jurisprudence on indigenous land rights.

In both *Amodu Tijani* and *Re Southern Rhodesia*, the JCPC held that a cession of territory to the British Crown did not affect the customary ownership rights of indigenous communities. But whereas in *Re Southern Rhodesia* such rights were deemed separate from private rights that the Crown should recognize, in *Amodu Tijani* indigenous land rights were to be respected by the Crown.[74] By taking indigenous title seriously and by accepting that native land tenure customs should be recognized despite their difference from English legal ideas, the ruling in *Amodu Tijani* served to soften the rigid ethnocentrism of *Re Southern Rhodesia. Amodu Tijani* therefore illustrates a key argument of this book: imperial justice served both to reify and contain colonial difference. At certain moments, the judgments issued by the Imperial Appeal Courts reinforced colonial notions of native difference and exceptionality, while at other times they softened differentiation and enhanced integration.

The contrasting decisions in *Re Southern Rhodesia* and *Amodu Tijani* may be explained in terms of the political conditions in the originating colonies. Southern Rhodesia was a settler colony, where colonial attitudes towards the social and economic value of land differed considerably from the non-settler colonies of West Africa. State control of land and the maintenance of Crown title were crucial to the colonial mining and concession economies of Southern Africa. In the peasant agricultural economies of West Africa, however, colonial commerce and imperial economic agendas were not threatened by native control of land.[75] In this regard, the JCPC's jurisprudence on Crown title and native land rights aligned with overarching imperial interests.

Amodu Tijani established an Empire-wide precedent for what constituted communal and customary land, both in cases against the government concerning Crown title and in land disputes between Africans. It became authoritative on two particular issues in British colonial administration: the effects of treaties ceding overseas territories to the British Crown, and the nature of African customary land tenures.[76] In the Swaziland land case of *Shobuza II v Millar* heard in 1926, the JCPC (referencing *Amodu Tijani*) affirmed the notion that individual ownership was foreign to African ideas and that land belonged to the community. The Board upheld that the native community had 'usufructuary' rights that placed certain limits on the Crown title. In the final analysis, however, the JCPC endorsed colonial Orders in Council which had the effect of dispossessing Africans of land.

[74] T. O. Elias, 'Nigeria's Contribution to Colonial Law' (1951) 33(3/4) *Journal of Comparative Legislation and International Law* 52–3.

[75] Silverstein, 'The Rule of Native Title', 69.

[76] Adewoye, 'The Tijani Land Case', 24.

The power of the Crown enabling the High Commissioner to acquire land and to make a Crown Grant, Lord Haldane stated in the judgment, was 'an Act of State which cannot be questioned in a Court of law'.[77]

Amodu Tijani was not only of precedential value to the courts in cases between natives and the government. It was also referenced extensively in land disputes among Africans. In *Sunmonu v Disu Raphael*, one of the questions before the JCPC was whether, in a marriage contracted under native customary law, property succession conferred title on individuals, or whether it benefited the entire family.[78] Affirming the principle in *Amodu Tijani*, Lord Haldane asserted that the native's right to land was primarily a usufructuary right that extended *prima facie* to the whole family. He recounted that although the JCPC noted in *Amodu Tijani* that modern influences had made it possible for individuals in West Africa to obtain land title through conveyance, the Board ultimately held that this practice could not be presumed to apply generally to natives.[79]

Beyond its legal significance, *Amodu Tijani* was also precedential in terms of Africans challenging the legal and political authority of colonial regimes. Chief Oluwa's victory at the JCPC ushered in other chiefly contestations of colonial authority. One of the most prominent of such appeals was the case of Chief Eshugbayi Eleko.

Contesting Authority: *Eshugbayi Eleko v The Government*

Eshugbayi Eleko v Officer Administering the Government of Nigeria[80], which was litigated at the JCPC twice, in 1928 and 1931, emerged from the same colonial context as *Amodu Tijani.* Eshugbayi Eleko was the paramount traditional ruler of Lagos, under whom Chief Oluwa was a sub-chief. The *Eleko* appeal concerned a turbulent power struggle between the colonial government and the Chief. It was also one of the outcomes of the *Chief Oluwa* land case.

The story of this constitutional dispute has been related elsewhere and is well preserved in the collective memory of the Yoruba people of Western Nigeria through oral history and folklore.[81] Most scholarly accounts of the episode focus on the political aspects of the case, and on the ways in which it shaped anti-colonial nationalism in the inter-war years. The discussion here is on the JCPC appeal

[77] *Sobhuza II v Allister Miller* [1926] AC 518 at 525.

[78] *Sunmonu v Disu Raphael* [1927] AC 881; Judicial Committee of the Privy Council, *Printed Papers in Appeal* (hereinafter JCPC PPA), Vol 27, 1927.

[79] *Sunmonu v Disu Raphael* [1927] AC 884; JCPC PPA, Vol 27, 1927.

[80] *Eshugbayi Eleko v Officer Administering the Government of Nigeria* [1931] AC 652; JCPC PPA, Vol 24 (1928) and Vol 26 (1931).

[81] See, for example, Patrick Cole, *Modern and Traditional Elites in the Politics of Lagos* (New York: Cambridge University Press, 1973); Adewoye, *The Judicial System in Southern Nigeria*; Sanya Onabamiro, *Glimpses into Nigerian History: Historical Essays* (Lagos: Macmillan, 1983); Richard L. Sklar, *Nigerian Political Parties: Power in an Emergent African Nation* (Princeton; Princeton University Press, 1963); T. N. Tamuno, *The Evolution of the Nigerian State: The Southern Phase 1898–1914* (London: Longman, 1972).

process and its relevance for our understanding of appellate judicial discourses on imperial universalism and colonial difference.

The antipathy between Chief Eleko and the colonial government of Nigeria began in 1915, when Eleko refused to cooperate with the government on the introduction of a new tax. In 1919, the government accused him of making certain political appointments without notifying the Governor, and subsequently suspended him.[82] The relationship deteriorated further in 1920, when Herbert Macaulay—in London with Chief Oluwa to witness the latter's land appeal at the Privy Council—gave interviews to the press, in which he criticized the government's treatment of Chief Eleko.[83] In an interview published by a British newspaper, Macaulay stated that Chief Eleko, 'acclaimed by seventeen million Nigerians as the titular king of Lagos' and the 'chief negro in a possession three times the size of Great Britain', whose grandfather ceded Lagos to the British government, was paid less than the lowest-paid European worker in Nigeria.[84] The authorities in Nigeria considered these statements misleading and an affront to the government, and subsequently called on Eleko to repudiate them 'fully and publicly'.[85]

Eleko protested to the government that he should not be held responsible for Macaulay's statements, but nonetheless sent a denial of the statements to all the newspapers in Lagos.[86] This gesture did not satisfy the government, which insisted that Chief Eleko send his bellman and town crier round the town to read a denial statement prepared by government officials. This was the only form of public repudiation the government would accept.[87] When Eleko refused to comply, the Governor issued a notice in 1925, deposing him as the paramount Chief of Lagos and ordering his deportation under the Deposed Chiefs Removal Ordinance.[88] A successor Chief from an opposing royal house was promptly appointed in his place.[89] Eleko was subsequently arrested, forcibly taken from Lagos, and sent into internal exile in the inland town of Oyo. This was done against the protests of most of the Lagos Chiefs who thought the deposition and deportation contravened customary law.[90]

The deportation order triggered one of the most hard-fought legal battles in West African colonial history; its ferocity and intensity was partly due to Eleko's popularity among the populace. The legal issues that involved both the original trial and subsequent appeals are complex, and space does not permit an exhaustive discussion here. It suffices to point out that the protracted case revolved around key questions of English law and native customary law—the writ of *habeas corpus* and

82 Cole, *Modern and Traditional*, 127.
83 *Daily Mail* (13 July 1920).
84 Hebert Macaulay to Lord Passfield, 13 January 1930, CO 583/173/10.
85 Henry Carr to Eshugbayi Eleko, 5 November 1920, NANI, CSO 33115 Vol 1.
86 Eshugbayi Eleko to H. C. Moorehouse, 14 October 1920, NANI, CSO 33115 Vol 1.
87 Henry Carr to Eshugbayi Eleko, 24 November 1920, NANI, CSO 33115 Vol 1.
88 W. F. Cowers, Gazette Notice Extract, 6 December 1920, NANI, CSO 33115 Vol 1.
89 Adewoye, *The Judicial System in Southern Nigeria,* 261.
90 Chief Obanikoro, Sworn Affidavit, *Eshugbayi Eleko v Officer Administering the Government of Nigeria*, NANI, CSO 33115, Vol 1.

the judicial ascertainment of customary law.[91] The central issue was whether a detained person could apply successively for a writ of *habeas corpus* to one judge after another, regardless of how many times it was refused.

From the beginning, Chief Eleko's legal team that included two leading African lawyers of the period, Eric Moore and J. Egerton-Shyngle, concentrated their attack on the government's deportation order. They petitioned for a writ of *habeas corpus*, requesting the court to order the appellant's presence at the hearing. They argued that under the provisions of the Deposed Chief Removal Ordinance, a magisterial investigation was a 'condition precedent' to an order of deportation.[92] This petition was refused on technical grounds. A second application for a writ of *habeas corpus* presented before Justice Webber of the Supreme Court was also refused on technical grounds.[93] Eleko's lawyers made a third application for a writ of *habeas corpus* before Justice M. L. Tew, who also refused it. The refusal followed the Attorney General's objection that the application was substantially the same as the one heard previously before Justice Webber and could therefore not be re-submitted to a judge of the same court.[94]

During each of these hearings the courts were packed with Lagosians who came to listen to the lawyers' attempts to bring back Chief Eleko. Many of those who attended the hearings were illiterate and hardly understood the esoteric proceedings. Even so, there was a general sense that the courts in Nigeria were using technicalities to shield the government and to prevent Chief Eleko from returning to Lagos. Hebert Macaulay, Eleko's leading supporter, was convinced that the people's salvation lay in the *habeas corpus* proceedings reaching the Privy Council. He wrote to Eleko's lawyer Egerton-Shyngle: 'I am anxious about the Habeas Corpus, as that is really what will appeal forcibly to the natives.' After Chief Oluwa's land case, the Privy Council had come to be regarded among the indigenous elite as the custodian of native liberties, and thus Macaulay was confident that the Privy Council would shield Eleko from the 'tyranny of the government'.[95] While agreeing with Macaulay that Eleko's chances of success were better at the Privy Council, Egerton-Shyngle reminded him that 'the writ of Habeas Corpus is a High Prerogative writ and bristles with technicalities'.[96] Both Macaulay and

[91] *Habeas corpus* refers to the legal action by means of which detainees can seek relief from unlawful imprisonment. The writ of *habeas corpus* has historically been an important common law instrument for the safeguarding of individual freedom against arbitrary state action.

[92] J. C. Howard, Solicitor General, Memorandum for use of the Respondent in *Eshugbayi Eleko v Officer Administering the Government of Nigeria*, 11 April 1930, NANI, CSO 33115, Vol 1.

[93] The second application for a writ of *habeas corpus* was refused on the grounds that there was a competent court of jurisdiction at Oyo, where Eleko was exiled, to which an application could have been made. Moreover, Justice Webber held that it was not essential that a person who had disobeyed an order to leave an area should be brought before a magistrate prior to an order of deportation being made. J. C. Howard, Solicitor General, Memorandum for use of the Respondent in *Eshugbayi Eleko v Officer Administering the Government of Nigeria*, 11 April 1930, NANI, CSO 33115, Vol 1.

[94] F. B. Marriman and Horace Douglas, 'Petition of Eshugbayi Eleko for Special Leave to Appeal to the Privy Council', 8 August 1925, NAUK, CO 583/177/A.

[95] *West Africa* (31 July 1931).

[96] Macaulay to Shyngle, 19 August 1925; Shyngle to Macaulay, 20 August 1925, HMP, III/4. Cited in Cole, *Modern and Traditional Elites in the Politics of Lagos*, 147.

Egerton-Shyngle came to the conclusion, however, that only the Privy Council could save the situation. 'Justice,' Egerton-Shyngle commented, 'is very wide awake here (in Lagos) instead of being blind.'[97]

After their appeal to the Supreme Court was dismissed in June 1926, Eleko's lawyers applied for special leave to appeal to the Privy Council. The first appeal to the JCPC was heard in 1928. The government considered the case of such importance that the Solicitor General for Nigeria, J. C. Howard, was dispatched to London to argue the government's case.[98] The JCPC overturned the decisions of the Supreme Court. Their Lordships declared that successive applications for a writ of *habeas corpus* could be made to different judges of the same court, and that it was up to each judge to consider the application on its own merit. On the basis of this finding, the JCPC remitted the case back to the Supreme Court in Nigeria.[99]

Successive re-hearings of the case at the Supreme Court went on between January 1929 and March 1930. In one hearing Justice Tew held that the court was not competent to decide the two key issues raised by Eshugbayi in his application: whether or not Eshugbayi was a 'Chief' under the Deposed Chiefs Removal Ordinance, and whether or not he had been properly deposed from office according to local customary law. It was also suggested that Eleko's deposition was 'an act of state' that could not be questioned by the courts.[100] At these hearings, the case for colonial difference was forcefully made. The Attorney General argued for the government:

> [W]hereas matters affecting the liberty of the subject are in England usually relegated to the ordinary courts of law . . . In comparatively underdeveloped countries, it may often be necessary to give powers to Executive Officers which would be regarded as extraordinary in England.[101]

At the end of the re-hearings in Nigeria, Eleko's legal challenge against deposition was dismissed and his *habeas corpus* application was refused. This warranted a second appeal to the Privy Council in 1931. At this point, it had become evident to many that the courts in Nigeria were unwilling to question the legality of the executive action to depose and deport Eleko.

At the JCPC hearing in 1931, the government's case rested partly on native custom, which was invoked to legitimize the decision to depose and banish Eleko. The government linked Eleko's deportation to the internal conflict within the ruling house of Lagos, claiming that it had merely sanctioned the deposition of an unwanted Chief as was the native custom. In pre-colonial times, that custom would

[97] Shyngle to Macaulay, 20 August 1925, HMP, III/4. Cited in Cole, *Modern and Traditional Elites in the Politics of Lagos*, 147.

[98] G. J. Lethem to Messers Burchells, 22 March 1928, NAUK, CO 583/166/2.

[99] Adewoye, *The Judicial System in Southern Nigeria*, 263.

[100] J. C. Howard, Solicitor General, 'Memorandum for use by the Respondent's Solicitors', 11 April 1930, NANI, CSO 33115, Vol 1.

[101] Referenced in W. B. Lloyd, Judgment of the Full Court of the Supreme Court of Nigeria, *Eshugbayi Eleko v Officer Administering the Government of Nigeria*, 3 March 1930, NANI, CSO 33115, Vol 1.

have warranted the death of a deposed Chief.[102] It was argued in defence of the government that while the fundamental principle underlying this custom had been preserved, its 'barbarous' features had disappeared under the influence of 'Christianity, British rule and the spread of enlightened and less primitive ideas'.[103] The custom could therefore only be enforced by the voluntary or compulsory removal of the deposed Chief, and the machinery for enforcing the custom was the Governor's power under the Chief Removal Ordinance.[104]

While the courts in Nigeria upheld these arguments, their Lordships roundly rejected them. Lord Atkin famously ruled that the court could not itself transform a barbarous custom into a milder one. 'If a custom stood in its barbarous character,' Lord Atkin stated, 'it must be rejected as repugnant to natural justice, equity and good conscience.'[105] The Board recognized that 'barbarous' ancient African customs may, under the influences of 'civilisation', become milder without losing their essential character of custom. But in such cases, it was essential for the party invoking custom to show that, in their milder form, such practices were still recognized in the native community as customs. It was the assent of the native community that gave a custom its validity, and therefore, barbarous or mild, it had to be proven to be recognized by the native community whose conduct it was supposed to regulate.[106]

It was also argued for the government that since the Governor had the prerogative authority to appoint Chiefs and had appointed Eleko as a Chief under that authority, the Governor could also remove him. Their Lordships were not persuaded by this argument, however. The Board was not convinced that prerogative instruments such as letters patent and Crown instructions to the Governor contained any such explicit provisions. They feared that these contentions would 'seriously affect the rights of natives in Nigeria'.[107] As Lord Blanesburgh put it: 'One is a little nervous of all cases affecting the liberty of the subject.'[108] Drawing analogy with the powers of the British Home Secretary to deport aliens, Lord Atkin stated in the judgment:

> In accordance with British jurisprudence, no member of the executive can interfere with the liberty or property of a British subject except on the condition that he can support the legality of his action before a court of justice. And it is the tradition of British justice that

[102] Evidence was provided in court that, under Yoruba customs, a deposed Chief was required to commit suicide by taking poison. If the Chief failed to do so, he had to be prepared to face civil war and fight for his throne. His life was effectively threatened if he did not commit suicide.

[103] M. L. Tew, Judgment of the Supreme Court in *Eshugbayi Eleko v Officer Administering the Government of Nigeria*, 6 August 1925, NANI, CSO 33115 Vol 1. Also see M. L. Tew, Judgment of the Supreme Court in *Eshugbayi Eleko v Officer Administering the Government of Nigeria*, 9 May 1929, NAUK, CO 583/166/2.

[104] M. L. Tew, Judgment of the Supreme Court in *Eshugbayi Eleko v Officer Administering the Government of Nigeria*, 9 May 1929, NAUK, CO 583/166/2.

[105] *Eshugbayi Eleko v The Officer Administrating the Government of Nigeria* [1931] AC 662.

[106] *Eshugbayi Eleko v The Officer Administrating the Government of Nigeria*, 662.

[107] *Eshugbayi Eleko v The Officer Administrating the Government of Nigeria*, 672.

[108] Privy Council, Eleko Case, 4th Day Proceedings, 9 February 1931, NAUK, CO 583/177/105, cited in Cole, *Modern and Traditional Elites in the Politics of Lagos*, 260.

judges should not shrink from deciding such issues in the face of the executive.... Their Lordships entertain no doubt that under the legislation in question, if the Home Secretary deported a British subject in the belief that he was an alien, the subject would have the right to question the validity of any detention under such order by proceedings in habeas corpus, and that it would be the duty of the Courts to investigate the issue of alien or not.[109]

In contrast to the Nigerian courts' unquestioned acceptance of the view that the Governor's orders to depose Eleko could not be subject to judicial investigation, their Lordships declared that the powers of the Governor under the Deposed Chiefs Ordinance were purely executive. It was the duty of the court in Nigeria 'to investigate the questions raised by the appellant's contentions and to come to a judicial decision'.[110] The Board rejected the notion that the deportation of Eshugbayi Eleko was 'an act of state', and ordered that the case should be remitted again to Nigeria, where it would be tried *ab initio*. It also spelt out in detail how the Nigerian courts should proceed in re-hearing the case.[111]

The JCPC's ruling was clearly an indictment of both the Nigerian government and judiciary. One legal officer in the Colonial Office described the judgment as the most critical of the proceedings of a local court that he had ever seen.[112] The judgment significantly weakened the government's case and was not well received by officials in Nigeria. Determined not to reinstate Chief Eleko, they explored several legal and executive options to prevent his re-instatement, including passing a special ordinance that would have effectively reversed the Privy Council's decision.[113]

In the end, the *Eleko* case was resolved through a political rather than judicial process. Upon his appointment as Governor of Nigeria in 1931, Sir Donald Cameron announced that the government would no longer pursue the *Eleko* case in the courts. Eleko's deportation order was withdrawn on the condition that he commits to be of 'good behaviour', and as long as 'peace and good order in Lagos' would not be disturbed by his return to Lagos.[114] Governor Cameron later admitted that there was a perception among Eleko's supporters that government had been weakened by the litigation and that the 'game was in their hands'. He explained to his superiors in Whitehall that he was compelled to resolve the matter 'out of court' in the public interest.[115]

Chief Eleko subsequently retuned to Lagos, and was reinstated to the throne amidst 'scenes of jubilation unprecedented in the history of Lagos'.[116] An unofficial public holiday was declared; shops, markets, and offices were closed and, for several weeks after his arrival, Lagos was in a festive mood. Several pamphlets were published chronicling the case, songs were composed, dances and plays were put

[109] *Eshugbayi Eleko v The Officer Administrating the Government of Nigeria*, 672.
[110] *Eshugbayi Eleko v The Officer Administrating the Government of Nigeria*, 670.
[111] *Eshugbayi Eleko v The Officer Administrating the Government of Nigeria*, 662.
[112] H. G. Bushe, 28 March 1931, NAUK, CO 583/177/A.
[113] J. W. Flood to A. J. Fiddian, 12 February 1931, NAUK, CO 583/177/A.
[114] Donald Cameron, Note by His Excellency the Governor, 29 June 1931, NAUK, CO 583/177/A.
[115] Donald Cameron to Lord Passfield, 16 July 1931, NAUK, CO 583/177/A.
[116] Cole, *Modern and Traditional Elites in the Politics of Lagos*, 149.

on showing its various aspects, all testifying to the personal involvement of those affected by the case. One newspaper contributor wrote triumphantly: 'Whenever in my hearings, Africans are accused of wanton litigiousness, I shall invite the critic to read up the history of the Eleko Case.'[117]

The *Eleko* case marked a turning point in anti-colonial politics in Nigeria, and embodied important elements of the larger question of self-determination. The government's treatment of Eleko endowed him with special symbolism.[118] It stimulated the creation of an alliance among the elite both traditional and modern, marking an era of mass involvement in politics. Chief Eleko's reinstatement was seen as a political victory for a nascent anti-colonial nationalism. Elites contributed funds to support Chief Eleko's legal appeal in Nigeria and England, and some mortgaged their homes and properties to support Eleko. Contributions and subscriptions also came from political and social groups in Lagos, including cultural associations, workers guilds, and market women's associations. The ability of Eleko and his supporters to raise funds for the expensive and protracted litigation puzzled and worried officials in Lagos and London.[119] 'It is extraordinary,' wrote one official in London, 'how Macaulay, by propaganda in his newspaper, by public meetings, public subscriptions and litigation has for so many years kept alive an agitation over Eshugbayi [Eleko].'[120]

As with Chief Oluwa's land case, Herbert Macaulay was at the forefront of the modern elites' support for Chief Eleko's cause. During the JCPC hearing, Macaulay sent a delegation to England in order to lobby members of the British parliament.[121] This appears to have had some effect, as several MPs raised questions regarding Eleko's case during parliamentary debates. In one instance, MP James Horrabin asked the Undersecretary of State for the Colonies to provide details about the deportation of Eshugbayi Eleko; also, what provisions had been made for him in exile, and whether the government intended to issue instructions for his release.[122] The British humanitarian organization, The League Against Imperialism, also took interest in the case and sent several supporting petitions to officials in Lagos and London.[123]

The *Eleko* case foreshadowed similar developments in Uganda in 1953, when the colonial authorities deposed and deported the King of Buganda, Kabaka Mutesa II. The government had accused the Kabaka of refusal to cooperate with the British government, and sought to reduce his influence in Ugandan politics. As in the case

117 *West Africa* (5 November 1931).

118 James S. Coleman, *Nigeria: Background to Nationalism* (Berkeley: University of California Press, 1958) 196.

119 J. E. W. Flood, Confidential Minute, 17 June 1929, NAUK, CO 583/166/2.

120 J. A. Calder, Internal Memorandum, 23 May 1930, NAUK, CO 583/173/10.

121 W. Birrell Gray to Chief Secretary of the Government of Nigeria, 28 February 1930, NAUK, CO 583/173/10.

122 The Undersecretary, William Lunn, provided details on the case but stated that, because the case was still under consideration by the courts, the Secretary of State was unable to take any action in the matter. House of Commons Debate, 5 November 1930, Vol 244, c846.

123 Reginald Bridgeman to Lord Passfield, 30 December 1930; Reginald Bridgeman to Under Secretary of State for Colonies, 12 January 1931, NAUK, CO 583/173/10.

of Chief Eleko, however, the deportation of the Kabaka did not stop the growing anti-colonial movement. On the contrary, it united the nationalist groups in Uganda, for whom the reinstatement of the Kabaka became a symbol of colonial resistance. The colonial authorities were compelled to restore the Kabaka to his throne in 1955.[124]

Apart from its political impact, the *Eleko* case was of precedential value in British imperial and Commonwealth jurisprudence. The JCPC's ruling that the right to apply for a writ of *habeas corpus* was not limited to a single application became *locus classicus* in questions of successive applications for *habeas corpus*.[125] The judgment also underscored a tendency on the part of the Imperial Courts to invoke universalist British standards on issues pertaining to the liberties of colonial subjects. In the *Eleko* case, the JCPC clearly enunciated the principles that would govern the application of the writ of *habeas corpus* in colonial territories. It also stipulated the right of a British subject in the colonies—as in England—to challenge executive action in the court.[126]

Arguments for native difference, which may have resonated with their Lordships on other cases, fell flat in *Eshugbayi Eleko.* The JCPC did not hesitate to apply British jurisprudence, and to draw British analogies when it found the local law on the scope of executive powers unclear.

Conclusion

The land and chieftainship disputes discussed in this chapter provide important insights into imperial universalism and colonial difference. Moreover, they attest to notions of imperial power and prestige. The dynamics of Empire were driven by prestige, and, in the colonies, prestige was considered more durable than power alone.[127] The possession of Empire was not only a matter of material interest; it held symbolic meaning both for the colonial subjects and the outside world. The victories of Chief Oluwa and Chief Eleko at the JCPC against the colonial government in Nigeria therefore held significant implications for imperial prestige. For the locally-situated colonial officials these rulings undermined the government's prestige, even if they did not seriously endanger the colonial order or subvert imperial agendas. Chief Oluwa's victory did not loosen British control over indigenous lands in Nigeria or elsewhere in the Empire. Chief Eleko remained politically marginalized in spite of his successful Privy Council appeals. Nevertheless, both legal appeals empowered African elites in their opposition to the government.

[124] Ramkrishna Mukherjee, *Uganda: An Historical Accident, Class, Nation, State Formation* (Trenton: Africa World Press, 1985) 245.

[125] Elias, 'Nigeria's Contribution to Colonial Law', 49–55; 'Successive Applications for Habeas Corpus' (1928) 66 *The Law Journal* 46.

[126] Elias, 'Nigeria's Contribution to Colonial Law', 49–55.

[127] Ronald Hyam, *Understanding the British Empire* (Cambridge: Cambridge University Press, 2010) 73.

The cases therefore show how colonial judicial processes enhanced the political awareness and influence of indigenous elites.

While the defeats suffered by the government at the Privy Council in the *Amodu Tijani* and *Eshugbayi Eleko* cases may have diminished the prestige of local officials, they certainly enhanced the prestige of the JCPC and the imperial judicial establishment. Given their antecedents, it is likely that Lords Haldane and Atkin would have had to persuade some of their more conservative colleagues of the correctness of their position in both cases. The JCPC's practice of not acknowledging or publishing dissenting judicial opinion, however, makes this a point on which one can only speculate. Although the JCPC was not entirely immune from political influence, the autonomy it enjoyed within the imperial system was evident in these cases. Local officials dreaded the spectre of successful native appeals against the government at the Privy Council. Traditional and modern African elites challenging the government placed great confidence in the Board and its ability to uphold justice at the centre of the Empire, where it had been denied in the colonies. This confidence in the JCPC would not endure, however. As colonial power waned in the mid-twentieth century, the Imperial Courts of Appeal's authority and legitimacy came under increased scrutiny by the colonial subjects. This marked the prelude to the courts' eventual demise as the next chapter shows.

6

Unknown God: The Limits of Imperial Justice

The story of the unknown god was a tale Lord Haldane liked to tell. In several speeches delivered over the course of his long career as a JCPC judge, he recounted the anecdote to underscore the imperial significance and influence of the JCPC. As Haldane told it, a traveller in India—a land of many gods—visited a remote part of the country, where he found a tribe offering sacrifices to an unknown god. He asked who the god was, to which the natives replied: 'We don't know, except that he is a very powerful god, because he interfered on our behalf against the government, and gave us back our land, which the government had taken. The only other thing we know is that the name of the god is the Judicial Committee of the Privy Council.'[1]

For Haldane, analogizing the JCPC with an Indian god served to draw attention to the pivotal imperial role of the Board, one that he, like many officials of the Privy Council, felt was less appreciated in Britain than in the colonies. In Haldane's story of the unknown Indian god, the emphasis is on the near transcendental esteem in which the JCPC was held by the natives in the colonies—extolling the god-like role that the Board came to assume in the affairs of imperial subjects in far-flung outposts of the Empire. Less emphasized in the anecdote, but no less poignant, is the image of the JCPC as a benevolent but *unknown* force. Through a century of dispensing imperial appellate justice from the centre of the Empire, the JCPC had indeed attained god-like status among some natives. However, it remained largely unknown and distant to the many colonial subjects over whose affairs the Board sat in judgment.

For all the devotion and awe unknown gods may inspire among faithful adherents, it was inevitable that a time would come when even the most doting devotee would question the mysteries of this unknown god and ponder the benefits of worshipping better known gods. In many parts of the British Empire, such anecdotal questions about the esteem and mystery of the JCPC lay at the centre of the challenges to the Board's influence and jurisdiction in the mid-nineteenth century. For more than a century, the JCPC played a crucial role as a link of the Empire. However, it was to be expected that such a link would feel the strain of dominions struggling for political autonomy and be correspondingly weakened as

[1] Lord Haldane, 'The Work for the Empire of the Judicial Committee of the Privy Council' (1922) 1(2) *The Cambridge Law Journal* 153. This story is also recounted in James Morris, *Pax Britannica: The Climax of an Empire* (London: Harcourt, 1979) 194.

they attained it.[2] It was inevitable that people of the subcontinent, as elsewhere in the Empire, would at some point be 'deprived of recourse to their great god'.[3]

This chapter examines the circumstances leading to the demise of the JCPC in British Africa. It explores the legal and political impulses that shaped the demands for the abolition of Privy Council appeals. It also examines the efforts made by British officials and politicians in the dominions and colonies to reform the JCPC to retain its relevance in the transition from Empire to Commonwealth, from the 1930s to the 1960s. In this transition most of the early debates centred on the JCPC's jurisdiction in the old dominions, notably the Irish Free States, Canada, and South Africa. The extension of the debate over the JCPC's jurisdiction to the rest of British Africa coincided with the post-war nationalist movement and the era of decolonization. Although the discussion in this chapter focuses on the abolition of the JCPC's jurisdiction in Africa, it begins by tracing the antecedents of the abolition of JCPC jurisdiction elsewhere in the Empire.

After a century of judicial influence, the demise of the JCPC's jurisdiction in Africa was precipitous. By the 1950s, the influence and jurisdiction of the JCPC and the regional colonial appeal courts had diminished significantly as a direct result of the anti-colonial movements. Between 1957 and 1966, several British colonies in Africa achieved independence and many of these new countries either immediately, or upon declaration of republican status, ended their appeals to the Privy Council. For many nationalist politicians in these countries, executive, legislative, and judicial sovereignty were inextricably interlinked. Delinking from the JCPC was therefore seen as a key step in the assertion of independence and sovereignty.[4]

The process of judicial delinking would turn out to be a complex and convoluted one. Although anti-colonialism and decolonization marked the defining moment in the demise of the JCPC in Africa as elsewhere within the British Empire, these developments in themselves did not necessarily make the JCPC's demise inevitable. In other parts of the Empire-Commonwealth, the influence and jurisdiction of the JCPC persisted for several decades after political independence was attained. Australia effectively abolished the right of appeal to the JCPC in 1986 and New Zealand in 2003. Sri Lanka abolished most appeals to the Privy Council in 1972, Malaysia in 1985, and Singapore in 1994. Most Caribbean countries continued appeals to the JCPC until 2001.[5]

[2] Anonymous, 'Decline of the Judicial Committee of the Privy Council. Current Status of Appeals from the British Dominions' (1947) 60(7) *Harvard Law Review* 1140.

[3] John de P. Wright, 'The Judicial Committee of the Privy Council' (2007) 10(2D) *Green Bag* 363.

[4] Graham Page, Adornment Debate, 29 June 1956, National Archives of the UK (hereinafter NAUK), CO/1026/114.

[5] Some former British Caribbean colonies and dependencies abolished the right of appeal to the Privy Council in 2001, when nations of the Caribbean Community voted to abolish the right of appeal to the Privy Council in favour of the Caribbean Court of Justice (CCJ). Patrick Robinson, 'The Monarchy, Republicanism and the Privy Council: The Enduring Cry for Freedom' (August 2012) *The Round Table* 7–8.

Table 6.1: Abolition of Privy Council Appeals in African Countries

Country	Independence	Abolition of Appeal
Botswana	1966	1966
Gambia	1965	1998
Ghana (Gold Coast)	1957	1960
Kenya	1963	1965
Lesotho	1966	1966
Malawi	1964	1965
Mauritius	1968	Appeals continue
Nigeria	1960	1963
Sierra Leone	1961	1961
Somalia (Somaliland)	1960	1960
South Africa	1910	1950
Swaziland	1968	1968
Tanzania (Tanganyika)	1961	1964
Uganda	1962	1962
Zambia	1964	1964
Zimbabwe	1980	1980

In contrast, most British ex-colonies in Africa had by 1966 abolished all appeals to the Privy Council, as Table 6.1 shows.[6] Most of them had also left the two main regional courts of appeal—the West African Court of Appeal and the East African Court of Appeal.

Arguments for sovereignty and judicial independence aside, the demise of the JCPC in Africa also had much to do with longstanding dissatisfaction with the unrepresentative composition of the JCPC bench. The right of appeal to a 'court' located overseas, made up mostly of English judges who were sometimes considered out of tune with local values was a sore point in the colonies even at the height of imperial power. This situation became even more untenable as imperial influence waned in the mid-twentieth century.

The Question of Colonial Representation

The question of colonial representation at the Privy Council and the JCPC in particular was always at the centre of imperial constitutional discourse. Although the jurisdiction of the JCPC as the highest court of appeal for the British Empire also extended to certain domestic matters, colonial appeals constituted the largest

[6] The abolition of appeals to the Privy Council also came relatively early in India, Burma, and Pakistan. India abolished the right of appeal to the Privy Council in 1949, a few years after it gained independence, while Pakistan abolished the right of appeal in 1950.

category of cases heard by the court in the twentieth century. In order to put the JCPC in a position to adjudicate appeals from the different legal systems within the Empire, reforms were introduced in the late nineteenth and early twentieth century, under which representative judges from all the colonies were eligible to sit on the JCPC if they were appointed as members of the Privy Council.[7] The need to provide the JCPC with guidance on the law of the colonial localities, from which legal appeals came, also prompted the provision for appointing Indian assessors under the 1833 Act which established the modern JCPC.

The Judicial Committee Act of 1871 provided for the appointment of four full-time judges who were judges of Superior Courts or the Chief Justices of the High Courts in Bengal, Madras, or Bombay. This was the first law that made exception to the principle that only members of the Privy Council could be appointed to the JCPC. It has been suggested that, by these changes, the JCPC lost part of its historical political significance, while assuming a decidedly more judicial character.[8] It is evident, however, that the intention behind the Act was to take advantage of the experience and expertise of long-serving colonial judges, rather than to open up the JCPC to indigenous judges. Indeed, the 1871 Act was very particular on who could be invited to the JCPC bench. It permitted only the invitation of those Privy Council members who, at the time of their appointments, had been judges of her Majesty's Superior Court at Westminster, Chief Justice of the High Court at Fort William in Madras and Bombay, or judges of the Supreme Court in Bengal. Such appointees were expected to attend the JCPC sitting in London when summoned for particular cases.

Although the JCPC occasionally included colonial judges since 1880s, their presence on the board was always a vexed issue. In 1895, the Judicial Committee Amendment Act provided for the appointment to the Privy Council, and then to the Judicial Committee, of any judge of a superior court in the Dominions and self-governing colonies. Further reforms introduced in 1908 and 1915 permitted representative judges from all British colonies to sit on the JCPC.[9] The first Dominion judge to sit on the JCPC under these terms was the English South African judge, Lord de Villiers, who was Chief Justice for the Cape Colony, and later the first Chief Justice of the Union of South Africa.[10]

The provisions aimed at ensuring more colonial representation had little practical effect, either in terms of diversifying the JCPC bench or increasing the range of the Committee's expertise. Most of the early Indian assessors appointed to the Committee were serving and retired English officials and judges who had worked in India. However, from 1909, South Asian judges began to have a major presence in the upper echelons of the imperial legal system with the appointment of Syed

[7] Imperial Conference 1930: Judicial Committee: Privy Council Proposed, National Archives of South Africa, Pretoria (hereinafter NASAP), BLO 88 PS12/2/24.

[8] J. J. Beauchamp, *The Jurisprudence of the Privy Council* (Montreal: Whiteford & Theoret, 1891) 14.

[9] Judicial Committee Act, 1915, NAUK, HL/PO/PU/1/1915.

[10] Z. Cowen, 'Notes on Constitutional Development in the Commonwealth' (1950) 32(3/4) *Journal of Comparative Legislation and International Law* 73.

Ameer Ali as the first South Asian judge on the JCPC.[11] Indigenous judges, such as Syed Ameer Ali and Dinshaw Mulla, who was appointed in 1930, played a crucial role in bringing indigenous perspectives to the jurisprudence of the JCPC, particularly in terms of their expertise and interpretations of Hindu and Islamic law.[12] The inclusion of African judges (outside of South Africa) would wait until 1962, when the Nigerian judge, Adetokunbo Ademola, was appointed to the Privy Council.

In spite of the theoretical composition of the JCPC, the three or five judges who sat to hear any one appeal were often persons in high judicial office in the United Kingdom.[13] There was also the occasional judge from Canada, Australia, or South Africa who sat on the Board by virtue of his appointment to the Privy Council. Sometimes, judicial assessors were also drawn from the ranks of retired colonial judges who provided advice on local laws and customs. Yet many, in both the metropole and the colony, considered this anomalous. A bench composed exclusively of English judges, critics argued, was ill equipped to effectively adjudicate appeals from different legal systems within the expanding Empire.[14] Although the most persistent calls for reforming the JCPC came from the colonies, there was also domestic pressure for a more representative JCPC or in some cases, an alternate Imperial Court of Appeal.

Questions over colonial representations in the JCPC echoed longstanding debates over judicial unity and cohesiveness within the British Empire. Commenting on the lack of adequate colonial representation on the JCPC bench in 1886, Lord de Villiers, then the Chief Judge of Cape Colony, wrote: 'There can be little sincerity in the desire generally avowed in England to draw closer ties, which join the Mother Country and the Colonies as long as an anomaly of this nature is allowed to exist.'[15] Such views were not limited to judicial officers in colonial outposts who wanted some influence in judicial decision-making at the imperial centre. Metropolitan politicians expressed similar views.

Writing against the backdrop of the Anglo-Boer War in 1900, Geoffrey Drage, a British member of parliament, bemoaned the lack of judicial cohesiveness within the British Empire and called for the establishment of an 'Imperial Council for Defence and Judicature' along the lines of the German Supreme Imperial Court in Leipzig. The Germans, he argued, had done a much better job of harmonizing and consolidating German imperial jurisprudence than Britain had done with the JCPC. The Imperial Council he advocated would represent not only English legal traditions but also the policy and legal opinion of the governments of India, Canada, Australia, South Africa, and other colonies. Apart from the benefit of

[11] For a history of Ameer Ali's pioneering role on the JCPC, see Muhammad Yusuf Abbasi, *The Political Biography of Syed Ameer Ali* (Lahore: Wajidalis, 1989); Shan Muhammad, *The Right Honourable Syed Ameer Ali: Personality and Achievements* (Delhi: Uppal, 1991).

[12] The Mulla who wrote the leading textbooks on Islamic and Hindu law for colonial India also decided several cases on personal law from British South Asia.

[13] Graham Page, Adornment Debate, 29 June 1956, NAUK, CO/1026/114.

[14] J. B. Nihill to K. Roberts-Wray, Confidential Memorandum, 20 May 1955, NAUK, CO/1026/114.

[15] Cited in S. S. Abrahams, Internal Memorandum to K. Roberts-Wray, Colonial Legal Service, NAUK, CO/1026/114.

fostering greater legal and judicial unity within the Empire, the Imperial Council would serve as a place to discuss 'great imperial questions', thus placing them out of the reach of local politics.[16]

Officials in Whitehall were not convinced of the need for broader provisions for colonial representation on the JCPC than was statutorily allowed already. They also did not see the benefit of a new Imperial Court of Appeal. At a time when the idea of an imperial federation was in vogue, Secretary of State for the Colonies Joseph Chamberlain and other British officials perceived the JCPC as an important element of imperial unity, and were reluctant to tinker with what was considered a less-than-perfect but stable judicial institution. However, bowing to pressure from the dominions, in 1901 the Colonial Office issued invitations to legal experts from the colonies for a conference in London to discuss proposals for an Imperial Court of Appeal for the Empire. Representatives came from Canada, Newfoundland, Australia, New Zealand, Natal, the Cape Colony, and India. Some of the delegates argued for creating an entirely new and more representative Imperial Court of Appeal to replace the JCPC. The Australian representative, Justice Hodges, argued that such imperial court was desirable because it would command the admiration and respect of the whole 'British race' in the dominions, and it would also be a powerful factor in the development of a closer union between all parts of the Empire.[17]

Others were not so convinced. Sir James Prendergast, the Chief Justice of New Zealand, opposed both the proposal for a new Imperial Court of Appeal and the appointment of colonial judges to the JCPC. He argued that there was no agreed scheme for colonial representation on the JCPC, and that in colonies, where the legal system was fundamentally the same as in England, he failed to 'find a logic and sufficient reason' for colonial representation.[18] In the end, the only consensus that the delegates could agree on was that legal appeals should continue to lie from the colonies to the Privy Council. Officials at Whitehall could not have hoped for a better outcome. In his report on the conference, Chamberlain noted almost gleefully that since no far-reaching alteration in the structure and constitution of the JCPC would be considered satisfactory by the colonies, the JCPC remained the best option for judicial governance within the Empire.

This was also the position of the Privy Council. When the idea of abolishing appeals was first broached in the dominions, the JCPC defended itself in a memorandum that stated: 'To abolish this controlling power and abandon each colony and dependency to a separate Court of Appeal of its own would be to destroy one of the most important ties connecting all parts of the Empire and to renounce the last and most essential mode of exercising the authority of the Crown over its possessions abroad.'[19]

However much British administrative and judicial officials may have wished to maintain the status quo, dissatisfaction with the unrepresentative composition of

[16] *The Times* (9 June 1900). [17] *The Times* (30 November 1901).

[18] *The Times* (30 November 1901).

[19] Dominion of Canada, 'Debates of the House of Commons Official Report' Vol 1 (Ottawa: Queen's Printer, 1939) 212.

the JCPC bench persisted. Questions remained about the ability of the JCPC to cope with the variety of cases from legal systems across the Empire without adequate representation from the colonies and dominions. It was frequently pointed out, for example, that few judges on the JCPC had any training in Roman-Dutch law which was applicable in Ceylon and the Cape Colony. This raised further concerns about judicial incompetence and miscarriage of justice. The main complaint was that, being composed almost entirely of United Kingdom judges, the JCPC could not match local practitioners in their knowledge of local law and conditions.

Disquiet in the colonies over the lack of their representation on the JCPC bench and the Council's capacity to effectively adjudicate cases from diverse legal systems contrasts with the celebratory attitudes towards the work of the JCPC from officials in Britain. In the nineteenth and early twentieth century, commentators in Britain tended to see the diversity of legal systems within the jurisdiction of the Privy Council as a source of pride rather than concern. Eulogizing the work of Lord Watson as a JCPC judge, Lord Haldane claimed that he never failed to endeavour to interpret the law according to the spirit of the jurisprudence, from which the appeal came. If it was a Cape appeal from South Africa, he acted as a Roman Dutch lawyer; if it was an Indian case of adoption, he entered into the religious reasons for the rule to be applied; if it dealt with a Quebecois case of substitution under the old French code or a Jersey appeal about the customs of Normandy, Watson equally embraced the role of a local judge.[20] Such judicial versatility, once a source of pride and influence, increasingly came to be questioned by the mid-twentieth century. Tumult abroad and uncertainties at home during the interwar years seem to have influenced the shift from assurance to uncertainty.

Cracks in the Imperial Judicial Edifice

The first cracks in the imperial judicial edifice appeared in the old dominions. The debate over the right of JCPC appeal informed discussions of dominion status in the 1920s and early 1930s following the Statute of Westminster which established legislative equality with the United Kingdom for the self-governing dominions of the British Empire. Most of the early discussion focused on strengthening representation from the old dominions of Canada, Australia, New Zealand, South Africa and, to a lesser extent, India. During this period, the JCPC arguably faced a crisis of relevance and legitimacy arising mainly from the demands in Canada and the Irish Free States for the abolition of the rights to Privy Council appeal. The political circumstances leading to the abolition of appeals in both countries foreshadowed the end of appeals in Africa and elsewhere in the Empire-Commonwealth.

In Canada, the role of the JCPC as the court of final appeal had long evoked complaints that the English judges on the Board were not sufficiently familiar with

[20] Lord Watson, 'The Appellate Courts of the Empire' (1900) 12 *Judicial Review* 5.

local affairs to properly decide difficult questions involving constitutional politics. One of the principal reasons behind the demands for abolition of the JCPC was dissatisfaction with the Board's treatment of the distribution of powers between the dominion government and the provinces. In the course of more than quarter of a century of adjudication, the JCPC, by its strict interpretation of the British North America Act, ascribed more powers to the provinces at the expense of the dominion government. By the 1920s, attitudes towards the JCPC in Canada ranged from measured criticism to vehement denunciation.[21]

Proponents of the JCPC argued that the Board played a constructive role in its interpretation of Canadian Constitutional law. The Provinces were recognized as authorities equal to the Dominion government, which resulted in censuses and contentment in the Canadian Constitution. Supporters of the JCPC also thought the Board's isolation from Canadian politics—rather than being an alienating factor—actually enhanced the objectivity of its decisions.

A host of critics disagreed with JCPC's decisions on key constitutional issues, however. They saw the JCPC's interpretations of the British North America Act as contrary to the vision of the Canadian Confederation's founding fathers. It was thought that JCPC judges were unduly swayed by the counsel appearing before them due to the judges' lack of personal experience with federal state affairs that left them unable to critically evaluate the quality of legal arguments presented to them.[22] Judges such as Lord Watson and Lord Haldane, who adjudicated several Canadian constitutional cases, were caricatured as bungling intruders who, either through malevolence, stupidity, or inefficiency, channelled Canadian development away from the centralized federal system that had been wisely created by the founding fathers.[23] Opponents of the JCPC also stressed that the adjudication of Canadian appeals by a court manned largely by United Kingdom judges was 'repugnant to Dominion sovereignty'.[24]

Such views were not limited to the dominions. Commenting on the JCPC and the need for a more representative Imperial Court of Appeal, the Scottish legal scholar Arthur Keith wrote in 1912:

> It is idle to deny that the taking of appeals to the Privy Council is a mark of inferior status and partial servitude.... The matter is essentially one of national feeling and status. The existence of a true Imperial Court would remove all difficulty on this score, while the maintenance of the present position is just and proper as long as the Dominions desire to remain dependencies. But to talk of free and autonomous nations and equal partners in the Empire under these circumstances is childish folly.[25]

[21] Alan C. Cairns, 'The Judicial Committee and its Critics' (1971) 4(3) *Canadian Journal of Political Science* 301.

[22] de P Wright, 'The Judicial Committee of the Privy Council', 368.

[23] Cairns, 'The Judicial Committee and its Critics', 301.

[24] W. R. Lederman, 'Notes on Recent Canadian Constitutional Developments' (1950) 32(3/4) *Journal of Comparative Legislation and International Law* 74.

[25] Arthur Berriedale Keith, *Responsible Government in the Dominions Vol 2* (Oxford: The Clarendon Press, 1912) 1102–4.

By the 1920s, the question of colonial appeals to the JCPC had become a key issue in British imperial politics. At the Imperial Conference of 1926, much attention was devoted to the problem of the relation between the emerging independence of the dominions and their continuing constitutional status as colonial dependencies. The conference ended with a declaration that 'it was no part of the policy of His Majesty's government that questions affecting judicial appeals should be determined otherwise than in accordance with the wishes of the part of the Empire primarily affected'.[26] In 1931, this principle was enacted into law in the Statute of Westminster, which effectively made it possible for dominions to abolish appeal to the JCPC. Canada subsequently abolished the right of appeal in criminal cases in 1933 and in all appeals in 1949.[27]

Following the Statute of Westminster, discussions about the abolition of Privy Council appeals in the colonies became more prominent during negotiations for the dismantling of the British Empire. With independence approaching, demands for an end to appeals amplified in the colonies. Associated with concerns about the lack of representation on the JCPC were longstanding complaints about the disconnect between the English judges who adjudicated colonial appeals in the comfort of Westminster, and the varied realities of life in the outposts of the Empire. A frequent complaint was that appeals to the JCPC involved inordinate expense and delay due to distance, and that the JCPC was a rich man's court where poorer litigants could not afford to go.

Even in the face of these criticisms, some, in both colony and metropole, were unconvinced of the need for radical changes to the composition or procedures of the JCPC. They argued for the continued relevance of the JCPC in the transitioning Empire to Commonwealth. Writing in 1923, Lord Haldane sought to dispel the notion of the JCPC's illegitimacy and inefficacy allegedly caused by physical distance from the colonies. 'The Judicial Committee of the Privy Council,' he argued, is 'not a body, strictly speaking, with any location.'

> The Sovereign is everywhere throughout the Empire in the contemplation of the law. He may as well sit in Dublin, or at Ottawa, or in South Africa, or in Australia, or in India as he may sit here, and it is only for convenience, and because we have a Court, and because the members of the Privy Council are conveniently here that we do sit here; but the Privy Councillors from the Dominions may be summoned to sit with us, and then we sit as an Imperial Court which represents the Empire, and not any particular part of it.[28]

Expressing a similar opinion on the question of JCPC procedures, Sir George Rankin, a former Chief Justice of Bengal and JCPC judge, noted that though the JCPC may sit in a Committee room in the House of Lords or in a Law Court in the Strand, its judges were cognizant of the need for judicial input from the colonies,

[26] David Swinfen, *Imperial Appeal: The Debate on the Appeal to the Privy Council, 1833–1986* (Manchester: Manchester University Press, 1987) 102.

[27] William S. Livingston, 'Abolition of Appeals from Canadian Courts to the Privy Council' (1950) 16(1) *Harvard Law Review* 107.

[28] (1923) 57 *The Irish Law Times and Solicitors' Journal* 173. Also see *Hull and Co. v McKenna* [1926] IR 402 at 404 (PC).

which they ensured through time-tested procedures.[29] Difficult colonial cases had warranted JCPC judges to use judicial assessors and hear appeals in the colony of origin; such as the Indian Division of the Committee, which occasionally heard appeals in India.[30]

Beyond the question of distance and representation, however, was also the general perception that the JCPC, regardless of the quality of judges that staffed its bench, was ultimately a second-class court. It was, after all, an appellate court constituted exclusively to adjudicate colonial cases; an Imperial Court situated in the imperial centre but with limited jurisdiction over metropolitan cases. The reluctance of British officials to contemplate having United Kingdom appeals heard by anyone else other than the House of Lords was taken as evidence that, with the Privy Council, the dominions and colonies were being subjected to an inferior court to which Britain did not subject her own citizens. Critics often made reference to the landmark case of *London Joint Stock Bank v McMillan*, in which it was held that the decisions of the JCPC were not theoretically binding in English courts, even if they may be deemed influential.[31]

Dominion politicians also drew attention to key procedural differences between the judicial work of the House of Lords and the Privy Council. The judgments of the House of Lords took immediate effect, while JCPC 'judgments' were, in fact, merely recommendations, upon which the Crown made the final decision in an Order in Council. This gave rise to doubts about the character of the Judicial Committee as a true court. The view that the JCPC was an inferior adjudicatory body designed for the colonies persisted in spite of assurances by officials in Whitehall that the Judicial Committee was indeed a court, and that the King in Council had no constitutional power to interfere in any way with its judgments.[32]

The image of the JCPC as a court for the colonial underclass was not easily shaken. If the JCPC was good enough for colonial subjects, why was it not also considered good enough for British citizens? This became a key argument against the retention of the right to JCPC appeals in the colonies. It echoed a sentiment expressed several years earlier by Lord Haldane who opposed the exclusion of United Kingdom from the jurisdiction of the JCPC: 'Though the Privy Council is considered good enough for the colonies, it is not allowed in Great Britain and Ireland to be good enough for us.'[33] Perhaps more than any other critiques of the JCPC, the view that the JCPC dispensed 'selective and inferior justice' most undermined the public's perception of its relevance and legitimacy in Africa.[34] At a time when the assertion of national sovereignty and claims about the 'equality of

[29] Visheshwar Kulshreshtha, *Landmarks in Indian Legal History and Constitutional History* (Lucknow: Eastern Book Co., 1960) 216.

[30] George Rankin, 'The Judicial Committee of the Privy Council' (1930) 7(2) *Cambridge Law Journal* 11–12.

[31] [1918] AC 777. For an analysis of this case, see H. H. Marshall, 'The Binding Effect of Decisions of the Judicial Committee of the Privy Council' (1968) 17(3) *International and Comparative Law Quarterly* 744.

[32] Kenneth Roberts-Wray, 16 May 1955, NAUK, CO/1026/114.

[33] Hansard, House of Commons, Vol 83 c 101, 14 May 1900.

[34] *West African Pilot* (2 July 1963) 6.

men and nations' were key messages of nationalist anti-colonial politicians, the idea of subjecting citizens of newly independent nations to 'selective and inferior justice' struck a chord in the colonies, and was strongly rejected.

It is noteworthy that much of the discussion over colonial representation centred on the inclusion of 'colonial judges'—white judges of European ancestry rather than indigenous judges from the 'tropical colonies'. In the early debates, there was very little talk of indigenous African representation on the Privy Council or on the JCPC. Apart from evident colonial racial barriers, this trend may be attributed to the absence of qualified indigenous legal personnel who could be called upon for high-profile judicial responsibilities in the JCPC. Moreover, British officials saw the inclusion of European colonial judges as a useful step in bringing the JCPC closer to colonial subjects. Making this case, the Secretary of State for the Colonies, Alan Lennox-Boyd, stated:

> The appointment of serving or retired colonial judges to the Judicial Committee of the Privy Council will have political value in the long run, in that members of the legal profession in the territories advancing towards self-government would probably look with more favour upon appeals to the Privy Council known to include such members.[35]

The appointment of more colonial judges to the JCPC between 1930 and 1950 did not, however, dampen the demands for indigenous representation on the JCPC bench. Such demands were occasioned by the significant changes in the legal and judicial landscape of British Africa from the 1930s onwards. The small but active group of Western-trained African lawyers who began to play an important role in the colonial legal system demanded greater inclusion in the colonial judiciary. The fact that these indigenous lawyers were not seriously considered as candidates for the JCPC bench until the 1960s, had more to do with the racial restriction imposed on non-white judges than with anything else. Their eventual engagement in the discussions about reforming the JCPC would foreshadow nationalist demands for the abolition of JCPC appeals in South Africa.

South Africa: The *Pearl Assurance* Case

In South Africa, the first legal initiative to abolish appeals to the Privy Council began with the enactment of the South Africa Act of 1909, which abolished the right of appeal from provincial courts, even as it allowed for appeal from the Supreme Court by special leave of the Privy Council.[36] The restriction on JCPC appeals was extended in 1920, when legislation was introduced granting citizens leave to appeal in civil cases. This legislation raised serious constitutional questions. It marked the culmination of a long history of constitutional challenges to the

[35] A. Lennox-Boyd to Viscount Kilmuir, Confidential Dispatch, 24 June 1955, NAUK, CO1026/144 and Proposals for the Secretary of State to Consider Appointment of Retired Colonial Judges to the Judicial Committee of the Privy Council, NAUK, CO 1026/144.

[36] Anonymous, 'Decline of the Judicial Committee of the Privy Council. Current Status of Appeals from the British Dominions' (1947) 60(7) *Harvard Law Review* 1140.

jurisdiction of the JCPC in the country, arising mainly from the assumption that the English judges sitting on the Committee were ill-equipped to adjudicate cases based on the Roman-Dutch law traditions of the country. Appeals from South Africa to the JCPC, which were never significant, declined considerably after 1920. Between 1920 and1933, there were only ten Privy Council appeals from South Africa, none of them particularly significant.[37] Most of these were commercial cases involving Afrikaners or Europeans settlers.

One such case, *Pearl Assurance Co. Ltd v Government of the Union of South Africa*, appeared before the JCPC in 1934. It provided the main impetus for the abolition of appeal in South Africa.[38] The case concerned questions regarding the amount of damages recoverable on a breach of contract under Roman-Dutch law and the onus of proof as to the amount of damage suffered. Before this case, it had been the established practice of the JCPC to grant a leave of appeal for South African cases only in far-reaching questions of law or on matters of dominant public importance. In *Pearl Assurance* however, the JCPC departed from this principle by granting leave on a question relating to the law of contract. This raised the prospects of almost unrestricted appeals to the JCPC. It also caused concern among local politicians over what was considered the unilateral expansion of JCPC jurisdiction in the country, which was then expressed in the South African parliament in 1935, when a motion was raised for the abolition of appeals to the Privy Council.[39]

Apart from criticism of the extension of the JCPC's jurisdiction to matters relating to private law, there was also opposition to the decision itself, which effectively overruled the judgment of the Supreme Court of South Africa. Some critics of the JCPC decision suggested that the judges of the Committee were charged with an impossible task of applying a system of law, with which they were only slightly acquainted.[40] This case brought to a head the longstanding disquiet among nationalist politicians over JCPC appeals, and gave strength to the movement for abolition.

Another argument for abolition was the feeling that the existence of the right of appeal to the Privy Council was inconsistent with the sovereign independent status of the Union of South Africa. The Nationalist Party in South Africa, which was at the forefront of the calls to abolish the right of appeal to the Privy Council, frequently pointed to the inequities inherent in the appeals process that, apart from being 'an undeserved slur' on South African judges, 'placed a powerful weapon in the hands of rich litigants'.[41]

The 'abolitionists', as the advocates for ending the JCPC appeals came to be known in the local press, pointed to the unsatisfactory nature of many decisions by the Privy Council composed of men unlearned in the Roman-Dutch law.[42] The case that came up most frequently was the 1930 case of *Estate Welsford v Estate*

[37] T. E. Water to Hertzog, 15 June 1933, NASAP, BLO 88 PS 3/3, 1933–1937.

[38] [1934] AC 570 at 579.

[39] Privy Council Acts: Imperial: Judicial Committee, NASAP, GG 1845 53/592.

[40] D. Malan, 19 January 1937, NASAP, GG 1845 53/592.

[41] Appeals to the Privy Council, Office of the Governor General, NASAP, GG 1845 53/592.

[42] Privy Council Acts: Imperial: Judicial Committee, NASAP, GG 1845 53/592.

Wright. There, the presiding judge—a well-known Roman-Dutch law authority—was bound to follow an earlier judgment of the Privy Council in a Roman-Dutch question of law, even though he was convinced that the judgment was not in accordance with Roman-Dutch law.[43]

Nationalist politicians claimed it was anomalous for a sovereign independent state to subject its own tribunals to the overruling jurisdiction of a court of another state over whose constitution it has no control. They contended that the Appellate Division of South African Supreme Court was the most suitable and most competent court to give judgment in cases relating to the South African law.[44] Proponents of the retention of JCPC appeal, mainly members of the pro-British Dominion Party, countered that calls for the abolition of the right of appeal related to anti-British nationalist politics rather than to the jurisprudence of the JCPC.[45] They pointed out that appeals to the Privy Council from the Union of South Africa had been rare, and that decisions of the JCPC had no demonstrable prejudicial effect on the administration of justice in the country.[46]

In the end, nationalists opposed to the retention of the right to Privy Council appeals won the argument. South African appeals to the JCPC were finally abolished in 1950 with the enactment of the Privy Council Appeals Act. The Act provided that there would be no future appeal to the King in Council, from any judgment or order of any court in the Union of South Africa or South-West Africa.[47] This, however, did not foreclose the continued efforts to rehabilitate the JCPC and assert its continued relevance in the transition from Empire to Commonwealth.

Salvaging the JCPC: A Peripatetic Commonwealth Court

Scholars of the JCPC have suggested that opposition to the jurisdiction of the Privy Council in Dominion and Commonwealth appeals was political rather than juridical.[48] Dissatisfaction with JCPC decisions fuelled longstanding legal and juridical opposition to the system of appeals. In his pioneering study of the debate over the abolition of Privy Council appeals, David Swinfen argued that the opposition to JCPC jurisdiction in colonial appeals was fundamentally founded on political grounds.[49] Opposition to the jurisdiction of the Privy Council was linked first with sovereigntist demands in the Dominions, and later with anti-colonial movements in Asia and Africa. The shrinking of JCPC jurisdiction

[43] *Estate Welsford v Estate Wright* [1930] Orange Free State Provincial Division 162 at 166, Appeals to the Privy Council, Internal Memorandum, Office of the Governor General in NASAP GG 1845 53/592.

[44] Appeals to the Privy Council, Office of the Governor General, NASAP, GG 1845 53/592.

[45] Edward Iwi, A Plea for an Imperial Council and Judicial Committee, 18 November 1937, NASAP, BLO 88 PS12/2/24.

[46] Appeals to the Privy Council, Internal Memorandum, Office of the Governor General, NASAP, GG 1845 53/592.

[47] Marshall, 'The Judicial Committee of the Privy Council', 705–6.

[48] Swinfen, *Imperial Appeal*, 12.

[49] Swinfen, *Imperial Appeal*, 12.

revolved around questions of sovereignty and the 'republican drift' of newly independent nations more than anything else.

While the evidence in this book largely supports this argument, additional underlying factors equally drove the political impulses behind the abolition of JCPC jurisdiction. Firstly, is not always possible to clearly distinguish political from juridical impulses, since juridical arguments for abolition of JCPC appeals were often shaped by political calculations. Arguments for judicial autonomy, for example, could not be entirely separated from demands for executive and legislative independence. Moreover, the core set of political arguments against the retention of JCPC appeals in Africa pivoted on the question of 'colonial alienation', which arose from the historically unrepresentative composition of the JCPC.

In many parts of British Africa, concern about judicial representation began with local courts. As national consciousness grew after World War I and many political cases came before the courts, the absence of Africans in the colonial judiciary looked oppressive to local elites, and created a feeling of helplessness. In the 1920s, Nigeria and the Gold Coast vigorously campaigned for a larger number of indigenous African lawyers to be appointed as judges and magistrates in the colonial courts.[50] The expectation was that some of these judges would gain appointments to the regional appeal courts and even the Privy Council. Although Africans were appointed to the lower ranks of the colonial judiciary mainly as magistrates and heads of native courts, the scope of these appointments did not meet the expectations of the local elites. By the 1940s, criticisms of the unrepresentative composition of the colonial and imperial judiciaries had grown more intense.

In the colonies, opinion on the retention or abolition of JCPC appeals was divided partly along professional lines. For the most part, the JCPC enjoyed high regard among indigenous elites in the legal profession as a tribunal composed of judges of ability and experience. There was also an appreciation of the quality of JCPC judgements that, some believed, centred on the 'the pursuit of justice with common sense and a distaste for mere technicalities'.[51] One Nigerian politician described the JCPC as a source of comfort to many, and an impartial arbiter of justice in the Commonwealth.[52] These views of the JCPC were, however, not widely shared. Many within the emergent class of Western-educated political elites remained critical of the JCPC.

In the African debates, three main arguments against the continuation of appeals were brought forward. First, the JCPC was regarded as a United Kingdom Court, whose continued jurisdiction was out of harmony with the status of independence. It was frequently pointed out that the Committee sits in far-away London, and, although some of its members were from other Commonwealth countries, none were indigenous African judges. The second argument was that the JCPC was out

[50] Omoniyi Adewoye, *The Judicial System in Southern Nigeria, 1854–1954: Law and Justice in a Dependency* (Atlantic Highlands, NJ: Humanities Press, 1977) 247.

[51] West African Court of Appeal Judgments, National Archives of Nigeria, Ibadan (hereinafter NANI) CSO 33115, Vol 1.

[52] Anthony Enahoro, *Fugitive Offender* (London: Cassell, 1965) 255.

of direct contact with local conditions in Africa as a result of its physical and jurisdictional distance. Unlike the practice in Indian appeals, for example, the adjudication of African cases drew little on the expertise of local assessors and judges. There was also criticism of the JCPC's inclination towards imperial legal uniformity—the tendency to apply the law of one country too readily to another country, largely disregarding local differences. The third main argument concerned the relevance of the JCPC in the post-Second World War period and the dwindling number of appeals from African jurisdictions.[53]

By the 1950s, the issue of colonial representations and the future of the JCPC had become a subject of growing public and parliamentary interest in Britain itself. The general sentiment was that the British government had not done enough to create an inclusive and representative JCPC, reflective of the transition from Empire to Commonwealth. In 1955, member of parliament Graham Page raised one of the many key questions:

> Why, when the Registrar of the Privy Council asks the Lord Chancellor's Department to nominate the Board for Hearing an appeal, is a commonwealth or Colonial Judge never nominated? Is there some difficulty about paying for their services? It really is little wonder that India, South Africa, Canada and Pakistan have broken away from this appellate jurisdiction. However brilliant our judges may be, one can understand the injury to political prestige which such nations would feel that they suffer in continuing to submit appeals to an entirely United Kingdom court... It is a trend that we need not continue if the former colonies now gaining their independence, could feel while they are still colonies that the Judicial Committee is *their* court that *their* judges are members of it.[54]

Graham Page went on to stress the continued relevance of the JCPC as an important pillar in the structure of the Commonwealth that had to be strengthened and adapted to meet modern standards. He was particularly critical of the practice of drawing members of the JCPC almost entirely from the ranks of high judicial officers in the United Kingdom. In his view more had to be done to dispel the notion—prevalent especially in the colonies—that the JCPC was a committee of 'rather old gentlemen sitting in Whitehall'.[55]

The calls for reform of the JCPC were in line with what many British officials considered a necessary strategic shift from sustaining an Empire that was clearly in decline to maintaining British influence in the emergent Commonwealth. By bringing about an orderly transfer of power, the government could secure an important role for Britain in the future of the ex-colonies. A strong and reformed JCPC or its successor was thought crucial to maintaining a strong union within the new Commonwealth of Nations.[56] Discussions within British officialdom about the inclusion of indigenous judges and the reforming of the JCPC were shaped by this shift in strategic policy. The goal was to stem the anticipated tide of abolition of JCPC jurisdiction as several African colonies were gaining independence.

[53] Kenneth Roberts-Wray, *Commonwealth and Colonial Law* (London: Stevens, 1966) 461.
[54] Graham Page, 29 June 1956, NAUK, CO/1026/114. Original emphasis.
[55] Graham Page, 29 June 1956, NAUK, CO/1026/114.
[56] A. Lennox-Boyd to Viscount Kilmuir, 24 June 1955, NAUK, CO 1026/114.

Throughout the period of decolonization in the 1950s and 1960s, British policy consistently favoured the retention of the Privy Council appellate system.[57] This was because it afforded an opportunity for Britain to exercise control over Empire-Commonwealth affairs. In the 1960s, this goal partly informed discussions of the establishment of the Commonwealth Court of Appeal as a successor institution to the JCPC. Like the JCPC, the new Commonwealth Court of Appeal would be a bastion for maintaining judicial standards in the Commonwealth. The old concept of imperial responsibility had taken on a new form. British officials came to believe that the continuation of the right of appeal from courts in the countries of the new Commonwealth to the Judicial Committee or to another new Commonwealth Court of Appeal would most effectively safeguard human rights and civil liberties in these countries. For a period of time discussions also revolved around a Commonwealth Bill of Rights, to be underwritten by the reformed appellate system.[58]

One of the suggested reforms to keep the JCPC relevant in an era of decolonization was the proposal to transform the Judicial Committee—in its general Commonwealth functions—into a new peripatetic or itinerant Commonwealth Court, with a membership more truly representative of the countries within its jurisdiction.[59] The court would be composed of Commonwealth judges who would hear and determine appeals from the courts of all Commonwealth countries, including the United Kingdom. Unlike the JCPC, the new court would cease to be closely identified with the United Kingdom, and would become more closely acquainted with local conditions. The anticipated increase in the number of appeals coming to the new Commonwealth Court would require the court to sit in multiple divisions and in multiple locations. These far-reaching changes, some officials thought, would address longstanding discontent about the JCPCs composition in the colonies. The fact that the proposed Commonwealth Court would have jurisdiction also over the United Kingdom would remove one of the major impediments to the legitimacy of the JCPC in the colonies—the notion that it was a second-class court with jurisdiction over colonial subjects but not the citizens of the United Kingdom.[60]

The proposal for a Commonwealth Court represented the revival of an old idea and marked the culmination of British attempts to regain some initiative in the matter of Commonwealth appeals. Addressing the Scottish Law Society in Edinburgh in 1900, Lord Haldane, then a practising lawyer and Queen's Counsel, spoke in glowing terms about the value of the right of appeal to the Privy Council; he perceived it as the most important aspect of the 'silken bonds' that held the British Empire together. Haldane then proposed a grandiose scheme to amalgamate the House of Lords and the JCPC into one great Imperial Appellate Tribunal in ways that foreshadowed the later calls for a Commonwealth Court of Appeal.[61]

[57] K. Roberts-Wray, Confidential Despatch, 4 July 1955, NAUK, CO 1026/114.
[58] Swinfen, *Imperial Appeal*, 12; Appeals to the Privy Council: Kenya in NAUK, DO 161/247.
[59] K. Roberts-Wray, Confidential Despatch, 4 July 1955, NAUK, CO 1026/114.
[60] Roberts-Wray, *Commonwealth and Colonial Law*, 461.
[61] Jean Graham Hall and Douglas F. Martin, *Haldane: Statesman, Lawyer, Philosopher* (London: Barry Rose Law Publishers, 1996) 176.

Another proponent of the Commonwealth Court of Appeal was the JCPC judge, Lord Normand. Writing in 1950, he acknowledged that the JCPC bench still had not been rendered representative enough of the Empire, and continued to lack judges from the colonies. 'There has been no thorough-going attempt,' he stated, 'to draw into the service of the Judicial Committee the wealth of legal experience and ability available within the Empire, or to make it truly representative of the King's dominions as a whole.'[62] To address this, Normand proposed transforming the JCPC into a peripatetic court that could sit anywhere within the Empire-Commonwealth. The JCPC didn't have to be fixed in Whitehall, but instead could sit in any part of the dominions as the convenience of the King's subjects may require.[63]

Similar proposals for a 'travelling Privy Council' were put forward by the Lord Chancellor Lord Simon. The travelling JCPC would go on circuit across the Empire-Commonwealth, and would accord a prominent place to colonial judges. Responding to these proposals, the president of the Eastern African Court of Appeal, Sir Barclay Nihill, suggested that anyone selected to represent the colonies should have experience of appellate work in Africa, given the increasing number of appeals from East Africa. He argued that the judicial needs of Africa should be a paramount consideration in any plans for reforming or transforming the JCPC.[64]

In making the case for the inclusion of East African judges on a reformed JCPC, Sir Nihill drew attention to the increased number of criminal and civil appeals from East African territories. Many of these cases involved complex questions of Hindu law, Islamic law, and native custom. Although the judges of the JCPC, 'with their great knowledge and experience', were equipped to deal with such cases, Nihill thought that assistance from judges with first-hand experience of local conditions would be beneficial. The inclusion of colonial judges would also serve to bolster the prestige of the colonial judiciary, and assure parties to an appeal that facts, motives, and circumstances brought out in the appeal would be readily understood in their local context.[65]

Although the calls for a peripatetic JCPC became especially strident in the 1950s, similar proposals had been made earlier. Politicians and judicial officers in the dominions expressed their longstanding demands for the JCPC to go on circuit to the great cities of the Empire, including Ottawa, Delhi, Sydney, and Wellington, instead of remaining in London. In a speech to the Canadian Bar Association in 1935, Justice (later Lord) Maugham persuasively made the case for a circuit-based JCPC comprised of dominion and colonial judges. He argued that the practical difficulties of the JCPC's rotations had been reduced with the technological advances in air travel and civil aviation. Two decades later, John Wyatt, the Attorney General for Kenya, made the exact same argument in a memorandum to the Colonial Office, suggesting the inclusion of the African cities of Lagos,

62 Cowen, 'Notes on Constitutional Development in the Commonwealth', 74.
63 Cowen, 'Notes on Constitutional Development in the Commonwealth', 74.
64 J. B. H. Nihill, Outward Despatch, 7 January 1955, NAUK, CO/1026/114.
65 J. B. H. Nihill to K. Roberts-Wray, 20 May 1955, NAUK, CO/1026/114.

Nairobi, and Salisbury in the JCPC circuit.[66] This, he argued, would serve two purposes. First, it would raise the prestige of the judiciary and the law in the colonies generally, and secondly it would be of educational value to the members of the local bar to be able to appear before the Lordships of the JCPC and see eminent judges in action.[67]

By the end of the 1950s, the debates seem to have diverged from reforming the JCPC to constituting a successor, the Commonwealth Court of Appeal. A key impetus in the creation of the Commonwealth Court of Appeal was the notion that it would be more acceptable for such a tribunal to adjudicate constitutional disputes—this incapacity had been one of the Achilles' heels of the JCPC. The hope was that the new court might become a forum for the settlement of justiciable disputes between the members of the expanded Commonwealth of Nations. Advocates of these changes drew an analogy with the newly established International Court of Justice in The Hague.[68]

Even proponents of a peripatetic JCPC or the Commonwealth Court of Appeal recognized the shortcomings of such a vision, however. They were apprehensive about the procedures for setting up such a court and staffing its bench. Many feared that allocating seats on the bench to particular countries, especially the newly independent ex-colonies, would compromise the high judicial standards historically maintained by the JCPC. The dominant view was that the ability of a country to provide judges of the requisite calibre should not be contingent on the size or importance of that country, but rather on the quality of its judicial establishment and the pool of judicial officers. It was also thought that a 'judicial circuit', which would involve extensive air travel and changes of climate, would be arduous for older, more experienced judges. Only 'younger men', with invariably less experience, would be left to undertake the work. These factors would restrict the selection of judges, and potentially impact the quality of the court as a result. Additionally, circuit travel and subsistence costs would make the court's operation extremely expensive. One critic also doubted whether countries, especially the newly independent states with limited judicial resources, would even agree to release their best judges for long periods of time to serve the Commonwealth.[69]

Another question raised was whether the countries visited on circuit by the court would have input in creating the panel of visiting judges. Some worried that the newly independent countries—eager to assert their political and judicial autonomy—might insist on having greater influence in the composition of visiting judges to invidious effect. Additionally, they feared it might prove difficult to secure the high standard of advocacy required for a supranational appellate court created on the model of the historic JCPC.

In the end, none of these arguments mattered. Many indigenous elites in the colonies and in the newly independent ex-colonies increasingly saw the JCPC as an

[66] John Watt, 21 April 1955, NAUK, CO/1026/114.

[67] J. Hyatt, 21 February 1955, NAUK, CO/1026/114.

[68] B. T Gilmore to J. Chadwick, 8 July 1965, NAUK, CO 1026/114.

[69] Roberts-Wray, *Commonwealth and Colonial Law*, 461.

anachronistic survivor from the days of the Empire. Indeed, even the idea of replacing the JCPC with a peripatetic Commonwealth Court of Appeal was considered to be a 'doomed undertaking' that had come at least half a century too late.[70] Although in the 1950s and 1960s interest in a revamped British Commonwealth bore fruit with the creation of the Commonwealth Secretariat and various other forms of intra-Commonwealth cooperation, the Commonwealth Court of Appeal proved to be a broadly unattractive idea.[71] In many African colonies, nationalist politicians continued to link the proposals for a new Commonwealth Court to the role of the JCPC in the colonial context and to the question of national sovereignty. Nevertheless, a small minority of legal professionals continued to envision a reformed and relevant JCPC or a successor institution in independent former colonies.

Independence and the Abolition of Appeals

In the era of African decolonization, official and public opinion over whether or not to retain the practice of appeals to the JCPC broke down along both ideological and professional lines. Senior members of the local Bar as well as some conservative politicians favoured an arrangement, where appeals could continue to a reformed and more representative JCPC after the attainment of independence. In contrast, indigenous nationalist politicians at the forefront of the anti-colonial movement sought a complete break from the Privy Council and the JCPC upon the attainment of independence. The Malawian nationalist politician, Kamuzu Banda, who became Prime Minster of the country at independence, spearheaded a vigorous campaign against the retention of JCPC jurisdiction in the country. He declared before the Malawian parliament in 1965: 'We are now an independent country and I see no need for having our cases reviewed outside our country 6000 miles away. It is an infringement on our sovereignty.'[72]

Tensions between indigenous legal professionals and nationalist elites over the role of the JCPC in independent countries arose frequently during the constitutional negotiations leading up to their political independence. These tensions were not unique to African colonies. In the discussions about the abolition of the right to Privy Council appeal in India, for example, several prominent lawyers extolled the JCPC, arguing for its continued relevance in independent India. The JCPC, one legal scholar argued, had been a great unifying force in the judicial administration of India. At a time when there were no Indian judges in the High Courts and the number of Indian lawyers was very limited, the JCPC had 'unravelled the mysteries of Hindu Law, enunciated the principles of Mohammedan Law and formulated with clarity the customs which were prevalent in the country with an absolutely detached mind'. Admittedly there had been occasional lapses and

[70] S. Voigt, et al, 'Improving Credibility by Delegating Judicial Competence: The Case of the Judicial Committee of the Privy Council' (2007) 82(2) *Journal of Development Economics* 365.

[71] Swinfen, *Imperial Appeal*, 22:.

[72] *The Times* (14 April 1965) 6.

mistakes, but the JCPC undeniably had been a great unifying factor and a 'bastion of those fundamental principles of law on which the administration of justice is based'.[73]

Even so, it must be pointed out that this nostalgia for the JCPC in India was not as evident in Britain's African colonies. This was probably because the Indian experience with the JCPC was very different from Africa. While there were no indigenous African judges on the JCPC bench until the 1960s, Indian appeals were distinctive in that Indian judges had been occasional members of the Board since 1909. Such judges also sat both as full members of the bench and as assessors, advising the Board on the disposition of appeals from India. To a certain degree this arrangement in India helped to overcome the common criticism that the Committee lacked the expertise to hear appeals from the colonies.[74]

The cases of Ghana, Nigeria, and Kenya demonstrate the practical implications of the debate surrounding the retention or abolition of the right to JCPC appeal as it played out in Africa in the decolonization period. In Ghana, it was evident from the early constitutional negotiations between British officials and indigenous politicians that the decline of JCPC jurisdiction was inevitable. Three years after independence was granted, the Constituent Assembly Act of 1960 was enacted, providing that no legal appeals could lie to any court outside Ghana. No reason for this provision was given during the parliamentary debates on the Bill; nevertheless, it is safe to assume that the decision was driven by the same nationalist and sovereigntist impulses that had shaped the earlier decision to abolish JCPC jurisdiction in the dominions. The President of the newly independent Ghana, Kwame Nkrumah, was an ardent socialist-leaning nationalist and pan-Africanist who was averse to maintaining colonial institutional linkages. He repudiated such links as emblematic of 'neo-colonialism', a term he coined to describe the continued socio-economic and political control that, as he believed, could be exercised by former European colonial powers to perpetuate economic subordination and cultural assimilation of formerly colonized peoples.[75]

Speaking at the Ghana Law School a few years after independence, Nkrumah called for a legal system that served the needs of an independent and developing country. Such a legal system would mark a departure from the old colonial system, as he illustrated by invoking the JCPC.

> In the old days, one case alone might go on appeal to the Privy Council two or even three times upon one or other aspect of the matter and perhaps take up to twelve years before a final decision was reached. In consequence, there was no certainty as to the legal position

[73] Marshall, 'The Judicial Committee of the Privy Council', 702.

[74] However, even in India criticisms were levelled against the JCPC for wanting to fossilize ancient practices on the one hand, and for being too readily dismissive of legitimate customary practices on the other. One Indian nationalist politician critiqued the Committee for presuming 'obsolete and uncivilized' many things under the personal law of the Hindus. See H. H. Marshall, 'The Judicial Committee of the Privy Council: A Waning Jurisdiction' (1964) 13(2) *International and Comparative Law Quarterly* 704.

[75] Kwame Nkrumah, *Neo-colonialism: The Last Stage of Imperialism* (New York: International Publishers, 1966).

and the revenues of the traditional authorities involved were wasted in the working of a fantastically cumbersome, expensive and dilatory process. . . . The land litigation of the past should serve as a warning of the disastrous consequences of attempting to apply English legal forms to issues for which they were never intended.[76]

In 1960, Nkrumah announced plans for a new constitution that would make Ghana a republic. He believed that the retention of the right to Privy Council appeal would be inconsistent with the newly acquired republican status of the country. The British and Ghanaian governments reached agreement on the matter of appeals registered in the Privy Council office before 1 July 1960, which would continue and eventually be disposed of.[77] This model of phased removal from JCPC jurisdiction was replicated in Kenya and Nigeria, where the question of the right to Privy Council appeals became intertwined with the politics of decolonization and the struggles for political ascendancy by nationalist elites in the post-colonial order.

Kenya: Property Rights and the Settler Factor

As in Ghana, independence in Kenya did not result in the immediate abolition of JCPC appeals. The Kenya Independence Act of 1963 and the Kenya Constitution provided for the continuation of Privy Council appeals, not to Her Majesty in Council, but specifically to the JCPC. These policies effectively made the JCPC a court constituted for Kenya.[78] Under this arrangement, applications for leave to appeal were made directly to the JCPC, rather than to the British Crown. JCPC decisions were conveyed in the form of an order granting the leave to appeal and directing the courts of origin (or the concerned local authorities) to take the necessary action. This process differed from the traditional Privy Council procedure, whereby appeals were addressed to the British Crown. Usually, JCPC decisions were conveyed as recommendations to the Crown who subsequently issued Orders in Council.[79] The new constitutional arrangement, which allowed for a modified role of the JCPC in independent Kenya, was the result of a tenuous political compromise between African nationalists desiring that the right to Privy Council appeal be abolished, and white settler politicians who were generally in favour of the retention of appeals. As Kenya moved towards independence, British officials were keen to ensure the retention of the right to Privy Council appeals. The push to retain JCPC jurisdiction proved more contentious in Kenya than in other African colonies.

A major concern of the British authorities in urging that the independent government of Kenya maintain appeals to the JCPC was the protection of British economic interests in the country. In the political and diplomatic discussions leading up to independence, such concerns were carefully couched in arguments highlighting the need to institute a judicial arrangement that would guarantee the

[76] Kwame Nkrumah, 'Ghana' (1962) 6(2) *Journal of African Law* 106.
[77] Marshall, 'The Judicial Committee of the Privy Council', 705–6.
[78] Section 6, Kenyan Independence Act in NAUK, DO 161/241.
[79] Appeals to the Privy Council from Nigeria, NAUK, DO 161/83.

constitutional protection of human rights in independent Kenya. At the Kenya Constitutional Conference in 1960, the Secretary of State for the Colonies stated that it was the 'firm view' of the British government that legal provisions should be included in Kenya's independence constitution, to provide for the judicial protection of human rights and for the protection of property rights specifically.[80]

The emphasis on property rights in the discussions about JCPC jurisdiction in independent Kenya reflects the deeper economic and political considerations that shaped decolonization in Kenya. As majority rule and the loss of European political power became increasingly inevitable, British officials and leaders of the European settler community refocused on setting up constitutional safeguards that would protect European economic interests in the independent state. Concerns in Britain over the property rights of European settlers in independent Kenya prompted assurances from the Colonial Office that the new Bill of Rights being proposed for the country would continue to guarantee that property could not be compulsorily acquired by the State, except for public purpose and upon the payment of full compensation. Assurances were also made that a right of appeal to the JCPC would continue to exist.[81]

British interests in maintaining appeals to the JCPC were also presented in terms of protecting minority rights, which, in this case, were mainly the rights of the white settler and Asian minorities. British officials expressed concern that the minorities in Kenya might feel 'dangerously uncovered' without the right of appeal to the JCPC. During the British parliamentary debate on Kenyan independence in 1962, one member of parliament concurred that it was 'wise in the home country of three races and many different tribes to include in the Constitution a Bill of Rights, enforceable by the courts, with an ultimate appeal to the Privy Council. . . '.[82]

There was, however, disagreement between the Commonwealth Relations Office and the Colonial Office about the ideal course of action in maintaining appeals to the JCPC after colonies became independent. The Commonwealth Relations Office favoured a bilateral agreement, which would represent a binding international agreement that could not be terminated unilaterally. On the contrary, the Colonial Office thought that the conclusion of such an agreement might later cause embarrassment in Kenyan-British political relations, if the Kenyan government wished to abolish appeals. In that case, the concurrence of the British government would be necessary before the agreement could be terminated and concurrence would appear to be sacrificing the interest of European and other minorities that the agreement was intended to safeguard. Officials at the Colonial Office also doubted that such an agreement could be effectively concluded at a time of tense political negotiations for independence. They preferred the entrenchment of constitutional provisions guaranteeing the retention of the right of appeal to the JCPC.[83]

[80] 'Kenyan Independence Conference', Confidential Memorandum, NAUK, CO 822/3113.

[81] Kenya: Appeals to the JCPC—Notes by Colonial Office, July 1963, NAUK, CO 822/3113.

[82] Lord Listowel, quoted in 'Kenya: Appeals to the JCPC—Notes by Colonial Office', July 1963, NAUK, CO 822/3113.

[83] Appeals to the Privy Council, Commonwealth Relation Office Memorandum, 18 March 1964, NAUK, DO 161/247.

In constitutional negotiations the Colonial Office pushed strongly to enact the right of appeal to the JCPC in the independence constitution, rather than through later bilateral agreements as Kenyan politicians had proposed. British officials considered the retention of appeals to the JCPC a crucial point that had to be addressed through constitutional rather than diplomatic means. Officials of the East African Department of the Colonial Office strongly advised against waiting until after the colonies became independent to negotiate the retention of JCPC jurisdiction in Kenya. The reason was, as one official put it, 'we cannot be sure that any agreements eventually concluded would cover all the cases in which we want appeals to lie to the Privy Council'.[84]

At the Lancaster House Conferences, in which Kenya's constitutional framework and independence were finalized, it was agreed that the scope of Privy Council appeals from Kenya be narrowed but not abolished entirely. Appeals from Kenya would continue to apply in specific classes of cases, including interpretation of the constitution and enforcement of the Bill of Rights.[85] Still, British officials harboured no illusions that the right of JCPC appeal would be retained once independence was achieved. It was evident in the constitutional negotiations that leading African politicians were opposed to the idea of retaining appeals.[86] The Minister of State for Colonial Affairs and Privy Councillor, Lord Colyton, saw the abolition of Privy Council appeals as inevitable under the circumstances. He acknowledged that the right of appeal to the Privy Council would likely disappear after independence, given the inclination of Kenyan politicians to move towards a republic upon attaining independence. He nevertheless stressed the need for Britain to do as much as possible to ensure that these rights were entrenched in the independent constitution.[87]

Apart from the political impulses against the retention of the JCPC's jurisdiction in Kenya, there were also legal arguments for abolition. As in South Africa, the main concern within the local political and legal establishment was that English judges who constituted the JCPC bench were ill-equipped to adjudicate complex matters arising from local customary, Islamic, and Hindu law. The case that was most frequently cited as proof of these shortcomings was the 1951 case of '*Bakhshuwen v Bakhshuwen*'.[88] The issue involved Islamic law, not English law, but the JCPC resolved that the courts of Kenya (and Zanzibar) were bound by a decision on the point given earlier in an appeal from India. In his judgment, Lord Simonds claimed that the decisions of the JCPC regarding the interpretation of Islamic law—heard on appeal from India—were not confined in their authority to India, but were binding also in the Court of Appeal for Eastern Africa. The alleged reason was that 'Islamic law as administered and applied in India is the same as that applied and administered in East Africa'.[89]

[84] 'Kenyan Independence Conference', Confidential Memorandum, NAUK, CO 822/3113.
[85] 'Kenyan Independence Conference', Confidential Memorandum, NAUK, CO 822/3113.
[86] R. M. Tesh, 7 January 1965, NAUK, DO 161/247.
[87] 'Kenyan Independence Conference', Confidential Memorandum, NAUK, CO 822/3113.
[88] *Fatuma binti Mohammed bin Bakhshuwen v Mohammed bin Salim Bakhshuwen* [1952] 1 AC 1.
[89] G. W. Bartholomew and J. A. Iliffe, 'Decisions' (1952) 1(3) *International and Comparative Law Quarterly* 392.

In Kenya, where the distinction between the practice of Islamic law in East Africa and in India had long been understood, officials voiced strong disagreement with this ruling.[90] The JCPC judgment was perceived as a simplistic and homogenous view of Islamic law, ignorant of the cultural contingencies and complexities of Kenya. Moreover, the Indian case that had provided the grounds for the JCPC decision in the Kenyan case was also severely criticized in India and eventually overruled by legislative act. Local critics of the Kenyan decision argued that the JCPC did not consider—and apparently did not have evidence for—the different course of historical development of Islamic law in India and East Africa. According to one contemporary legal scholar, the ruling in the *Bakhshuwen* case amounted to applying judicial precedent in such a way that extended the judicial errors of one country to make them law in another.[91]

Discontent over cases like these, where local opinion thought JCPC decisions were wrong or undesirable, combined with nationalist sentiments and prompted demands for judicial independence—specifically the abolition of the right to Privy Council appeals. In 1965, new legislation ending all Kenyan appeals to the Privy Council was introduced, bringing an end to a century of JCPC jurisdiction in that part of East Africa.

Nigeria: Judicial Activism and Power Politics

As in Kenya, demands for the abolition of Privy Council jurisdiction in Nigeria were partly driven by feelings of dissatisfaction with the JCPC's decisions in a number of high-profile cases. However, unlike in Kenya, where the debates centred more on disagreements with the judicial reasoning, the debate in Nigeria focused primarily on political issues. The JCPC's decisions in numerous constitutional cases just prior to or immediately after the country's independence were unpopular among local politicians and ruling elites. They thought the judgments were political or law-making in nature, and therefore considered them an interference with the constitutional structure of the country. In many ways, the debate over JCPC appeals in Nigeria mirrored the Canadian debate, where opponents of the JCPC saw its decisions as distortions and variations of the country's constitutional vision and its established institutions. In the end, in both Nigeria and Canada the jurisdiction of the JCPC was removed, mainly because the Committee had reached decisions that were out of step with the local political leadership.[92]

[90] For example, in the case of *Talibu bin Mwijaka v Executors of Siwa Haji*, Justice Hamilton stated: 'The Mahommedan law in East Africa has not been subjected to the same modifying influences as in India and remains the same as when the Min Haj was written in the sixth century of the Hejira'. *Talibu bin Mwijaka v Executors of Siwa Haji* [1907] EALR 33.

[91] Bartholomew and Iliffe, 'Decisions', 392.

[92] See *Attorney General for Ontario v Attorney General for Canada* [1937] AC 355 at 53. J. W. Katende and George W. Kanyeihamba, 'Legalism and Politics in East Africa: The Dilemma of the Court of Appeal for East Africa' (1973) 43 *Transition* 45.

Nigeria became independent of British rule in 1960; its republican constitution of 1963 made the Supreme Court of the Federation the highest appeal court for the country. This provision effectively ended the JCPC's jurisdiction in the country. The decision to abolish the rights of appeal to the JCPC was quite contentious, however. Significant difference of opinion regarding the abolition of JCPC appeals fractured Nigeria's political and legal establishment, particularly because some high-profile political cases were still before the Committee. The pivotal case was *Akintola v Adegbenro*[93]—a protracted and highly charged constitutional case involving two of the country's most influential politicians from opposing political parties.

The case revolved around the interpretation of sections of the Constitution of the Western Region of Nigeria, which provided that the Governor could only remove the Regional Premier from office when it 'appears to him' that the Premier had lost the support of the majority of House of Assembly members.[94] Exercising this power, the Governor of the Western Region in Nigeria had dismissed the Regional Premier on the basis of a letter signed by some opposition members of the regional parliament, who had stated they no longer supported the Premier.

The Regional High Court, which first heard the case, resolved that the Governor could not dismiss the Premier, except on the basis of an adverse vote against him taken on the floor of the House as dictated in British parliamentary convention. This decision was upheld on appeal by the Supreme Court of Nigeria. Upon appealing to the JCPC, however, the Supreme Court's decision was reversed. Their Lordships held that the Constitution of Western Nigeria was a written one, and thus its wording could not be overridden by the 'extraneous principles of other constitutions which were not explicitly incorporated into it', in this case, the British constitutional convention relating to the sovereign's right.[95] The broader legal principle enunciated was that, in cases where it is desired to incorporate a British rule or convention in the constitution of a Commonwealth country, it must be done expressly in order to have legal effect.

This decision overruled the Nigerian courts and was contrary to the wishes of the Nigerian Federal government. It was also poorly received by the ruling politicians who felt threatened by the removal of the Governor's power implied in the JCPC's decision.[96] Equally dissatisfied with the decision were those who assumed that conventions of the British Constitution, which had not been expressly excluded from the Nigerian Constitution, could be invoked in interpreting the provisions relating to a British-style parliamentary system of government adopted by the country at independence.[97] The result was a rushed amendment to the constitution that took away the power of the Regional Governor, and subsequently that of the

[93] [1963] AC 614.

[94] T. O. Elias, 'The Commonwealth in Africa' (1968) 31(3) *Modern Law Review* 291.

[95] [1963] AC 614.

[96] J. Chadwick, Internal Memorandum, Commonwealth Relations Office, 16 July 1963, NAUK, 1026/114.

[97] 'British Constitution' here refers to the set of laws and principles under which the United Kingdom is governed rather that a single constitutional document.

Head of State, to dismiss a Premier (or the Prime Minister) except on the basis of an adverse vote to that effect taken on the floor of the house of parliament.

Another incident that stoked opposition to the JCPC in Nigeria never even reached the JCPC. Soon after the *Adegbenro* case of 1963, two opposition politicians, Anthony Enahoro and Obafemi Awolowo, who were being prosecuted by the ruling government, explored the possibility of appealing to the Privy Council. Enahoro had been accused of treasonable felony and arrested in Britain at the request of the Nigerian government. He then initiated several legal appeals against his arrest, which, to the irritation of Nigerian authorities, delayed his extradition to Nigeria.

Several members of the British parliament who believed that Enahoro would not receive a fair trial in Nigeria also objected to his extradition. In order to reassure the sceptical members of parliament, the British Attorney General publicly stated that if Enahoro were tried and convicted in Nigeria, he could still seek justice by appealing to the JCPC.[98] This commentary generated heated discussions in Nigeria, where officials interpreted them as aspersions on the country's judicial system. In a letter to the JCPC judge, Lord Evershed, the Chief Judge of Nigeria stated:

> It seems to me a pity that members of the House of Commons have shown a remarkable degree of irresponsibility by their utterances and uncalled for criticisms of the Judiciary in Nigeria. We are very resentful indeed of what some of them have said, and although our Judiciary may not claim perfection—I wonder which is perfect—we at least can say that we are free from interference from the executive and we can claim to be independent. Much has been said to mar the friendly relations between your country and mine. Our Prime Minister, who as you know is a level headed man has taken all these much to heart, and he was telling me the other day that the sooner Nigeria declares itself a republic and opts out of the Judicial Committee of the [Privy Council], the better, after all that has been said.[99]

The Enahoro affair and the JCPC ruling in the *Adegbenro* case intensified the calls for the abolition of appeals to the JCPC, particularly from regional officials who saw the decision as a threat to regional political autonomy and to political stability. Michael Okpara, the Premier of Eastern Nigeria, stated that the JCPC's ruling 'had exposed the absurdity of an independent country like Nigeria leaving her destiny in the hands of foreigners 4,000 miles away to toy with irrespective of the demands of order and good government'. He described the Privy Council as a 'capricious anachronism which should be excised from Nigeria immediately'.[100]

The decision in the *Adegbenro* case also generated critical commentary in the local press. The dominant opinion was that it was no longer acceptable for Nigeria to have the decision of its Supreme Court annulled by a body of non-Nigerian jurists sitting in London.[101] The leading newspaper, the *West African Pilot*, editorialized that the *Adegbenro* case had demonstrated the failures of the 'Daniels of the British realm' and emphasized the need to discontinue all appeals to the Privy

[98] J. Chadwick, Internal Memorandum, Commonwealth Relations Office, 16 July 1963, NAUK, 1026/114.

[99] A. Ademola to R. Evershed, 3 April 1963, NAUK, DO 161/83.

[100] Legal Department: Questions on the Privy Council, NAUK, CO 1026/223.

[101] V. C. Marin to J. O. Moreton, 19 August 1963, NAUK, DO 161/83.

Council.[102] The *Morning Post* called for an immediate and complete break with further appeals from Nigerian Courts to the Privy Council in London. It argued that the JCPC decision undermined and ridiculed the country's status as a sovereign nation. It stated: 'We are proud of our judges and magistrates because they have shown transparent impartiality and fair play in the administration of justice. Why must we continue to flirt with the dangers of entrusting some of our affairs to foreigners whose real aims are often difficult to define?'[103]

At a time when British policy was to push for the retention of Privy Council appeals in the newly independent ex-colonies, these criticisms of the JCPC were of concern to British officials. In a memorandum to London in 1960, one British diplomat in Nigeria expressed his worry that senior government officials, who were normally well informed and balanced on legal matters, were unable to see that the Privy Council was acting as the ultimate court of appeal under the Nigerian Constitution and not as an instrument of the British government left over from the days of colonial rule.[104] Prominent among the government officials critical of the JCPC was the Attorney General and Minister for Justice, Taslim Elias, who put forward political and legal arguments against the retention of JCPC appeals.[105] Nevertheless, the British High Commissioner Robert Fowler, under instructions from the Colonial Office, unsuccessfully tried to convince the government to continue non-constitutional appeals to the Privy Council.[106]

Although the tide of official and public opinion was against the retention of Privy Council appeals, some officials held out hope that a reformed JCPC could still play a role in the country's judicial system. Some of these officials preferred the strengthening rather than weakening of the legal and judicial ties with Britain. British officials were quick to identify such pro-JCPC officials as local allies in the push to keep JCPC jurisdiction in Nigeria. Perhaps the most prominent of these local allies was the Nigerian judge Sir Adetokumbo Ademola.

A firm advocate of British legal traditions, Sir Adetokumbo was knighted by Queen Elizabeth in 1957, and was appointed the first Chief Judge of independent Nigeria in 1960. Shortly after his appointment as Chief Judge, he was appointed to the Privy Council and to the JCPC in 1963, as part of an attempted transition of the JCPC from an imperial institution to a Commonwealth Court. Sir Adetokumbo thereafter became a passionate supporter of the retention of the JCPC's jurisdiction in Nigeria and other Commonwealth countries.[107] He envisioned a reformed JCPC that would continue its historically key role in fostering legal uniformity and upholding a common standard of appellate justice within the Commonwealth. Writing to his British counterparts in 1963, Sir Adetokumbo stated that the 'great thing' he would like to see happen was for the JCPC to travel

102 *West African Pilot* (2 July 1963) 6.

103 *Morning Post* (27 August 1963) 3.

104 B. T. Gilmore to J. Chadwick, 8 July 1965, NAUK, 1026/114.

105 B. T. Gilmore to J. Chadwick, 8 July 1965, NAUK, 1026/114.

106 R. Fowler to J. Chadwick, NAUK, DO 161/83; Appeals to Privy Council from Nigeria, NAUK, CO 1026/223.

107 Legal Department: Questions on the Privy Council, NAUK, CO 1026/223.

to Commonwealth Countries that still retained the link.[108] Rather than being simply a Court of Appeal, the JCPC could metamorphose into a Commonwealth International Court to settle any disputes that might arise between members of the Commonwealth.[109]

Even as the officials of the Lord Chancellor's Office worked with supporters like Sir Adetokumbo to advocate for the retention of Privy Council appeals from Nigeria and other newly independent Commonwealth countries, their Lordships themselves seemed less keen about this course. After the JCPC's judgment in the *Adegbenro* case and the harshly critical reaction it generated in Nigeria, several JCPC judges expressed disinclination to continue adjudicating constitutional matters from independent jurisdiction.[110]

In the end, even the appointment of a sympathetic Nigerian judge, Sir Adetokumbo, could not change the tide of public opinion against the retention of Privy Council appeal. The right to Privy Council appeal from Nigeria was soon formally abolished with the adoption of the Republican Constitution in October 1963. The same year, one disillusioned British diplomat in Lagos noted that '[m]any people here are proud that Ademola has been appointed to the Privy Council but I fear that the changes that have been made so far have not been sufficient to persuade Nigerians that the JCPC is a Commonwealth institution'.[111] There was recognition that the reform of the JCPC had simply not kept up with the pace of change in the Commonwealth.[112]

The regional Imperial Courts of Appeal did not fare any better than the JCPC. The West African Court of Appeal disappeared by a process of erosion as the territories under its jurisdiction gained independence. Ghana severed ties with the court at independence in 1957, followed by Nigeria, Gambia, and Sierra Leone. The EACA was retained in Kenya, Tanzania, and Uganda under the auspices of the East African Community established by these countries at the time of their independence. Under this arrangement, the court was transformed into the East African Court of Appeal. The East African Community and the court were eventually abolished in 1977, partly due to internal disagreement about the scope of the court's jurisdiction in member countries. As with the JCPC, a key factor in the disintegration of the EACA were complaints over the unrepresentative and unbalanced composition of the court. Kenyan dominance of the court both at the bench and in the docket caused tension among the member counties, leading to the court's disintegration.[113]

108 Legal Department: Questions on the Privy Council, NAUK, CO 1026/223.

109 Appeals to the Privy Council from Nigeria, NAUK, DO 161/83.

110 N. Aspin, Confidential Memorandum, 31 July 1963, NAUK, CO 822/3113.

111 Bob Fowler to John Chadwick, 1 August 1965, NAUK, DO 161/83.

112 R. Cox, Confidential Dispatch, 9 July 1963, NAUK, DO 161/83.

113 Frans Viljoen, 'The Realisation of Human Rights in Africa through Sub-Regional Institutions' in *African Yearbook of International Law Vol 7*, ed, Abdulqawi A. Yusuf (The Hague: Kluwer Law International, 1999) 192.

Conclusion

Half a century after the abolition of Privy Council jurisdiction in Africa, similar concerns about sovereignty, judicial independence, and the lack of representation on the JCPC bench re-emerged in Jamaica—one of the last Commonwealth countries that still recognized the Privy Council as its court of final appeal. Debates about the abolition of Privy Council appeal in Jamaica surfaced in the early twenty-first century. Writing in 2012, the Jamaican jurist Patrick Robinson argued for replacing the monarchy in Jamaica with a republican form of government and the Privy Council with an independent Caribbean Court of Justice. In his view, the right to JCPC appeal in independent Jamaica had negative implications for the identity and self-image of the Jamaican people.[114] Republican status and judicial independence, Judge Robertson argued, is the 'natural and logical culmination of the process of emancipation and the attainment of national independence'. As he put it:

> Replacing the (Privy Council) is about acknowledging the struggle of our ancestors... We say to them: you did not struggle in vain; it will be the final vindication of their struggle; fail to relinquish and replace those ties, and we fail them; not to grasp the plenitude of sovereignty and independence available to us would be an abnegation and a grave betrayal of their hopes and aspirations.[115]

The Privy Council, Judge Robertson argued, was not accessible to the vast majority of Jamaicans. The right to appeal to the Privy Council was therefore illusory, because most Jamaicans could not afford the '5,000-mile trek for justice'.[116] Consequently, only a few people could seek justice at the JCPC, those who were relatively well off and those accused of murder who received pro bono help from English lawyers. 'It was only the wealthy and the wicked who go to the Privy Council', Robinson reasoned.[117]

Remarkably, the arguments advanced by Judge Robertson and by the new generation of critics of the JCPC in the Caribbean echo those put forward elsewhere in the mid-twentieth century. Discontentment with the cost of bringing appeals to London, the lack of representation on the JCPC bench, and the implications of JCPC jurisprudence for national sovereignty were among the issues raised. Developments in Jamaica in many ways mirrored earlier debates in Africa: the urge to abolish JCPC jurisdiction was equally fostered both by a sense of dissatisfaction with the institution and by nationalist sentiments. The general feeling was that the JCPC—once a necessity in the age of Empire—was an anachronism in a period of decolonization and independence.[118] In spite of the promise of reform, the JCPC had failed to reform fast enough in transitioning from Empire to Commonwealth. Ultimately, it succumbed to the growing feeling in the newly independent ex-colonies

114 Robinson, 'The Monarchy, Republicanism and the Privy Council', 1–8.
115 Robinson, 'The Monarchy, Republicanism and the Privy Council', 7–8.
116 Robinson, 'The Monarchy, Republicanism and the Privy Council', 6.
117 Robinson, 'The Monarchy, Republicanism and the Privy Council', 6.
118 Marshall, 'The Judicial Committee of the Privy Council', 709.

that the right of appeal to a court composed of foreign judges overseas was a derogation of national sovereignty that effectively placed executive and judicial officers in a position of subordination. The right to Privy Council appeal, however excellent and valuable it may have been in the colonial days, was considered incompatible with the dignity and responsibility of an independent sovereign state.

The central challenge that confronted the JCPC in the age of decolonization was transitioning from its historic task of managing colonial differences to the new mission of managing national differences. In managing and adjudicating colonial differences in the British Empire, the JCPC and the regional appellate courts operated within a framework of imperial, political, and normative cohesiveness. Colonial otherness could easily be accommodated and managed against the background of overriding imperial legal and judicial standards, which were cast in universalist terms. The aspiration towards judicial standardization and normative legal cohesiveness effectively legitimized the work of the JCPC, and validated the accommodation of colonial differences.

Safeguards such as the repugnancy doctrine placed substantive limits on the legal expression of difference. Local invocations of Islamic and customary law and their judicial recognition in imperial courts posed no serious threat to the goal of upholding basic standards of British law. As the Empire disintegrated, however, the political and normative framework for maintaining legal and judicial conformity also fell apart. The notion of univeralist imperial justice could no longer provide constraints on the expression of colonial differences. Attempts to reform the JCPC, transitioning it into a Commonwealth Court of Appeal, could not resolve the problems of relevance and legitimacy. A new effort to link the retention of JCPC appeals to the protection of constitutional human rights in the Commonwealth resulted from these debates. Even so, it could not legitimize the ongoing existence of the JCPC. Without the homogenizing power of the Empire, the JCPC became insular and unrepresentative, falling into irrelevance amidst the varied and autonomous judicial systems of the newly independent nations of the Commonwealth.

7
Conclusions

The post-colonial scholar Partha Chatterjee has argued that the history of the global phenomenon of modern empire, from the eighteenth to the twentieth century, has been fundamentally shaped by the unprecedented problems posed by the rule of European states over Asiatic and African peoples. These myriad problems, as well as the ways both colonizers and the colonized sought to address them, have defined the norms and practices of the modern nation-state. Modern empire, Chatterjee suggests, was not an aberrant supplement to the history of modernity, but rather its central constituent part.[1]

The relationship between empires and modern nation-states was not simply one of succession or displacement. Rather, the logic and processes of Empire remain immanent in the construct of modern nation-states and contemporary global political systems. What imperial powers did in their colonies was closely linked with their self-perception as European nation-states. Similarly, what colonial subjects did in their engagement with and opposition to Empire stemmed from their notion of modernity and sovereignty.[2] Empires and their legacies, therefore, remain relevant to our understanding of the contemporary world order, particularly given the shifts towards supra-nationality, regional integration, confederation, and globalization, all of which echo old imperial forms of layered sovereignty and centre/periphery relations. As some have suggested, we may indeed be returning to a neo-imperial age.[3]

The story of imperial control of the administration of justice in Africa is intricately linked with the unfolding history of the post-colonial state. The tension between universalist imperial legal agendas and the adjudication of colonial difference also bears relevance to the contemporary history of globalization. I have addressed some of these connections in the introductory chapter of this book. Here, I examine the key legacies of the imperial justice as administered by the JCPC

[1] Partha Chatterjee, *The Black Hole of Empire: History of a Global Practice of Power* (Princeton: Princeton University Press, 2012) xi.

[2] Partha Chatterjee and Ayca Cubukcu, 'Empire as Practice of Power', *Humanity Blog*, 28 August 2012, <http://www.humanityjournal.org/blog/2012/08/empire-practice-power-empire-inseparable-part-modern-political-theory>.

[3] Given the endurance of empires in human history, it has been suggested that the nation-state may be a blip on the historical horizon whose hold on the world's political imagination may well prove partial or transitory. Jane Burbank and Frederick Cooper, *Empires in World History: Power and the Politics of Difference* (Princeton: Princeton University Press, 2010) 3.

and regional appeal courts, and offer an interpretation of their relevance to understanding contemporary globalism and legal cosmopolitanism.

A key argument of this book is that imperial courts were central to the construction and contestation of colonial difference as well as to the subsequent management of tensions between native exceptionalism and imperial universalism. The adjudication of imperial difference inevitably manifested the contradictions of British law. Imperial Appeal Courts operating beyond the direct influence of provincial colonial officialdom served as alternate locales for debates revolving around questions of inclusion and exclusion, power and restraint.

The main legacy of these imperial courts is that the precedents they established in upholding imperial legal universalism and adjudicating colonial difference continue to shape legal and judicial cultures in post-colonial societies. Case law provides vital and potent examples of the lasting power of colonial institutions. Most of these cases are still being applied in courtrooms in common law jurisdictions in Africa and beyond. The judgments of the JCPC, the WACA, and the EACA preserved in several overlapping Law Reports continue to provide guiding judicial precedence. The history of the JCPC and the African regional appeal courts also holds important lessons in the promise and limitation of supranational adjudications and the globalization of legal cultures.

Cases dealing with the judicial interpretation of customary law examined in this book typify a central paradox in colonial legal systems in Africa: a tension between imperial universalism and local exceptionalism and between the maintenance of fundamental principles of British justice, which became the basis for legitimizing empire, and recognizing local African customs that were also considered indispensable to achieving justice. In effect, colonial judicial culture contained two contrasting tendencies: an aspiration towards homogeneity and a measured accommodation of 'native' difference. In law as in culture, colonial policy in the civic sphere was based on the principle of cultural authenticity and assimilation premised on a certain universalist idealism. In contrast, legal and cultural policy in the customary sphere was underpinned by the principle of difference.[4] These two agendas were not always contradictory or mutually exclusive but were sometimes complementary in furthering the goals of the colonial state.

The overriding divide in colonial law was racial and cultural. In adjudicating colonial difference, the dominant themes in the work of the Imperial Appeal Court were similarly race and culture. This is evident from many of the cases involving the interpretation of customary law discussed in this book. However, there were other sites of difference and 'otherness' that had to be managed in the courts. These include the questions of ethnicity, religion, class, and gender. Imperial Courts of Appeal were also called upon to adjudicate these subordinate constructions of colonial difference. Is it correct then, to argue—as has been said of colonial medicine—that an overriding 'politics of difference' lay at the heart of administration of imperial appellate justice?[5]

[4] Mamood Mamdani, *When Victims become Killers* (Princeton: Princeton University Press, 2001) 26.
[5] See, for example, Megan Vaughan,*Curing their Ills* (California: Stanford University Press, 1991) 13.

Not quite. The politics of difference was certainly evident in imperial appellate justice, but so was the politics of homogeneity and conformity. The judgments of the JCPC were as informed by notions of native difference as they were by a commitment to a common standard of British justice.

Neither the accommodation of native difference, nor the aspiration towards legal conformity can be explained wholly in terms of liberal imperialism. The Fabian socialist inclinations of JCPC judges like Lord Haldane may have influenced their liberal interpretations of colonial laws, but both particularistic and universalist approaches to the adjudication of difference were imperial necessities. To endure through its expansionist encounters, British imperialism had to be responsively accommodating.[6] Imperial legal and judicial systems needed to recognize and accommodate local differences in order to survive and thrive. Tolerating colonial difference was seen as central to achieving the redemptive prospects of British justice and the larger goal of bringing the colonized within the fold of civilization.[7] Imperial law needed to be flexible, extendable, and modifiable, not in spite of the civilizing mission but because of it. The natives had to become the same as the 'civilized' colonists, yet remain inalterably different from them. This unsettled paradox permeated the colonial space.

The universalist impulse of colonial law and justice was driven as much by the civilizing agenda as it was by colonial exigencies. To adjudicate cases from across the Empire, the JCPC and the regional appeal courts were expected to serve and function no less than the courts in England. Their purpose was to deal with cases of conflicts with clear-cut rights and duties established by objective investigation of only those events deemed relevant to each case. The colonial laws that the Law Lords of the JCPC and the colonial judges of the WACA and the EACA were called upon to interpret had commonalities that allowed for a certain uniformity in imperial justice. This uniformity was ensured by case law and the doctrine of precedence.

Legal uniformity was also achieved through the British practice of modelling laws in one colony on those already enacted in another part of the Empire. Sometimes, whole statutes were incorporated into the law of the borrowing colonial territories. For example, several Indian statutes were imported wholesale into East African law. The East Africa Order in Council of 1897, which provided the legal framework for colonial governance in the East African Protectorate, was modelled after a similar law enacted in Bombay.[8] The New Zealand Chattels Transfer Act of 1924 was copied word-for-word, and enacted in Kenya in the 1930s. Criminal Codes were similarly replications of enacted templates. The Northern Nigerian Criminal Code of 1904 derived from the Queensland (Australia) Code of 1901, with modifications from the Gold Coast Code of 1892. The Queensland Code

[6] Peter Fitzpatrick, 'Terminal Legality: Imperialism and the (de)composition of Law' *Law, History, Colonialism: The Reach of Empire*, Diane Kirkby and Catharine Coleborne, eds (Manchester: Manchester University Press, 2001) 9–25.

[7] Fitzpatrick, 'Terminal Legality', 19.

[8] Thomas R. Metcalf, *Imperial Connections: India in the Indian Ocean Arena, 1860–1920* (Berkeley: University of California Press, 2008) 52.

itself was based on the Italian Penal Code of 1888, with provisions taken from the New York Penal Code. The Gold Coast Code of 1892 was modelled on earlier enactments in Jamaica and St Lucia. Finally, when the Nigerian Code was revised in 1959, it was replaced by a code based on the Sudan Code, which had been based on the Indian Penal Code.[9]

As I have attempted to demonstrate in this book, the imperial imperative and universalist idealism that underpinned colonial law were also evident in the establishment and regulation of the institution of 'native assessors'. The law providing for native assessors in the judicial system derived from the Indian Evidence Act, just as the provisions of the East African Criminal Procedure Codes were taken directly from the Indian Code of Criminal Procedure.[10] Thus, in terms of legal procedures, Indian legal codes rather than extant English laws from which these codes may originally have derived provided the required imperial standards. The unification of the Colonial Administrative Service on the eve of the Second World War and, specifically, the creation of a unified Colonial Legal Service in 1933, was also an important part of the homogenizing and universalizing process. Although the main goal of unifying the Colonial Legal Service was the standardization of conditions of employment, it also strengthened imperial standards in the realms of law and justice administration.[11]

These legal connections were not one-directional. Just as statutes developed in India and the Dominions were replicated in African colonies, so too did JCPC judgments in cases appealed from Africa influence jurisprudences elsewhere in the Empire-Commonwealth. Some of these landmark African cases, such as *Re: Southern Rhodesia* and the *Amodu Tijani* case relating to indigenous land rights, and the *Eshugbayi Eleko* case relating to *habeas corpus*, provide examples of the precedential value of African appeals in imperial jurisprudence.[12] The circulation of legal knowledge transformed the colony and post-colony as well as the metropole. The European 'self' was in many ways defined by the assumptions about and encounters with the 'native other'.[13] Consequently, even though in principle the JCPC and the regional Courts of Appeal adjudicated cases based on the local laws of the territories from which the appeals came, the similarities in these laws invariably generated a degree of uniformity in appellate judicial interpretation.

[9] J. N. Matson, 'The Common Law Abroad: English and Indigenous Laws in the British Commonwealth' (1993) 42(3) *The International and Comparative Law Quarterly* 758.

[10] John Gray, 'Opinion of Assessors in Criminal Trials in East Africa as to Native Custom' (1958) 2(1) *Journal of African Law* 8.

[11] Jerry Dupont, *The Common Law Abroad: Constitutional and Legal Legacy of the British Empire* (London: F.B. Rothman Publications, 2001) xvii.

[12] *Amodu Tijani v The Secretary, Southern Nigeria* [1921] 2 AC 399; *Eshugbayi Eleko v The Officer Administering the Government of Nigeria* [1931] AC 662.

[13] This argument is a central thesis of Edward Said, *Orientalism* (New York: Pantheon, 1978). Also, Sally Merry, 'From Law and Colonialism to Law and Globalization' (2003) 28 *Law & Social Inquiry* 578.

The Imperative of Colonial Difference

Colonial aspiration towards legal and judicial conformity was mediated by the notion of native difference in complex and unstable ways. Parallel to the imperial ideal of British justice was a conscious effort to moderate the impact of colonial laws imported from England or India by recognizing pre-existing local customs that had traditionally regulated African lives. Imperial legal culture could accommodate such customs to the extent that they were not patently incompatible with English law or 'repugnant' to notions of justice, equity, and 'good conscience' that had been cast in universal terms. The logic was self-evident: desirable as it was to extend more 'civilized' English legal cultures to natives in the colonies, local circumstances made such wholesale imposition impractical. The colonial courts were therefore expected to enforce a curious blend of English common law and local African customary law—adhering to the framework of imperial notions of morality and natural justice—rather than England's own law. As one colonial judge argued in 1906, 'it is not *law* that is required to be applied [by the courts] in Africa but *Equity*: the complex laws of England are unsuited to the primitive conditions under which people live in Africa'.[14]

Colonial officials recognized that the principles on which European style courts operated differed from existing African notions of law and justice. After all, imperial appeal courts were not expected to apply the Common Law in its English purity. Rather, the adjudication of cases was to be guided by the specific laws enacted in the colonies from which the cases came, as long as such laws did not negate fundamental standards of British justice. Paradoxical assumptions about the primacy of British justice and the essential difference of the colonized 'other' were inherent in the work of the JCPC and the regional appeal courts. The paradox was further amplified by colonial anthropologists and legal scholars.[15] Unlike the English-style courts, they argued, African notions and systems of justice followed a peculiar logic. Under the traditional African systems, the goal of a judicial process was the amicable resolution of a dispute, rather than the strict adherence (or defence of) to the legal rights of the involved parties.[16] The duty of the chiefly authorities administering this form of native customary law in settling disputes was to 'assuage injured feelings, to restore peace, to reach a compromise acceptable to both disputants'.[17]

[14] Quoted in *The Lagos Weekly Record* (21 April 1906).

[15] See, for example, Max Glauckman, *The Judicial Process Among the Barotse of Northern Rhodesia* (Manchester: Manchester University Press, 1955).

[16] W. C. E. Daniels, *The Common Law in West Africa* (London: Butterworth, 1964); A. N. Allott, *Essays in African Law* (London: Butterworth, 1960); Robert L. Kidder has made similar arguments about pre-colonial India. See Robert L. Kidder, 'Western Law in India: External Law and Local Responses' in Harry M. Johnson, ed, *Social System and Legal Process* (San Francisco: Jossey-Bass, 1978) 159–62.

[17] J. N. Matson, 'The Supreme Court and the Customary Judicial Process in the Gold Coast' (1953) 2(1) *The International and Comparative Law Quarterly* 48.

Colonial legal re-ordering was founded on the idea that the maintenance of social harmony and equilibrium was the dominant objective of African legal proceedings. A government memorandum issued in 1957 with the purpose of regulating the activities of the local courts in Tanganyika stated: 'whereas amongst Europeans the stress is on the individual and his rights, amongst the Bantu it is upon the community, upon the family or clan, and its continuing solidarity'.[18] The emphasis on native difference notwithstanding, the legitimacy of the European-style legal systems introduced in the colonies continued to rest on their perceived relevance to Africans and on a certain imperial universalist idealism.

Both British official and African elites shared the notion that in order to implement justice effectively in the colonies, both English legal principles and colonial statute laws had to be interpreted in ways that reflected native difference. This view was well articulated by Judge De Silva of the JCPC in a case involving the interpretation of African customary land law. 'In a proceeding in a Native Court,' he stated, 'too much importance cannot be attached to the failure to observe a point of [legal] practice.'[19] Although such assumptions about native difference were constantly questioned and sometimes repudiated, they stood at the core of the adjudication of colonial difference in the courts of Empire.[20]

The paradox of accommodating native difference, while at the same time upholding imperial standards of law and justice, was not easily resolved. Colonial law may have accommodated African difference, but the imperial universalism that underpinned it required that the 'difference' be at least partially contained as well. Colonial appellate judges were often called upon to interpret the fundamental principles of colonial law in the context of local expediencies. In the *Dhalamini* case discussed in Chapter 3, for example, the JCPC insisted that the statutory provisions, requiring the opinion of African assessors in criminal trials to be given in an open court, could not be disregarded on the grounds of African difference or native exceptionality. To do so would be to compromise the principles of judicial transparency, which were considered to be the bedrock of British justice.[21] Significantly, the JCPC insisted on the strict interpretation of legal codes relating to native assessors and native customs—cases about which judicial attitudes were typically laissez-faire. In *Dhalamini*, the JCPC came down rather firmly on the side of imperial universalism regarding the question of transparency and openness of

[18] Tanganyika Local Government Memoranda No 2 (Local Courts), Dar es Salam, Government Printer, 2 in Colonial Legal Service and Cognate Matters, KNAN, AP 1/1693.

[19] *Kwame Mensah otherwise Nana Akwamuhene v Kojo Abrokwa and another* [1961], in Olisa Chukura, Olisa, ed, *Privy Council Judgments: Opinions of the Judicial Committee of the Privy Council in appeals from West Africa, 1841 to 1973* (London: Gilford, 1981) 856.

[20] Sally Falk Moore has argued that the 'social equilibrium' presentation of African disputation logic is a mixture of African self-idealization and colonial/anthropological political theory. Although this interpretation is not entirely without merit, it is a well-edited version of the facts. There is ample ethnographic evidence in anthropological works written during both the colonial and post-colonial periods of inner struggles within groups. Sally Falk Moore, 'Treating Law as Knowledge: Telling Colonial Officers what to say to Africans about running "their own" Native Courts' (1992) 26(1) *Law and Society Review* 32.

[21] *Mahlikilili Dhalamini and others v R* [1942] AC 583 at 593 (hereinafter, *Dhalamini v R*).

judicial proceedings. It upheld the principles of British justice instead of, rather than supporting, claims about African difference.

At the same time, however, it would appear that the judges of the JCPC also recognized that the much vaunted universalist ideals of British justice could only be achieved in the colonies if some allowance was made for the proper recognition of African customs in judicial proceedings. In its judgment in *Dhalamini*, for example, the JCPC stressed that the law requiring the use of native assessors in trials involving Africans could not be invoked simply as an aid to the judge. It must also be construed as a 'safeguard to natives' accused of crimes and as a guarantee to them that their customs and traditions are not being misunderstood or misapplied by an 'alien court'. Such concerns that inflexible application of English law could distort the customary order and result in miscarriage of justice in African societies were commonplace.[22]

The attentiveness of imperial and colonial judges to native difference was driven both by imperial political exigencies and by judicial philosophies. Scholars of British colonial legal policies have argued that the legal philosophies of prominent British judges on the JCPC, such as Chief Justice Richard Burton and Lord Haldane, were influenced by early twentieth-century beliefs in the existence of a 'natural' African community. This notion arose from a 'complex web of radical liberal, neo-Hegelian and Fabian socialist thought'.[23]

The judicial philosophy of Lord Haldane, the emblematic JCPC judge, is particularly instructive. Evidently, it reflected the Calvinist theology of his Scottish upbringing. Haldane brought this 'missionary zeal' to his judicial work, which was further influenced by his interpretations of Hegelian philosophy centred on the belief in the importance of the state.[24] A firm believer in the greater state—the Empire—he advocated some autonomy for each dominion and colony within the British realm. Haldane's close association with the representatives of colonial governments during his early legal career convinced him that the two key tenets of the Empire's preservation were the Crown and the Law. Specifically, he believed that political autonomy in the colonies could be mediated through the universally 'civilising influence' of the English law. Most significantly, he also thought that the JCPC—strengthened with permanent representation from the colonies—should epitomize the only form of centralized power over the Empire.[25]

Apart from providing insight into the strategies colonial appellate judges used to reconcile the tension between imperial universalism and the 'othering' of colonial subjects in the realm of law, the cases reviewed in this book tell another story. They provide some context for understanding the cosmopolitan nature of British imperial legal culture and the ideological hybridities that shaped it. They equally show

[22] *Dhalamini v R*, 592.

[23] M. P. Cowen and R. W. Shenton, 'British Neo-Hegelian Idealism and Official Colonial Practice in Africa: The Oluwa Land Case of 1921' (1994) 22(2) *Journal of Imperial and Commonwealth History* 217.

[24] Jean Graham Hall and Douglas F. Martin, *Haldane: Statesman, Lawyer, Philosopher* (London: Barry Rose Law Publishers, 1996) 43.

[25] Hall and Martin, *Haldane*, 43.

how unsure, tentative, and expediential colonial rule was. Far from being the culmination of some grand vision of colonists, colonial legal culture was the product of a complex interplay of personalities, policies, and institutions in both the colonies and metropole.

The Persistence of Hegemony

Most scholars of Empire now agree that colonialism can no longer be viewed simply as a process of imposition by a single European metropole onto a monolithic colonized space. Rather, colonialism must be seen as tangled layers of political relations, lines of conflicting projections, and domestications that converged in specific local misunderstandings, struggles, and representations. Social action in colonial Africa or elsewhere cannot be reduced to the polarities of metropole/colony or colonizer/colonized, or to balanced narrative plots of imposition and response or hegemony and resistance. Such narratives, however refigured and nuanced, limit our appreciation of the complexities and contradictions that are opened up through sustained research in the fields and archives.[26] Therefore, the focus must be as much on the tensions and ambiguities of Empire as on its crushing power and triumphs.[27]

Within the context of the history of law and justice in colonial Africa, this approach requires a reconfiguration of the discourse beyond what has been described as the paradigm of 'domination and legitimisation'.[28] Studies undertaken within this paradigm often proceed from the premise that colonial law and justice were 'centres of power and privilege, feared sites, replete with structures of patronage and favouritism'.[29] The courts and the justice they dispensed were not ends in themselves, but instruments for legitimizing colonial rule, fostering the hegemony of the colonial state, or privileging emergent African elites at the expense of underprivileged Africans. Underneath the rhetoric of legal rights and objective justice lay an overriding need to maintain social order on a scale conducive to colonial interests.[30]

While this approach which views colonial law primarily as an instrument of power systems provides useful insights into how colonial legal systems furthered the ascendancy of dominant groups, it obstructs a fuller understanding of the creative tensions between and within European and African legal cultures in syncretic

[26] Nancy Rose Hunt, *Gendered Colonialisms in African History* (Oxford: Blackwell, 1997) 4.

[27] Frederick Cooper and Ann Stoler, eds, *Tensions of Empire: Colonial Cultures in a Bourgeois World* (Berkeley: University of California Press, 1997).

[28] Bonny Ibhawoh, 'Stronger than the Maxim Gun: Law, Human Rights and British Colonial Hegemony in Nigeria' (2002) 72(1) *Africa: Journal of the International African Institute* 55–6.

[29] Maurice Nyamanga Amutabi, 'Power and Influence of African Court Clerks and Translators in Colonial Kenya' in Benjamin N. Lawrence, Emily Lynn Osborn, and Richard L. Robert eds, *Intermediaries, Interpreters, and Clerks: African Employees in the Making of Colonial Africa* (Madison, WI: University of Wisconsin Press, 2006) 203.

[30] Martin Lynn, 'Law and Imperial Expansion: The Niger Delta Courts of Equity, *c.* 1850–85' (1995) 23(1) *Journal of Imperial and Commonwealth History* 28–39.

processes that produced new hybrid cultures. Others have shown that, rather than being simply arenas of colonial power and elite domination, colonial courts often turned into battlegrounds on which were contested the access to resources and labour, the relationships of power and authority, and interpretations of morality and culture.[31] In this process, local people encountered the realities of colonialism; subsequently, both they and the Europeans shaped the laws and institutions, relationships and processes, meanings and understandings of the colonial period itself. For example, as I have shown in this book, the roles of African lawyers, local Chiefs, 'native assessors', and other indigenous employees of the colonial state shaped the interactions of subject populations with European officials. Their roles blurred colonial dichotomies and created key intersections of power, authority, and knowledge.[32] Such a blurring of dichotomies led to the creation of hybrid legal cultures shaped by European powers and also by the initiatives and responses of Africans involved in the administration of justice.[33]

The central argument of this book is that the JCPC and the regional appeal courts were crucial sites for the construction and contestation of colonial difference and also the crucibles of the production of new hybrid legal cultures that shaped both the colonial and post-colonial order in Africa. This is evident in the ways that ideologies of colonial inclusion and differentiation were challenged by people acting within the political structures of the Empire and by those outside the legal and political space. Still, the emphasis on imperial liberal universalism, dialogue, and hybridities here should not overshadow the real hegemonic power relations which, for the most part, defined the interactions between the colonizer and the colonized within the imperial legal system. While the JCPC and the regional Appeal Courts sometimes effectively protected the colonial subjects from colonial excess and inequities, treading the fine line between imperial universalism and colonial difference, such interventions never seriously threatened the imperial order. Even though it was sometimes necessary to soften differentiation within the 'substructure' of the Empire, its 'superstructure' remained firmly premised on the essential difference of the colonized 'other'.

To argue that the adjudication of Empire embodied a tension of universalism and difference, and a process of hybridization, is not to deny the brutal domination and conflict that defined the colonial order. Rather, it is to draw attention to the complex ways in which the imperial judicial system was constructed and

[31] This point has been made in several studies of colonial law in Africa. See, for example, Kristin Mann and Richard Roberts, eds, *Law in Colonial Africa* (Portsmouth: Heinemann, 1991); Martin Chanock, *Law, Custom, and Social Order: The Colonial Experience in Malawi and Zambia* (Portsmouth: Heinemann, 1998); Sally Falk Moore, *Social Facts and Fabrications "Customary" Law on Kilimanjaro, 1880–1980* (Cambridge: University of Cambridge Press, 1986); Margaret Jean Hay and Marcia Wright, *African Women and the Law: Historical Perspectives* (Boston: Boston University Press, 1982); Lawrence, Osborn, and Roberts, eds, *Intermediaries, Interpreters, and Clerks*.

[32] Benjamin N. Lawrence, Emily Lynn Osborn, and Richard L. Roberts, 'African Intermediaries and the "Bargain" of Collaboration' in *Intermediaries, Interpreters and Clerks*, eds Lawrence, Osborn and Roberts, 4.

[33] D. A. Westbrook, 'Colonial Discourse Theory' in Robin W. Winks, ed, *The Oxford History of the British Empire, Vol 5* (Oxford: Oxford University Press, 1999) 609.

maintained. Such an argument also illuminates the often overlooked role of colonized Africans in shaping imperial jurisprudence. As John Comaroff has noted, 'the historical fact that there were these "tensions of empire" did not make imperialism any the less exploitative. Or coercive. Nor did it soften the inequalities that saturated colonial societies everywhere; if anything, it sharpened them.'[34] If there was a dialogue about universalism and difference in the imperial appeal courts, it was a dialogue premised on and suffused by power inequality. This power inequality was the most basic working principle of Empire—a racialized inequality between the British ruling class and the subject populations that was most evident in the settler colonies of Eastern and Southern Africa. Still, for the colonized, the tensions and contradictions of Empire sometimes opened up opportunities to resist, subvert, and negotiate colonial power. While imperial tensions and hybridities did not diminish the coercive power of British imperialism, it gave the colonized material from which to fashion their own understandings of European overrule.

Indeed, it is instructive that none of the cases examined in this book were potentially threatening to the colonial social and political order. This may well explain the tone and substance of the liberal juridical dialogue they engendered. In the *Amodu Tijani* and *Eshugbayi Eleko* cases discussed in Chapter 5, the colonial government in Nigeria suffered embarrassing defeats at the JCPC. The victorious African Chiefs and their supporters relished their victories, and were empowered in their opposition to government policies. However, these judgments did not seriously endanger the colonial order or significantly alter colonial agendas. After all, the 'intransigent' Chief Eshugbayi Eleko who sought to make Lagos 'ungovernable' for British authorities in Nigeria remained politically marginalized despite his successful JCPC appeal against his deposition and deportation.

Similarly, the victory of Chief Oluwa in *Amodu Tijani* at the JCPC did not loosen British control over indigenous lands in Nigeria or elsewhere in the British Empire. True, the case redefined indigenous land title in a way that imposed certain limits on the scope of state authority; however, it did not alter the basis of British control of land in the colonies. In the landmark case of *Shobuza v Millar*, the JCPC held that a declaration of land grant by the Protectorate government of Swaziland was an exercise of power by 'Act of State', unchallengeable in any British court.[35] In another land case, the JCPC pointed out that the Treaty of Cession by which the Chiefs of Lagos purportedly granted their lands to the British Crown was 'an Act of State by which the British Crown acquired full rights and sovereignty over Lagos'. Under these circumstances, the JCPC held, the 'Courts of Law will not take it upon themselves to construe the Treaty'.[36]

Judicial debates over legal universalism were much more constrained, if not muted, in appeal cases that had the potential of seriously threatening the imperial

[34] John Comaroff, 'Colonialism, Culture and the Law: A Foreword' (2001) 26 *Law and Social Inquiry* 313.

[35] *Sobhuza II v Allister Miller* [1926] AC 518 at 526.

[36] *Adeyinka Oyekan v Musendiku Adele* [1957] 2 All ER 785 at 790.

order. In the Mau Mau trials of Jomo Kenyatta and other officials of the Kenyan African Union in 1957, the colonial courts in Kenya found all the defendants guilty and pronounced the maximum sentence of seven years' hard labour. Remarkably, in what has been described as a 'scandalous miscarriage of Justice', the JCPC refused the defendants leave to appeal the decision, even though their defence rested on an appeal to emergent universal human rights jurisprudence.[37] In East Africa where the Privy Council had long been viewed as a white man's court, it is likely that the JCPC's apparent desire to detach itself from passing on the pleas of those imprisoned in Kenya during the Mau Mau emergency further undermined the Board's claim to justice rather than political expediency. The conclusions that this book makes about imperial universalism, colonial difference, dialogue, and legal hybridities in the adjudication of Empire therefore must be firmly located within the framework of the contested but overarching power relations in the colonial state.

The Legacies of Imperial Justice

Many parts of our globalizing moment are fundamentally intertwined with imperialism; the seismic cultural and intellectual transformations enacted by colonialism are central to any understanding of globalization over the long run.[38] Imperial knowledge systems have, in many ways, defined the cosmopolitan intellectual traditions of the twentieth and twenty-first centuries. The history of the administration of imperial justice through the JCPC and the regional African Appeal Courts offers important lessons for contemporary trends in the globalization of legal culture.

European empires acted as powerful agents of globalization, appropriating new territories and new sources of revenue, moving people, commodities, and ideas from colony to colony as well as between the imperial centre and constituent peripheries. Similarly, the age of globalization has ushered in an unprecedented transfer of legal ideas and institutions from one society to another around the world. As in the imperial era, the flow of law, knowledge, and expertise takes place among countries and peoples of vastly unequal power and resources. We are now witnessing an era of global legal transplants carried out in the name of democracy, human rights, and the rule of law.[39] Today's reformers see themselves as promoting a better, more just, and more 'civilized' society. Yet, the legitimating narratives of the present are not dissimilar from those of the colonial past. Both incorporate normative ideas of civilization, evolution, and social progress. Where colonialism

[37] Ronald Hyam, *Britain's Declining Empire: The Road to Decolonization 1918–1968* (Cambridge: Cambridge University Press, 2000) 191.

[38] Tony Ballantyne, 'Empire, Knowledge, and Culture: From Proto-Globalization to Modern Globalization' in A. G. Hopkins, ed, *Globalization in World History* (London: W.W. Norton, 2002) 117.

[39] Merry, 'From Law and Colonialism to Law and Globalization', 588.

emphasized Christianity and civilization, contemporary globalism emphasizes democratization and human rights.[40]

Contemporary shifts toward global jurisprudence and supranational adjudication bear resemblance to the historical role of the JCPC and the imperial regional appeal courts of Africa.[41] In the post-World War II era, several such supranational judicial organizations have emerged, reflecting the increasing globalization of legal and judicial culture. These include institutions such as the International Criminal Court, the International Court of Justice, the European Court of Human Rights, the Inter-American Court of Human Rights, the African Court on Human and Peoples' Rights, and the International Centre for the Settlement of Investment Disputes.[42] Imperial Courts of Appeal are, in some sense, the historical antecedent of these supranational judicial arrangements, where nation-states delegate judicial competence beyond their national borders.[43]

Like the JCPC and other colonial appellate courts, the jurisdiction of these supranational judicial organizations cuts across national and cultural boundaries. They are staffed by judges and adjudicators who, like imperial judges, often have limited knowledge of the cultures and customs of the disputants who come before them. As with earlier imperial appeal courts, they too must struggle to find the right balance between promoting contemporary universalist ideals of human rights and transnational justice, while allowing for some degree of local autonomy and difference.

There are, of course, important distinctions between the Imperial Courts of Appeal—the subject of this book—and contemporary supranational courts. The British Empire was no world government and the JCPC was no world court. Empires had law codes and courts based on domestic models, which they sought to impose on colonized societies. In contrast, globalization, when defined as supra-territoriality, involves transnational codes and institutions. Empires imposed and sustained national codes in distant places; globalization assails national codes and sovereignty.[44] Distinctions can also be made between the procedures and processes of the imperial courts and those of contemporary supranational

[40] Merry, 'From Law and Colonialism to Law and Globalization', 588.

[41] The term 'supranational adjudication' as used here refers to the adjudication by courts or other judicial organizations sitting above, rather than within or between, states. For a discussion on the concept of supranational adjudication, see Alex Mills and Tim Stephens, 'Challenging the Role of Judges in Slaughter's Liberal Theory of International Law' (2005) 18 *Leiden Journal of International Law* 4.

[42] For a discussion of the development of supranational adjudicatory institutions see Laurence R. Helfer and Anne-Marie Slaughter, 'Toward a Theory of Effective Supranational Adjudication' (1997) 107(2) *Yale Law Journal* 276–80; S. Choudhry, 'Globalization in Search of Justification: Towards a Theory of Comparative Constitutional Interpretation' (1999) 74 *Indiana Law Journal* 819, 819–27; Kanishka Jayasuriya, 'The Rule of Law in the Era of Globalization: Globalization, Law and the Transformation of Sovereignty; The Emergence of Global Regulatory Governance' (1999) 6 *Indiana Journal of Global Legal Studies* 425, 432–3.

[43] S. Voigt, M. Ebeling, and L. Blume, 'Improving Credibility by Delegating Judicial Competence: The Case of the Judicial Committee of the Privy Council' (2007) 82(2) *Journal of Development Economics* 348–73.

[44] John Weaver, 'Empires' *in Globalization and Autonomy Online Compendium*, 9 September 2011, <http://www.globalautonomy.ca/global1/servlet/Glossarypdf?id=CO.0066>.

adjudicatory institutions. Indeed, as the highest court of appeal for the British Empire, the JCPC was a uniquely imperial way of delegating judicial authority.

Despite the distinctions between the imperial appeal courts and today's supranational courts, there are significant parallels as well. In both cases, adjudication requires discretion and compromise to achieve order. It is now commonplace in many jurisdictions for courts to refer extensively to the decision of the courts of foreign jurisdictions when interpreting domestic and international human rights guarantees. The judgments of supranational courts are studied and invoked in courtrooms around the world. Increasingly, we have the sense of living in an interdependent global legal system, marked by economic globalization and an emergent universal human rights order. Advocates of universal human rights strive to solidify the human rights legal system as coherent, unified, and codified, and to suppress its fragmentary, provisional, and inventive qualities.[45]

In this increasingly interdependent and globalizing world, supranational courts play a vital role in fashioning and upholding a nascent universal legal culture founded on international human rights law, both within and beyond states. Yet, like the JCPC and imperial regional appeal courts, these new institutions must grapple with the inevitable tensions between aspirations towards universal legal standards and persistent assertions of local difference. The work of the European Court of Human Rights (ECtHR) provides the clearest example of this tension. From the perspective of European Union Law, where the interpretation of rights differs from country to country, national courts are asked to renounce the constitutional scope of protection in favour of the scope defined in the European Convention on Human Rights. Like the JCPC, the ECtHR has become a supranational judicial authority charged with upholding common judicial standards on questions of human rights, while taking into consideration the varying socio-political and legal cultures of the states from which cases arise. Like the JCPC, the ECtHR has sought to strike this delicate balance through what has been described as a process of 'judicial dialogue' specifically aimed at legitimizing judicial decision-making at a supranational level.[46]

The processes and outcomes of such supranational juridical dialogue invariably engender new legal and jurisprudential universalisms, as well as contested constructions of globality. This creates conformity, as well as dissent and discontent. Those sceptical of legal globalism and supranational adjudication worry about sacrificing local culture, national sovereignty, and autonomy for supposedly universal legal and human rights standards.[47]

Historians are in a unique position to contribute to these debates by looking back at the tensions between imperial universalism and local difference in colonial legal and judicial cultures. This marks a contribution to our knowledge of the

[45] Merry, 'From Law and Colonialism to Law and Globalization', 584.

[46] Aida Torres Pérez, *Conflicts of Rights in the European Union: A Theory of Supranational Adjudication* (Oxford: Oxford University Press, 2009).

[47] See Michael P. Scharf, 'The Politics Behind U.S. Opposition to the International Criminal Court' (1999) 6(1) *The Brown Journal of World Affairs* 97–104.

imperial past, fostering a better understanding of the challenges of contemporary legal globalization. There is much that we can learn about law and globalization today from revisiting past imperial systems of law and justice. Empires—the principal antecedents of globalization—will figure centrally in constructing the history of contemporary globalization, when the time comes for that history to be written.[48] My hope is that by providing insight into the adjudication of empire, this book offers a guide to understanding the benefits and challenges that will inevitably come with adjudicating globalization.

[48] John Weaver, 'Empires' in *Globalization and Autonomy Online Compendium*.

Bibliography

MANUSCRIPT COLLECTIONS

Herbert Macaulay Papers, University of Ibadan, Nigeria.
Kwame Nkrumah Papers, Public Records and Archives Administration Department, Ghana.
Mensah Sarbah Papers, Public Records and Archives Administration Department, Ghana.
Papers of Richard Burdon Haldane, 1st Viscount Haldane of Cloan, Edinburgh University, UK.
Tom Mboya Papers, Hoover Institution on War, Revolution, and Peace, Stanford University, USA.

GOVERNMENT DOCUMENTS

a. United Kingdom

Constitutional Progress in the Federation of Nigeria (No R 3172).
Corfield, FD, *Historical Survey of the Origins and Growth of the Mau Mau* (Cmnd 1030, London: HMSO, 1960).
Facts about the Federation of Nigeria (No R 3222, Feb. 1957).
The Future of the East African Commission Services. Report of the London Discussions, June 1961 (Cmnd 1433, London: HMSO, 1961).
Jones, G. I., *Basutoland Medicine Murder: A Report on the Recent Outbreak of 'Diretlo' Murders in Basutoland* (London: HMSO, 1958).
Kenya Independence Conference 1963 (Cmnd 2156, London: HMSO, 1963).
Native Courts and Native Customary Law in Africa (London: HMSO, 1957).
Nigeria Constitutional Order in Council, 1951 (No 1172, London: HMSO, 1951).
Office of Commonwealth Relations, *Hearing by the Judicial Committee of the Privy Council of Appeals from Courts or Judges in Ghana, Exchange of Letters between the Government of the United Kingdom and the Government of Ghana* (London: HMSO, 1960).
Printed Papers in Appeal 1906–1956, The Judicial Committee of the Privy Council, (London) [Multiple volumes].
Proposed Constitution of Ghana, (Cmnd 71, London: HMSO, 1957).
Report of the Conference on the Nigerian Constitution held in London in July and August, 1953 (Cmnd 8934, London: HMSO, 1954).
Reports of the Kenya Constitutional Conference 1962 (Cmnd 1700, London: HMSO, 1962).
Tanganyika (Legislative Council) (Amendment) Order 1959 (No 1048, London: HMSO, 1959).

b. Ghana

Constitution of the Republic of Ghana (Accra: Government Printing Office, 1957).
The Ghana (Constitution) Order in Council, Gold Coast Gazette No 13, 1957.
Judgments of the Judicial Committee of the Privy Council on Appeal from the Gold Coast Colony 1874–1928 (Accra: Government Printing Office, 1929).

c. Kenya

Butterfield, Harry Robert Frederick, *Index Digest of the Reported Cases Determined by the Court of Appeal for Eastern Africa and on Appeal Therefrom by the Judicial Committee of the Privy Council, 1900–1952* (Nairobi: Government Printer, 1954).

The Constitution of Kenya (Amendment) Act 1964, Kenya Gazette Supplement 155, Act No 28, 1964.

The Constitution of the Republic of Kenya (Nairobi: Government Press, 1963).

Court of Appeal for Eastern Africa, *Eastern African Court of Appeal Orders in Council and Rules* (Nairobi: Government Press, 1954).

Court of Appeal of Eastern Africa Annual Reports 1954–1960 (Nairobi, 1960).

Gazette of the Colony and Protectorate of Kenya, 1 July 1925.

Hamilton, Robert William, Pickering, George Hunter, and Sheridan, Joseph Alfred, *Law Reports of Kenya: Containing Cases Determined by the Supreme Court, Kenya Colony and Protectorate, and by the Court of Appeal for Eastern Africa, and by the Judicial Committee of the Privy Council on Appeal from that Court* (Nairobi: Government Printer, 1967).

Hamilton, Robert William, *The Origin and Growth of British Jurisdiction and of the Judicial System of the East African Protectorate* (Nairobi: Government Printer, 1918).

Law Reports Containing Decisions of the Court of Appeal for Eastern Africa and of the Judicial Committee of the Privy Council on Appeal from that Court (Nairobi: Government Press, 1954).

Report of the Bushe Commission of Inquiry into Justice (Nairobi: Government Press, 1933).

d. Nigeria

Constitution of the Federal Republic of Nigeria (Lagos: Government Printer, 1963).

Selected Judgments of the West African Court of Appeal, vol 12 (Lagos: Government Print Department, 1946).

West African Court of Appeal, *Selected Judgments of the West African Court of Appeal* (Lagos: Government Print Department, 1952).

e. Sierra Leone

The West African Court of Appeal Rules (Freetown: Government Printer, 1937).

f. South Africa

Lagden, Godrey Yeatman, *South Africa: Report of the Commission, with Annexures and Appendices,* South African Native Affairs Commission, Cape Times (Limited Government Printers, 1905).

g. Tanzania

Tanzania Presidential Commission Report (Dar es Salaam: Government Printer, 1965).

NEWSPAPERS AND MAGAZINES

Ashanti Times

Daily Mail (UK)

Daily Telegraph (Nigeria)

Daily Telegraph (South Africa)

Daily Times (Nigeria)
The East African Standard
The Gold Coast Observer
The Gold Coast Times
The Independent (UK)
The Indian Advocate
Lagos Weekly Record
The Times (UK)
West Africa
West African Pilot

PRIMARY

Bing, Geoffrey, *Reap the Whirlwind: an Account of Kwame Nkrumah's Ghana from 1950 to 1966* (London: MacGibbon and Kee, 1968).
Enahoro, Anthony, *Fugitive Offender* (London: Cassell, 1965).
Foster, Joseph (ed), *The Register of Admissions to Gray's Inn, 1521–1889, together with the Register of Marriages in Gray's Inn Chapel, 1695–1754* (London: private printing, 1889).
Gandhi, M. K., *An Autobiography: Or, the Story of my Experiments with Truth* (Ahmedabad: Navajivan Publishing House, 1969).
Joscelin, Elspath and Huxley, Grant, *Four Guineas: A Journey through West Africa* (London: Chatto & Windus, 1957).
Macgeagh, Henry F. and Sturgess, H. A. C. (eds), *Register of Admissions to the Honourable Society of the Middle Temple: From the Fifteenth Century to the Year 1944*, vol 2 (London: Butterworth & Co, 1949).
Nkrumah, Kwame, *The Autobiography of Kwame Nkrumah* (Edinburgh: Thomas Nelson & Sons, 1957).
Nkrumah, Kwame, *I Speak of Freedom: A Statement of African Ideology* (Surrey: Heinemann, 1961).
Nyerere, Julius, *Freedom and Unity: A Selection from Writings and Speeches 1952–1965* (London: Oxford University Press, 1967).
Piggott, Theodore, *Outlaws I have Known and Other Reminiscences of an Indian Judge* (Edinburgh: William Blackwood and Sons, 1930).
Records of the Honorable Society of Lincoln's Inn, vol II (London: Lincoln's Inn, 1896).
Setalvad, Motilal C, *My Life: Law and Other Things* (London: Sweet and Maxwell, 1971).
Sturgess, H. A. C., *The Middle Temple Bench Book, being a register of Benchers of the Middle Temple: From the earliest records to the present time* (London: not listed, 1958).

SECONDARY

Abbasi, Muhammad Yusuf, *The Political Biography of Syed Ameer Ali* (Lahore: Wajidalis, 1989).
Abel, Richard L., *The Legal Profession in England and Wales* (Oxford: Basil Blackwell, 1988).
Abun-Nasr, Jamil M. and Spellenbert, Ulrich, and Wanitzek, Ulrike (eds), *Law, Society, and National Identity in Africa* (Hamburg: Helmut Buske, 1990).
Adewoye, Mooneye, *The Judicial System in Southern Nigeria, 1854–1954: Law and Justice in a Dependency* (Atlantic Highlands: Humanities Press, 1977).
Adewoye, Mooneye, *The Legal Profession in Nigeria, 1865–1962* (Ikeja: Longman, 1977).

Afigbo, A. E., *The Warrant Chiefs: Indirect Rule in South Eastern Nigeria 1891–1929* (New York: Humanities Press, 1972).

Allott, A. N., *Essays in African Law* (London: Butterworth, 1960).

Anderson, David G., *Histories of the Hanged: The Dirty War in Kenya and the End of Empire* (New York: WW Norton & Company, 2000).

Anyebe, A. P., *Customary Law: The War Without Arms* (Enugu: New Dimension, 1995).

Asch, Michael, *Aboriginal and Treaty Rights in Canada: Essays on Law, Equity, and Respect for Difference* (Vancouver: UBC Press, 1997).

Ashforth, Adam, *The Politics of Official Discourse in Twentieth-Century South Africa* (Oxford: Clarendon Press, 1990).

Ạsiwaju, A. I., *Western Yorubaland under European rule, 1889–1945: A Comparative Analysis of French and British Colonialism* (Atlantic Highlands: Humanities Press, 1976).

Bayly, C. A., *The Birth of the Modern World, 1780–1914: Global Connections and Comparisons* (Malden: Blackwell, 2004).

Beauchamp, J. J., *The Jurisprudence of the Privy Council* (Montreal: Whiteford & Theoret, 1891).

Benton, Lauren, *Law and Colonial Cultures: Legal Regimes in World History, 1400–1900* (Cambridge: Cambridge University Press, 2002).

Bilder, Mary Sarah, *The Transatlantic Constitution: Colonial Legal Culture and the Empire* (Cambridge: Harvard University Press, 2004).

Bing, Geoffrey, *Reap the Whirlwind: An Account of Kwame Nkrumah's Ghana from 1950 to 1966* (London: MacGibbon & Kee, 1968).

Boğaç, Ergene, *Local Court, Provincial Society and Justice in the Ottoman Empire: Legal Practice and Dispute Resolution in Çankırı and Kastomonu 1652–1744* (Leiden: Brill, 2003).

Brantley, Cynthia, *The Giriama and Colonial Resistance in Kenya, 1800–1920* (Berkeley: University of California Press, 1981).

Brantlinger, Patrick, *Rule of Darkness: British Literature and Imperialism, 1830–1914* (Ithaca: Cornell University Press, 1990).

Brougham, Henry, *Lord Brougham's Speeches in 1837 & 1838* (London: Ridgway, 1837).

Brougham, Henry, *Speeches of Henry Lord Brougham upon Questions Relating to Public Rights, Duties, and Interests* (Edinburgh: A&C Black, 1838).

Burbank, Jane and Cooper, Frederick, *Empires in World History: Power and the Politics of Difference* (Princeton: Princeton University Press, 2010).

Burns, Alan, *Colonial Civil Servant* (London: Allen & Unwin, 1949).

Campbell, Robert M, et al, *The Real Worlds of Canadian Politics: Cases in Process and Policy* (Peterborough: Broadview Press, 2004).

Chanock, Martin, *Law, Custom, and Social Order: The Colonial Experience in Malawi and Zambia* (Cambridge: Cambridge University Press, 1985).

Chanock, Martin, *The Making of South African Legal Culture 1902–1936: Fear, Favour, and Prejudice* (Cambridge: Cambridge University Press, 2001).

Chatterjee, Partha, *The Nation and its Fragments; Colonial and Postcolonial Histories* (Princeton: Princeton University Press, 1993).

Chatterjee, Partha, *The Black Hole of Empire: History of a Global Practice of Power* (Princeton: Princeton University Press, 2012).

Chukkol, Kharisu Sufiyan *Supernatural Beliefs and the Criminal Law in Nigeria: A Critical Appraisal* (Zaria: Ahmadu Bello University, 1981).

Chukura, Olisa (ed), *Privy Council Judgments: Opinions of the Judicial Committee of the Privy Council in Appeals from West Africa, 1841 to 1973* (London: Gilford, 1981).
Cohn, Bernard S., *Colonialism and its Forms of Knowledge: The British in India* (Princeton: Princeton University Press, 1996).
Cole, Patrick, *Modern and Traditional Elites in the Politics of Lagos* (New York: Cambridge University Press, 1973).
Comaroff, Jean, *Body of Power; Spirit of Resistance: Culture and History of a South African People* (Chicago: University of Chicago Press, 1985).
Comaroff, Jean and Comaroff, John L., *Christianity, Colonialism and Consciousness in South Africa*, vol 1, *Of Revelation and Revolution* (Chicago: University of Chicago Press, 1991).
Comaroff, Jean and Comaroff, John L., *The Dialectics of Modernity on a South African Frontier*, vol 2, *Of Revelation and Revolution* (Chicago: University of Chicago Press, 1997).
Comaroff, John L. and Roberts, Simon, *Rules and Processes: The Cultural Logic of Dispute in an African Context* (Chicago: University of Chicago Press, 1981).
Coombes, Annie E., *Rethinking Settler Colonialism: History and Memory in Australia, Canada, Aotearoa, New Zealand and South Africa* (Manchester: Manchester University Press, 2006).
Cooper, Frederick, *Colonialism in Question: Theory, Knowledge, History* (Berkeley: University of California Press, 2005).
Cooper, Frederick and Stoler, Ann Laura (eds), *Tensions of Empire: Colonial Cultures in a Bourgeois World* (Berkeley: University of California Press, 1997).
Coss, Peter (ed.), *The Moral World of the Law* (Cambridge: Cambridge University Press, 2000).
Crabbe, Azu, *John Mensah Sarbah 1864–1910, His Life and Works* (Accra: Ghana Universities Press, 1971).
Crozier, Anna, *Practising Colonial Medicine: the Colonial Medical Service in British East Africa* (New York: IB Tauris, 2007).
Daniels, W. C. E., *The Common Law in West Africa* (London: Butterworth, 1964).
Danquah, Joseph Buaki (ed), *Cases in Akan Law: Decisions Delivered by the Honourable Nana Sir Ofori Atta, KBE* (London: Routledge and Sons, 1928).
Darby, Philip, *The Three Faces of Imperialism* (New Haven: Yale University Press, 1987).
Darian-Smith, Eve and Fitzpatrick, Peter (eds), *Laws of the Postcolonial* (Ann Arbor: University of Michigan Press, 1999).
Dirks, Nicholas (ed), *Colonialism and Culture* (Ann Arbor: University of Michigan Press, 1992).
Dirlik, Arif, *Global Modernity: Modernity in an Age of Global Capitalism* (Boulder: Paradigm Publishers, 2007).
Dundes, Alan and Renteln, Alison Dundes (eds), *Folk Law: Essays in the Theory and Practice of Lex non Scripta* (Madison: University of Wisconsin Press, 1995).
Dupont, Jerry, *The Common Law Abroad: Constitutional and Legal Legacy of the British Empire* (Buffalo: S. Hein & Co., 2001).
Eagleton, Terry, et al (eds), *Nationalism, Colonialism and Literature* (Minneapolis: University of Minnesota Press, 1988).
Edsman, Björn M., *Lawyers in Gold Coast Politics c. 1900–1945: From Mensah Sarbah to J. B. Danquah*. Acta Universitatis Upsaliensis, Studia Historica Upsaliensia 111 (Uppsala: University of Stockholm, 1979).
Elias, Taslim Olawole, *Groundwork of Nigerian Law* (London: Routledge & Kegan Paul, 1954).

Elias, Taslim Olawale, *Nigerian Land Law and Custom* (London: Routledge & Kegan Paul, 1962).

Elias, Taslim Olawole, *The Nigerian Legal System* (London: Routledge & Kegan Paul, 1963).

Elias, Taslim Olawole, *Law in a Developing Society* (Benin City: Ethiope Publishing Corp., 1972).

Elkins, Caroline, *Imperial Reckoning: The Untold Story of Britain's Gulag in Kenya* (New York: H. Holt, 2005).

Epstein, A. L., *Juridical Techniques and the Judicial Process: A Study in African Customary Law*. Rhodes-Livingstone Papers, no 23 (Manchester: Manchester University Press, 1954).

Evans-Pritchard, E. E, *Witchcraft, Oracles and Magic among the Azande* (London: Oxford University Press, 1937).

Fisher, Michael, *Counterflows to Colonialism: Indian Travellers and Settlers in Britain 1600–1857* (Delhi: Permanent Black, 2006).

Fitz Roy, Almeric William, *The History of the Privy Council* (London: John Murray, 1928).

Fyfe, Christopher, *A History of Sierra Leone 1400–1787* (Cambridge: University Press, 1962).

Gandhi, M. K., *The Law and the Lawyers* (Ahmedabad: Navajivan Publishing House, 2004).

Geary, William, *Nigeria under British Rule* (London: Frank Cass, 1965).

Ghai, Yash, *Public Law and Political Change in Kenya: A Study of the Legal Framework of Government from Colonial times to the Present* (New York: Oxford University Press, 1970).

Gibson, Dale and Pue, W. Wesley (eds), *Glimpses of Canadian Legal History* (Winnipeg: Legal Research Institute, University of Manitoba, 1991).

Gluckman, Max, *The Judicial Process among the Barotse of Northern Rhodesia* (Manchester: Manchester University Press, 1955).

Haldane, R. B., *Selected Addresses and Essays* (London: Murray, 1928. Reprint, Freeport: Books for Libraries Press, 1970).

Hall, Catherine and Rose, Sonia O. (eds), *At Home with the Empire: Metropolitan Culture and the Imperial World* (Cambridge: Cambridge University Press, 2006).

Hall, Jean Graham and Martin, Douglas F., *Haldane: Statesman, Lawyer, Philosopher* (London: Barry Rose Law Publishers, 1996).

Harris, John H., *The Greatest Land Case in British History: The Struggle for Native Rights in Rhodesia before the Judicial Committee of His Majesty's Privy Council* (London: Anti-Slavery and Aborigines Protection Society, 1918).

Hay, Douglas and Craven, Paul (eds), *Masters, Servants, and Magistrates in Britain and the Empire, 1562–1955* (Chapel Hill: University of North Carolina Press, 2004).

Hay, Margaret Jean and Wright, Marcia, *African Women and the Law: Historical Perspectives* (Boston: Boston University Press, 1982).

Hobley, C. W., *Ethnology of Akamba and other East African Tribes* (Cambridge: The University Press, 1910).

Hobley, C. W., *Bantu Beliefs and Magic with Particular Reference to the Kikuyu and Kamba Tribes of Kenya Colony* (London: HF & G Witherby, 1922).

Hobley, C. W., *Kenya: From Chartered Company to Crown Colony, Thirty Years of Exploration and Administration in British East Africa* (London: Frank Cass, 1928).

Hobsbawm, Eric J. and Ranger, Terence O., *The Invention of Tradition* (Cambridge: Cambridge University Press, 1983).

Hodgkin, Thomas, *Nationalism in Colonial Africa* (London: Frederick Muller, 1956).

Hollander, Barnett, *Colonial Justice: The Unique Achievements of the Privy Council's Committee of Judges* (London: Bowes and Bowes, 1961).

Hooker, M. B., *Legal Pluralism: An Introduction to Colonial and Neo-Colonial Laws* (Oxford: Clarendon Press, 1975).

Hopkins, Anthony (ed), *Globalization in World History* (London: WW Norton, 2002).

Howell P. A., *The Judicial Committee of the Privy Council, 1833–1876: Its Origins, Structure, and Development* (Cambridge: Cambridge University Press, 1979).

Hunt, Nancy Rose, *Gendered Colonialisms in African History* (Oxford: Blackwell, 1997).

Hussain, Nasser, *The Jurisprudence of Emergency: Colonialism and the Rule of Law* (Ann Arbor: University of Michigan Press, 2006).

Hyam, Ronald, *Britain's Declining Empire: The Road to Decolonization 1918–1968* (Cambridge: Cambridge University Press, 2000).

Ibhawoh, Bonny, *Imperialism and Human Rights: Colonial Discourses of Rights and Liberties in African History* (Albany: State University of New York Press, 2007).

Karibi-Whyte, A. G., *The Relevance of the Judiciary in the Polity: A Historical Perspective* (Lagos: Nigerian Institute of Advanced Legal Studies, 1987).

Keith, Arthur Berriedale, *Responsible Government in the Dominions*, vol 2 (Oxford: The Clarendon Press, 1912).

Kirkby, Diane Elizabeth and Coleborne, Catharine (eds), *Law, History, Colonialism: The Reach of Empire* (Manchester: Manchester University Press, 2001).

Kirk-Greene, A. H. M., *Britain's Imperial Administrators, 1858–1966* (New York: St Martin's Press, 2000).

Kolsky, Elizabeth, *Colonial Justice in British India: White Violence and the Rule of Law*, Cambridge Studies in Indian History and Society (Cambridge: Cambridge University Press, 2011).

Lauer, Helen and Kofi Anyidoho (eds), *Reclaiming the Human Sciences and Humanities through African Perspectives*, vol 1 (Accra: Sub-Saharan Publishers, 2012).

Lawrence, Benjamin, et al, *Intermediaries, Interpreters, and Clerks: African Employees in the Making of Colonial Africa* (Madison: University of Wisconsin Press, 2006).

Lazarus-Black, Mindie and Hirsch, Susan F. (eds), *Contested States: Law, Hegemony, and Resistance* (New York: Routledge, 1994).

Lewis, Geoffrey, *Lord Atkin* (London: Butterworth, 1983).

Lieck, Albert (ed), *Trial of Benjamin Knowles* (Edinburgh: William Hodge & Co., 1933).

Likhovski, Assaf, *Law and Identity in Mandate Palestine* (Chapel Hill: University of North Carolina Press, 2006).

Luongo, Katherine, *Witchcraft and Colonial Rule in Kenya, 1900–1955* (Cambridge: Cambridge University Press, 2011).

MacGillivray, Alex, *A Brief History of Globalization: The Untold Story of Our Incredible Shrinking Planet* (London: Robinson, 2006).

MacKenzie, John M. (ed), *Imperialism and Popular Culture* (Manchester: Manchester University Press, 1986).

Mamdani, Mahmood, *Citizen and Subject: Contemporary Africa and the Legacy of Late Colonialism* (Princeton: Princeton University Press, 1996).

Mamdani, Mahmood, *Beyond Rights Talk and Culture Talk: Comparative Essays on the Politics of Rights and Culture* (New York: Palgrave Macmillan, 2000).

Mamdani, Mamood, *When Victims become Killers* (Princeton: Princeton University Press, 2001).

Mann, Kristin and Roberts, Richard (eds), *Law in Colonial Africa* (Portsmouth: Heinemann, 1991).
Mbembe, Achille, *On the Postcolony* (Berkeley: University of California Press, 2001).
McClintock, Anne, *Imperial Leather: Race, Gender, and Sexuality in the Colonial Contest* (New York: Routledge, 1995).
McGilchrist, John, *The Life and Career of Henry, Lord Brougham* (London: Cassell, Petter & Galpin, 1868).
McMillen, Christian W., *Making Indian Law: The Hualapai Land Case and the Birth of Ethnohistory* (New Haven: Yale University Press, 2007).
McQueen, Rob and Pue, W. Wesley (eds), *Misplaced Traditions: British Lawyers, Colonial Peoples* (Annandale: Federation Press, 1999).
Meek, Charles Kingsley, *Land Law and Custom in the Colonies* (London: Frank Cass, 1946).
Merry, Sally Engle and Milner, Neal (eds), *Popular Justice, Community Mediation, and Social Transformation* (Ann Arbor: University of Michigan Press, 1993).
Middleton, John, *The Ethnographic Survey of Africa: East Central Africa*, vol V (London: International African Institute, 1950).
Mommsen W. J. and De Moor J. A., eds, *European Expansion and Law: The Encounter of European and Indigenous Law in 19th and 20th Century Africa and Asia* (New York: Berg, 1992).
Moor, J. A. and Mommsen, Wolfgang J., *European Expansion and Law: The Encounter of European and Indigenous Law in 19th- and 20th-Century Africa and Asia* (Oxford: Berg, 1992).
Moore, Karl and Lewis, David, *The Origins of Globalization* (New York: Routledge, 2009).
Moore, Sally Falk, *Law as Process: An Anthropological Approach* (London: Routledge & Kegan Paul, 1978).
Moore, Sally Falk, *Social Facts and Fabrications: 'Customary' Law on Kilimanjaro* (Cambridge: Cambridge University Press, 1986).
Morris, H. F., *Some Perspectives of East African Legal History* (Uppsala, Norway: The Scandinavian Institute of African Studies, 1970).
Morris, H. F. and Read, James, *Indirect Rule and the Search for Justice: Essays in East African Legal History* (Oxford: Clarendon Press, 1972).
Murray, Colin and Sanders, Peter, *Medicine Murder in Colonial Lesotho: The Anatomy of a Moral Crisis* (Edinburgh: Edinburgh University Press, 2005).
Murray, J. H. P. (ed), *Papua or British New Guinea* (London: T. Fisher Unwin, 1912).
Nabudere, D. Wadada, *Imperialism in East Africa,* 2 vols (London: Zed Press, 1981).
New, Chester William, *The Life of Henry Brougham to 1830,* vol 1 (London: Clarendon Press, 1961).
Nuamah, H. A., *Murder in the Palace at Kibi: An Account of the Kibi Ritual Murder Case* (Accra: Educational Press, 1985).
Nwabueze, B. O., *The Machinery of Justice in Nigeria* (London: Butterworths, 1963).
Nwabueze, B. O., *Judicialism in Commonwealth Africa: The Role of the Courts in Governance* (New York: St Martin's Press, 1977).
Ollennu, Nee Amaa, *The Principles of Customary Land Law in Ghana* (London: Sweet and Maxwell, 1962).
Omu, Fred I., *Press and Politics in Nigeria, 1880–1937* (London: Longman, 1978).
Onabamiro, Sanya, *Glimpses into Nigerian History: Historical Essays* (Lagos: Macmillan, 1983).
Pérez, Aida Torres, *Conflicts of Rights in the European Union: A Theory of Supranational Adjudication* (Oxford: Oxford University Press, 2009).

Pratten, David, *The Man-Leopard Murders: History and Society in Colonial Nigeria* (Edinburgh: Edinburgh University Press, 2007).

Prestholdt, Jeremy, *Domesticating the World: African Consumerism and the Genealogies of Globalization* (Berkeley: University of California Press, 2008).

Pue, W. Wesley and Sugarman, David (eds), *Lawyers and Vampires: Cultural Histories of Legal Professions* (Oxford and Portland: Hart, 2003).

Rathbone, Richard, *Murder and Politics in Colonial Ghana* (New Haven: Yale University Press, 1993).

Risk, Richard, *The Privy Council and its Scholars* (Manitoba: Canadian Legal History Project, University of Manitoba, 1992).

Roberts, Andrew (ed.), *The Colonial Moment in Africa: Essays on the Movement of Minds and Materials, 1900–1940* (Cambridge: Cambridge University Press, 1990).

Roberts, Richard L., *Litigants and Households: African Disputes and Colonial Courts in the French Soudan, 1895–1912* (Portsmouth: Heinemann, 2005).

Robertson, Claire and Berger, Iris (eds), *Women and Class in Africa* (New York: Africana Publishing Company, 1986).

Roberts-Wray, Kenneth, *Commonwealth and Colonial Law* (London: Stevens, 1966).

Rosen, Lawrence, *The Anthropology of Justice: Law as Culture in Islamic Society* (Cambridge: Cambridge University Press, 1989).

Rosen, Lawrence, *Law as Culture: An Invitation* (Princeton: Princeton University Press, 2006).

Sachs, A., *Justice in South Africa* (Berkeley: University of California Press, 1973).

Said, Edward W., *Orientalism* (New York: Pantheon, 1978).

Said, Edward W., *Culture and Imperialism* (New York: Knopf, 1994).

Sarbah, John Mensah, *Fanti Customary Laws: A Brief Introduction to the Principles of the Native Laws and Customs of the Fanti and Akan Sections of the Gold Coast, with a Selection of Cases thereon decided in the Law Courts* (London: William Clowes and Sons, 1897).

Sarbah, John Mensah, *Fanti Law Reports of Decided Cases on Fanti Customary Law* (London: William Clowes and Sons, 1904).

Sarbah, John Mensah, *Fanti National Constitution: A Short Treatise on the Constitution and Government of the Fanti, Asanti, and other Akan Tribes of West Africa* (London: Frank Cass and Co, 1906).

Shamir, Ronen, *The Colonies of Law: Colonialism, Zionism and Law in Early Mandate Palestine* (Cambridge: Cambridge University Press, 2000).

Singha, Radhika, *A Despotism of Law: Crime and Justice in Early Colonial India* (Delhi: Oxford University Press, 1998).

Smith, Robert Sydney, *The Lagos Consulate, 1851–1861* (Berkeley: University of California Press, 1979).

Snyder, Francis G., *Capitalism and Legal Change: An African Transformation* (New York: Academic Press, 1981).

Snyder, Francis G. and Hay, Douglas (eds), *Labour, Law, and Crime: A Historical Perspective* (London: Tavistock, 1987).

Stoler, Ann Laura, McGranahan, Carole, and Perdue, Peter, *Imperial Formations* (Santa Fe: School for Advanced Research Press, 2007).

Swinfen, David, *Imperial Control of Colonial Legislation, 1813–1865: A Study of British Policy towards Colonial Legislative Powers* (Oxford: Clarendon Press, 1970).

Swinfen, David, *Imperial Appeal: The Debate on the Appeal to the Privy Council, 1833–1986* (Manchester: Manchester University Press, 1987).

Tamuno, Tekena, *The Evolution of the Nigerian State: The Southern Phase, 1898–1914* (London: Longman, 1972).
Thornberry, Patrick, *Indigenous Peoples and Human Rights* (Manchester: Manchester University Press, 2002).
Uche, U. U., *Contractual Obligations in Ghana and Nigeria* (London: Routledge, 1971).
Vaughan, Megan, *Curing their Ills: Colonial Power and African Illness* (Stanford: Stanford University Press, 1991).
Vaughn, Frederick, *Viscount Haldane: The Wicked Step-Father of the Canadian Constitution* (Toronto: University of Toronto Press for the Osgoode Society for Canadian Legal History, 2010).
Watson, Bruce, *Sacco and Vanzetti: The Men, the Murders, and the Judgment of Mankind* (New York: Viking Press, 2007).
Weaver, John, *The Great Land Rush and the Making of the Modern World, 1650–1900* (Montreal: McGill-Queen's University Press, 2003).
Weeramantry, C. G., et al (eds), *Legal Visions of the 21st Century: Essays in Honour of Judge Christopher Weeramantry* (The Hague: Martinus Nijhoff Publishers, 1998).
Wiener, Martin, *An Empire on Trial: Race, Murder, and Justice under British Rule, 1870–1935* (New York: Cambridge University Press, 2009).
Winks, Robin W. (ed), *The Oxford History of the British Empire*, 5 vols (Oxford: Oxford University Press, 1999).
Wolf, Eric, *Europe and the People without History* (Berkeley: University of California Press, 1982).
Zoë, Laidlaw, *Colonial Connections, 1815–45: Patronage, the Information Revolution and Colonial Government* (Manchester: Manchester University Press, 2005).

Table of Cases

Index

An italic *f* following a page reference indicates the presence of a figure; an italic *t* indicates the presence of a table.